Arizona

A Journey of Discovery

2005   2004   2003   2002   10   9   8   7   6   5   4

First Edition, ©2000 by Gibbs Smith, Publisher

Maps, graphs, and original art ©2000 by Gibbs Smith, Publisher

Cover photographs © by Tom Till: Slot Canyon, near Glen Canyon National Recreation Area, and Yeibichei Rocks, Monument Valley

Other photograph credits are listed at the back of the book.

Editorial Director, Susan A. Myers
Also edited by Amy M. Wagstaff and Courtney J. Thomas
Design by Ray Cornia

Published by
Gibbs Smith, Publisher
P.O. Box 667
Layton UT 84041
1-800-748-5439
text@gibbs-smith.com
www.gibbs-smith.com/textbooks

Printed and bound in China

ISBN 0-87905-856-0

Arizona

A Journey of Discovery

Jay Wagoner

SALT LAKE CITY

Contents

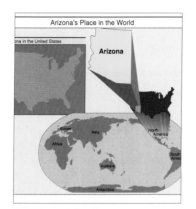

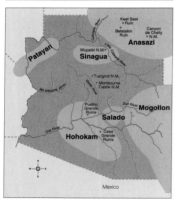

Maps

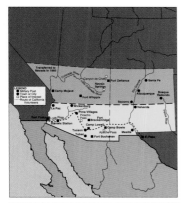

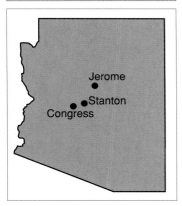

THE TIME
Millions of years ago
to the present

PLACES TO LOCATE
Grand Canyon
Four Corners
Mogollon Rim
Natural Bridge
Meteor Crater
Petrified Forest
Monument Valley
Humphreys Peak
Mount Bangs
Chiricahua Peak
Mount Graham
Mount Lemmon
Picacho Peak
Baboquivari Peak
Kitt Peak
Tucson Mountains
White Mountains
Salt River Valley

A Timeline of Arizona's Geologic History
Note: MYA means millions of years ago

600 MYA	500 MYA	400 MYA

Precambrian Era
(85% of the earth's time period)

Paleozoic Era (550–200 MYA)
Shallow seas cover Arizona.
Trilobites, amphibians, and reptiles live in seas.
Coal, oil, gas, and salt form.

Natural Arizona

Geology and Geography

The Colorado River winds through Grand Canyon National Park. (Photo by Tom Till)

TERMS TO UNDERSTAND
geography
sediment
geology
prehistoric
elevation
chaparral
exterminate
cauterize
silt
irrigation
foliage
commerce
urbanization
aqueduct
evaporative
smelter

300 MYA	200 MYA	100 MYA	PRESENT

Mesozoic Era (200–70 MYA)
Shallow seas, then sandy deserts cover the land.
Sedimentary rock is formed.
Dinosaurs and primitive mammals appear.
River systems exist.
Dinosaurs disappear.

Cenozoic Era (70 MYA to present)
Mammals live here.
Mountains are formed.
Plateaus rise.
Volcanoes erupt.
Copper, gold, and other minerals
   occur in rock.
Ice Age glaciers in North America
   change Arizona's climate.
Humans appear.

3

A Bird's-Eye View of Arizona

YOU ARE ABOUT to take a *geography* field trip in a hot air balloon! We lift off at the Mexican border, and zigzag north across the state to the Utah state line.

Feel the warm air rising from the desert floor? Watch out for that giant saguaro (suh WAH row)—its arms stretch out to grab us. Take a peek at that copper mine with those huge trucks winding their way out of the open pit. And over there—see that long green valley with the largest pecan grove in the country? Tucson is coming up. Fix your attention on the beautiful San Xavier Mission now in view. We'll have to climb to get over that grand "Sky Island Oasis" known as Mount Lemmon, just past Tucson.

Listen! Hear the hum of all those cars whizzing along the interstate to Phoenix? Don't try to count all the city folk. There must be five million of them. "What's that volcanic mountain rising out of the desert?" you ask. It's Picacho Peak, once a Butterfield stagecoach stop. The Yankees and Rebels fought a Civil War battle there.

Get ready! We're about to glide over Roosevelt Dam and Roosevelt Lake. Cast your eagle eye on those boats and fishermen.

We're heading for the Mogollon Rim (muggy YONE rim). Time to climb again. Nice little mountain shower, isn't it? The air smells refreshing, and get a whiff of the ponderosa pines. What a magnificent forest. It stretches east into the White Mountains and west all the way to Flagstaff.

The wind is right, so let's follow the railroad tracks into Flagstaff. Enjoying the pleasantly cool weather? It's all right to stare at the amazing sights you are about to see. Keep a sharp lookout for Sunset Crater, the last volcano to erupt in Arizona. You can't miss Humphreys Peak. See how it towers above everything else? In winter the Snow Bowl will resound with the happy yells of skiers.

We're heading north now and dropping down to the desert. Suddenly you see a long wide crack in the flat land. "Is that the Grand Canyon?" you ask excitedly. Yes, that's the world's most famous natural wonder. Takes your breath away, doesn't it? Notice how the view keeps changing. The light and shadows are dancing around on the colored canyon walls. Awesome!

The wind carries us across the canyon to the North Rim and over the Kaibab National Forest with its shady pines, firs, and quivering aspens. Take a glance at the buffalo herd on the House Rock Valley Ranch and those graceful deer in the meadow.

It's been an exciting ride, but it's time to land and drive home. Now, as you travel through the pages of this book, you will get an even better picture of the places and people of Arizona.

Physical Arizona

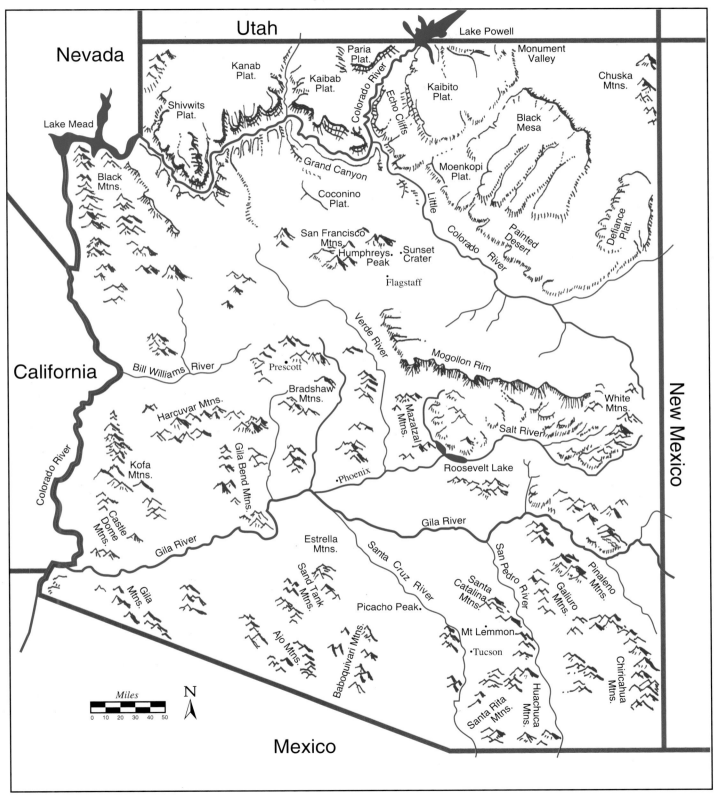

Nevada

Utah

Lake Powell

Paria Plat.

Kanab Plat.

Kaibab Plat.

Colorado River

Echo Cliffs

Kaibito Plat.

Monument Valley

Chuska Mtns.

Shivwits Plat.

Lake Mead

Black Mesa

Black Mtns.

Grand Canyon

Moenkopi Plat.

Coconino Plat.

Little

Colorado River

Painted Desert

Defiance Plat.

San Francisco Mtns.

Humphreys Peak

Sunset Crater

Flagstaff

California

Bill Williams River

Prescott

Verde River

Mogollon Rim

White Mtns.

New Mexico

Bradshaw Mtns.

Harcuvar Mtns.

Mazatzal Mtns.

Salt River

Kofa Mtns.

Gila Bend Mtns.

Phoenix

Roosevelt Lake

Colorado River

Castle Dome Mtns.

Gila River

Gila River

Gila River

Estrella Mtns.

Santa Cruz River

San Pedro River

Pinaleno Mtns.

Gila Mtns.

Sand Tank Mtns.

Santa Catalina Mtns.

Galiuro Mtns.

Picacho Peak

Mt Lemmon

Ajo Mtns.

Baboquivari Mtns.

Tucson

Chiricahua Mtns.

Santa Rita Mtns.

Huachuca Mtns.

Miles

0 10 20 30 40 50

N

Mexico

A Changing Land

ARIZONA'S LAND HAS NOT always been like it is today. Scientists say that for millions of years our region was under water except for a couple of small islands. The seas were teeming with animal life. Tiny shelled animals, larger clams, crabs, and fish that looked like sharks lived in the water and left their shells and bones behind. Gradually, dry land formed. The flooding and drying out of the land happened over and over again.

The sand and other *sediment* from the seas later turned into the rock layers of sandstone, shale, and limestone that you see today. Coal, formed deep under the ground from the remains of swamp plants, lay hidden for millions of years. As the earth's crust shifted and cracked, openings in the surface, called faults, occurred. Sea water deposited minerals such as copper and gold in the cracks of rock.

In other places, streams often flooded and uprooted trees. Huge logs were washed downstream and buried under thousands of feet of silt. The trees had no chance to decay as dissolved minerals in the groundwater seeped into the trunks, filling the wood cells with minerals that hardened into stone. The logs were petrified for all time.

Geologists **are scientists who learn about the earth's history by studying rocks and land formations.**

Nothing in nature changes Arizona's land quite as much as running water. It cuts through earth and rock to make canyons, carries sediment and deposits it in other areas, sometimes floods land, and makes for spectacular scenery. The photo shows Grand Falls, on the Little Colorado River.
(Photo by Tom Till)

Mountains and Plateaus Were Formed

Pressure from inside the earth and the weight of adjoining land regions pushed up mountain ranges and plateaus. Immediately wind and water erosion began to cut down into the mountains and plateaus, giving Arizona its present look. Rain swept tons of soil from the Mogollon Mountains to the lowlands, carrying uranium to what is now the Navajo Indian Reservation. Volcanoes erupted, building up high peaks and spreading lava over the land.

Prehistoric Animals

Even before the mountains and plateaus were formed, many kinds of *prehistoric* animals roamed our land. Dinosaurs were huge reptiles that once walked through the swamps in northern Arizona. The diplodocus and the brontosaurus were the largest dinosaurs. Those plant eaters had long necks and very small brains. In a fight, the plant eaters were no match for the larger meat-eating tyrannosaurus. That beast could stand on its hind legs. It was able to bite and claw the huge, clumsy plant eaters to death.

For reasons that scientists don't agree on, the dinosaurs all died and have never lived on the earth again. Their bones and tracks, however, are still being discovered. Today, tracks of a three-toed dinosaur can be seen on the Hopi Indian Reservation.

The inland seas disappeared along with the dinosaurs. As time passed, new forms of life appeared. New plants, freshwater fish, birds, and mammals moved over the land.

Fossils

Fossils are formed when minerals interchange with the organic (living) matter of a plant or animal after it has died, turning it into rock. Crab-like trilobites, shellfish, a fish that resembled a shark, and other sealife have been found in limestone at the Grand Canyon. They were fossilized when Arizona was under water.

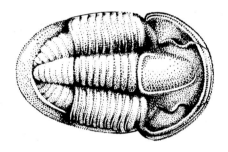

trilobite

Tyrannosors were rare in the Southwest.

ammonite

Giant Camels

Camels lived in North America, their place of origin, for millions of years. Though small in size at first, geologists have found fossilized bones of giant camels at Keams Canyon on the Navajo Reservation, in the San Pedro Valley, and near Wickiup. Why do you think camels became extinct in North America?

Keams Canyon •

• Wickiup

San Pedro Valley •

The Ice Age

Four times during the last million years a huge glacier covered most of North America. The glaciers never reached as far south as the land we now call Arizona, but they affected the weather here. Temperatures got colder and more rain fell. There was plenty of lush green vegetation for wild animals to eat.

The dinosaurs had disappeared and mammals then populated our region. Camels and antelopes ate tall grass in the Prescott area. Miniature horses galloped over the plateau north of Payson. Large bison, ground sloths, and tapirs lived all over North America. Huge mammoths were still here when the first people came. We know the people hunted mammoths for food because mammoth bones have been found with arrow points stuck in them.

Saber-toothed tiger   Camel   Bison   Mammoth   Sloth

Geography and History

GEOGRAPHY IS THE STUDY of the earth and its mountains, plateaus, valleys, deserts, rivers, and lakes. It is also the study of where and how people and animals live on the earth. What is Arizona's land like? Where do the people live, and why? How does our environment help us meet our needs for food, clothing, shelter, transportation, energy, jobs, and even our need for beauty and peace of mind? That is the study of Arizona's geography.

History is an account of what has happened in the past. How do the features of a place affect people and events? Why did people come here? What were their lives like? How did they help make Arizona what it is today? These are some of the questions geographers and historians try to answer.

Location: Where in the World is Arizona?

THE GRAND CANYON, the desert, cowboys, Indians, Wyatt Earp, Barry Goldwater, western movies—these are some of the images that many foreigners and even other people in the United States have of Arizona.

What would the foreigners say if asked to locate Arizona? A person in South America likely would call Arizonans *Norte Americanos*, meaning those who live on the continent of North America. Outsiders living anywhere would probably agree that Arizona is a state in the western part of the United States. Some people might say that Arizona borders Mexico, or that the Colorado River forms our boundary with California. Maybe a surveyor would pinpoint our northern boundary

Arizona's Place in the World

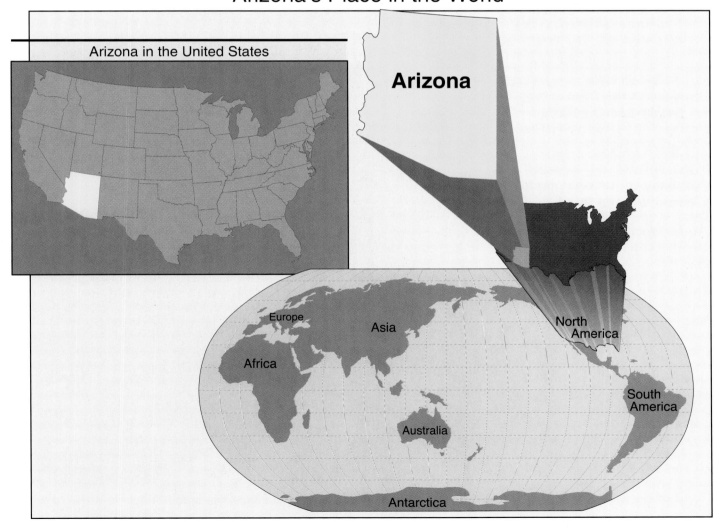

Arizona in the United States

Arizona

Europe
Asia
Africa
North America
Australia
South America
Antarctica

Edward Abbey, environmentalist and author, had a way of discouraging people from moving here. He wanted the place to himself:

"Ninety percent of my state is an appalling burnt-out wasteland, a hideous Sahara oasis, a grim, bleak, harsh sun-blasted inferno. Arizona is the native haunt of the scorpion, . . . the sidewinder, the tarantula, the vampire bat, . . . the centipede and three species of poisonous lizards: the Gila Monster, the land speculator, and the real estate broker. . . . In Arizona the trees have thorns and the bushes spines . . . I am describing a place I love. Arizona is my natural native home. Nobody in his right mind would want to live here."

with Utah at 37 degrees north latitude.

All of these descriptions tell us something about Arizona's location. From the various answers we see that location can be **absolute**—exact as to latitude and longitude, or it can be **relative** to another place—north of Mexico or west of New Mexico, for example.

Place: What Kind of a Place is Arizona?

ALL LOCATIONS ON earth have physical features that make them different from other places. The physical features of a place include things that are natural to the environment such as mountains, deserts, soil, plant and animal life, and bodies of water. Climate is another natural feature of a place.

Human characteristics are also part of a place. Pioneers built adobe and log homes and log fences for their cattle. They dug irrigation ditches to bring water to their farms. Today, small reservoirs, huge man-made lakes, freeways, tall city buildings, and homes in subdivisions are examples of human characteristics.

Many of Arizona's newcomers are ambitious, educated young people looking for jobs in high-tech manufacturing or other professions. Arizona is also a place where thousands of older people from other places retire. Retirement cities with names like Sun City, Green Valley, Leisure World, and Sun Lakes have sprung up here. Both the young and the old help make Arizona the kind of place it is.

Human characteristics such as cities help define a place. This is downtown Tucson, with the Catalina Mountains in the background. (Photo by Ric Nielson)

Climate

One characteristic of a place is its climate. Climate is the general pattern of weather over a long period of time. Arizona has a wide variety of climates. The main reason is the big difference in *elevation* from place to place. In general, the higher the elevation, the cooler the temperature. More rain falls on the mountains than on the low desert and this also affects the temperature.

This state has some of the hottest and coldest temperatures in the United States. In the White Mountains the thermometer can drop to 40 degrees below zero in the winter. Desert towns along the Colorado River have summer heat records soaring over 120 degrees.

The good news for desert dwellers is that summer nights in places away from big cities can be cool. The bad news is that nights are getting hotter in urban areas. Houses, high-rise buildings, and concrete shopping centers absorb heat during the day. At night they radiate the heat that doesn't escape into the atmosphere as it should. Instead, the heat waves hit the "pollution dome" that hovers over the big cities. The heat bounces back to the ground.

Dry and sunny most of the year, Arizona also has two rainy seasons. During the winter, winds bring moisture from the Pacific Ocean. These rains often take the form of a slow drizzle that lasts for several days. The moisture soaks into the soil with little runoff.

Late summer is the thunderstorm or "monsoon" season. Winds bring moist air from the Gulf of Mexico. Lots of thunder and lightning are common. A cloudburst may drop several inches of rain in a few minutes. Roads and rivers are flooded. Sometimes drivers who don't use caution have to be rescued by helicopter.

Snow falls mainly at altitudes above 4,500 feet. The surprise snowstorm that gave Tucson, at a low 2,389 feet, a white Christmas in 1987 was a rarity. Because of the warm temperatures, any snow at this level usually melts as soon as it hits the ground. The average annual snowfall in Flagstaff, at a very high altitude of 6,903 feet, is 97 inches, or about 8 feet.

Highs and Lows

- Highest point: Humphreys Peak near Flagstaff (12,633 feet)
- Lowest point: South of Yuma (138 feet)
- High elevations: cooler and wetter
- Low elevations: hotter and drier

Cooler temperatures and more moisture are found in the higher mountain elevations. Early spring snow fell at Oak Creek, Coconino National Forest.

(Photo by Tom Till)

Hotter temperatures and less moisture are characteristics of the lower desert elevations. The giant saguaro lifts its arms to the desert sun.
(Photo by Maryella Cundick)

A mature saguaro may be 150 years old and is about thirty-five feet tall.

Hedgehog cactuses bloom in the spring.
(Photo by Maryella Cundick)

Evergreen junipers were important to the American Indian people, who used them for strong fence posts. Nuts from the pinyon are prized by the Navajos.

A Dry Land

One word describes much of Arizona—dry. Water has long been precious here. "What the Indians worship most is water," wrote a Spanish diarist more than 400 years ago. "They say it makes the corn grow and sustains life." Today the Hopi people perform snake dances to bring the rain.

A Hopi Prayer
by Harrison Conrad

Rain! Rain!
For the growing grain,
For the high white mesa, the pale wide plain!
For the gods that fly
For the clouds in the sky
Child of the Snake Woman, run with our cry! . . .
Then the Gods will know
That the wind should blow
The black clouds up from far below, . . .
Rain! Rain!
For the dying plain:
For the sad, pale melon, the squash, and the grain!

Plant Life

AT LEAST 3,500 SPECIES of plants grow in Arizona. The plant life is as varied as the climate and elevation. The ponderosa pine is a beautiful and useful tree. Lumber sawed from this tree is soft but durable. The ponderosa grows best at high elevations. At lower elevations with less rainfall grow juniper, pinyon, and a variety of scrub oaks and brush thickets known as *chaparral*.

Grasslands are found at still lower elevations. The largest solid grass areas are in Cochise County. Geronimo once said that during his warrior days he could easily hide in the tall grasses. Short grasses and sagebrush grow in the higher deserts of northern Arizona.

In the Sonoran Desert many unusual plants survive with very little water. Desert cacti come in all shapes and sizes. The giant saguaro survives on water stored in its large fluted columns during rainy seasons. It grows slowly. In fact, the white saguaro blossoms, the official state flower of Arizona, do not appear until the cactus is close to eight feet tall and nearly sixty years old. It is like a condominium for the Gila woodpecker, elf owl, and other birds.

The thorny mesquite tree has been both useful and a nuisance. Pioneers used mesquite wood for roof timbers, fence posts, and firewood. After cattle overgrazed the ranges in the 1880s, mesquite began

The palo verde is the state tree of Arizona. It grows in the higher levels of the desert. In the spring the palo verde bursts forth with clumps of yellow blossoms. (Photo by Thomas Wiewandt)

to take over. Its roots took in so much water that the grasses couldn't survive. In recent years, however, the mesquite has become a popular tree for desert landscaping in cities.

In the spring, after ample winter rainfall, desert wildflowers may burst forth in a dazzling display of beauty. The blooms of golden Mexican poppies, blue lupine, purple owlclover, and many other flowers adorn the desert for only a few weeks. But, while the spectacle lasts, people come from hundreds of miles away to photograph, paint, or just enjoy the desert's moment of glory.

Arizona's State Symbols

Flower: saguaro blossom
Tree: palo verde

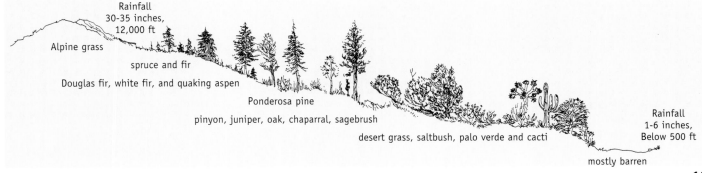

Rainfall 30-35 inches, 12,000 ft
Alpine grass
spruce and fir
Douglas fir, white fir, and quaking aspen
Ponderosa pine
pinyon, juniper, oak, chaparral, sagebrush
desert grass, saltbush, palo verde and cacti
Rainfall 1-6 inches, Below 500 ft
mostly barren

Natural Arizona

Arizona's Wildlife

There are no grizzlies left in Arizona but black bears are plentiful in the high country. Other big game animals are the elk, pronghorn antelope, mule deer, white-tailed deer, javalina, bighorn sheep, mountain lion, and buffalo. Buffalo are kept on two ranches managed by the Arizona Game and Fish Department. Preserving buffalo in Arizona seems fitting—they roamed the Grand Canyon area thousands of years ago.

The coyote, whose name means "barking dog," is the most adaptable animal in the state. Coyotes live anywhere—on the desert, in high pine country, or at the edges of cities. They hunt smaller animals at night and will eat insects, plants, and garbage. They sometimes kill sheep or calves. Ranchers and the government have tried to *exterminate* them, but coyotes continue to multiply.

The Wily Coyote

Of wild animals the coyote is the smartest of all.
He has thrived against odds with his back to the wall.
His cousin, the wolf, has near been dispersed,
But the coyote lives on while shot at and cursed.

—from an old ballad

Reptiles

Arizona has a wide assortment of snakes, lizards, turtles, and other reptiles. The only poisonous snakes are the rattlesnake and the coral snake. The diamond-backed rattler has caused the most human deaths.

The slow-moving Gila monster is the only poisonous lizard in the United States. Its skin looks like a pattern of black and yellowish beads. The Gila monster minds its own business if left alone. It is protected by state law. Another large lizard, the chuckwalla, hides by wedging its body in a crevice and inflating it with air. Indians, who enjoyed the chuckwalla's tender meat, used a pointed stick to puncture the lizard's hide and pry it loose.

Which of the animals pictured here is no longer found in Arizona?

In 1906, Charles Jesse "Buffalo" Jones brought a herd of buffalo to House Rock Valley north of the Grand Canyon. Jones hoped to interbreed the buffalo with domestic cattle, but his "cattalo" experiment failed.

Bighorn Sheep
(Photo by Gil Kenny)

Javalina with babies

Desert Tortoise
(Photo by Lynn Chamberlain)

Gila Monster Bites Rancher

The best-known victim of a Gila monster bite was Walter Vail. He and his partners owned the huge Empire Ranch south of Tucson. In 1890 Vail was on a spring roundup. One morning he killed a Gila monster, or thought he did, and tied it on the back of his saddle. He wanted to show it to a friend who had never seen one.

Back at the roundup camp, Vail dismounted, grabbing both ends of the saddle as he got down. The monster, still alive, clamped its strong jaws on one of Vail's fingers and began slowly chewing venom into the flesh.

"Take a stick and pry its mouth open," Vail shouted to the cowboys. They did just that.

Feeling weak from the terrible pain and swelling in his hand, Vail caught a train at the telegraph station for the ride to Tucson. There, Dr. John C. Handy cleaned and *cauterized* the wound and prescribed a remedy to make Vail sweat. Vail recovered from the bite.

This Gila Monster lives in the desert near the Superstition Mountains.

Birds

Arizona's birds range in size from the small hummingbird to the Merriam wild turkey. The turkey is listed as a big game species in Arizona. Other popular game birds are quail and doves. The "coo kuk coo cooah" sound of the dove is very pleasant. The long-tailed roadrunner is Arizona's most comical bird. It would rather run than fly, and sometimes races cars along the roadside. Unlike most birds, the roadrunner eats lizards and snakes.

This poem was written by Sharlot M. Hall, a pioneer poet and historian in Prescott.

Fishing is a popular outdoor sport in Arizona. About sixty species of fish inhabit the well-stocked lakes and streams, though the Arizona trout is the only native game fish. Fishermen catch bass (bigmouth, striped, and smallmouth), rainbow trout, catfish, crappie, bluegill, and others.

Roadrunner

Out of the western chaparral where the raw, new highways run,
He flashes swift as a rainbow flame and races the morning sun.
He perks and preens with lifted crest, he dances, heel and toe.
He will jig and flirt in the roadway dirt, then—off like a shot he'll go.

Roadrunner

Regions: They Don't Stop at State Lines

AREGION CAN BE A PART OF one state or include several states. Physical regions, such as the Colorado Plateau and the Sonoran Desert, have nothing to do with state boundaries. They have to do with types of land.

Arizona has three large land regions. They are the high Plateau Region, the central Mountain Region, and the low Desert Region. Each region is made up of one main kind of landform. Although each region has contrasts in scenery, certain things (such as high pine-covered mountains) can be found in all three regions.

Landforms of Arizona

Mountain

Plateau

Desert

PLATEAUS ARE HIGH, wide, flat landforms that often end with steep cliffs. They look like tables or wide steps many miles across. Sometimes they are called "table lands." Wind and water often cut deep canyons or strange shapes into plateaus.

Mountains are very high land formations. A long line of mountains is a mountain range. They are very important for our water supply because melting winter snow fills up mountain lakes and reservoirs. The water eventually joins streams and rivers that run down to the valleys. Most of our forests are in the Mountain Region.

Deserts are low, relatively flat areas of land that are usually surrounded by mountains or plateaus. Arizona's largest cities are in the flat Desert Region, next to mountains or plateaus.

Regions and Landforms of Arizona

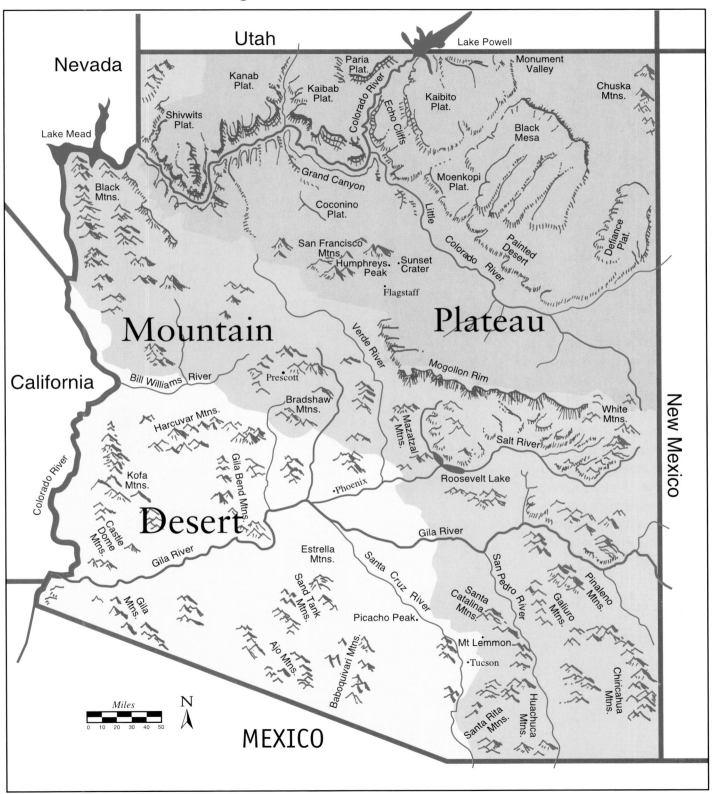

Nevada

Utah

Lake Powell

California

New Mexico

MEXICO

Mountain

Plateau

Desert

Lake Mead

Black Mtns.

Shivwits Plat.

Kanab Plat.

Kaibab Plat.

Paria Plat.

Colorado River

Echo Cliffs

Kaibito Plat.

Monument Valley

Chuska Mtns.

Black Mesa

Moenkopi Plat.

Grand Canyon

Coconino Plat.

San Francisco Mtns.

Humphreys Peak

Sunset Crater

Flagstaff

Little Colorado River

Painted Desert

Defiance Plat.

Verde River

Mogollon Rim

White Mtns.

Bill Williams River

Prescott

Bradshaw Mtns.

Harcuvar Mtns.

Kofa Mtns.

Gila Bend Mtns.

Mazatzal Mtns.

Salt River

Roosevelt Lake

Phoenix

Colorado River

Castle Dome Mtns.

Gila River

Gila Mtns.

Gila River

Estrella Mtns.

Sand Tank Mtns.

Ajo Mtns.

Santa Cruz River

Picacho Peak

Baboquivari Mtns.

Gila River

San Pedro River

Santa Catalina Mtns.

Galiuro Mtns.

Pinaleno Mtns.

Mt Lemmon

Tucson

Santa Rita Mtns.

Huachuca Mtns.

Chiricahua Mtns.

Miles

0 10 20 30 40 50

N

Plateau Region

The Plateau Region

The Plateau Region is part of the vast Colorado Plateau that was uplifted 30 million years ago. In general, the plateau is fairly level. But there are mountains, especially the San Francisco Peaks near Flagstaff, that rise above the plateau. The Colorado and Little Colorado Rivers have cut great canyons through the plateau. The Mogollon Rim, a steep rock cliff about 200 miles long, marks part of the plateau's southern edge.

Lumbering, cattle ranching, sheep raising, tourism, and the Santa Fe Railroad are important industries in the Plateau Region. Flagstaff, the chief city, depends on all these ways of making a living. It is also a trade center and the home of Northern Arizona University.

Tourists from all over the world come to see the plateau's natural wonders. The Grand Canyon, Sunset Crater, Meteor Crater, the Petrified Forest, and Monument Valley are the most famous.

"Whenever I am away from Arizona, I miss the sense of vast space and distance, the cumulus clouds floating across the bluest of skies, the presence of a horizon, and the dry desert winds. All these things remind me how great is our universe and how small we are — that self-reliance is important in this enormous world of ours."

—Justice Sandra Day O'Connor
United States Supreme Court

Flash floods occur during summer thunderstorms in Monument Valley.
(Photo by Tom Till)

ARIZONA: A Journey of Discovery

A Wild Car Ride in a 1907 Reo

George H. Smalley, a former editor of the *Tucson Citizen*, longed to see the Tonto Natural Bridge:

With five-gallon cans of gasoline strapped to the running board of my two-cylinder Reo, extra lengths of chain, and stacks of inner tubes, we started our hazardous journey . . .

There was a steep grade from the Mogollon Plateau down to the Natural Bridge . . . my oil-soaked brakes failed. Faster and faster the car sped, bouncing perilously about the curves in the mountain road. The top of the car was down and I had no windshield.

Ethel in the rear seat cried 'Bank it! Bank it!' I suddenly saw a slide of gravel ahead near a curve. . . . I shot the car up the slide . . . and when it started to slide back I let down the chug [brake bar]. The sharp steel end of the bar dug into the ground a few feet from the rim of Dead Man's Canyon.

Thankful to be alive, we all clasped hands and silently walked down the road where a farmer stood. 'Where can I find the Natural Bridge?' I asked.

With a proud sweep of his hand, he replied, 'You are standing on it!' My Reo was the first auto to reach the Natural Bridge.

Kanab Point, North Rim,
Grand Canyon National Park
(Photo by Tom Till)

The Grand Canyon

Arizona's Grand Canyon is the world's most famous natural wonder. The Grand Canyon is the best place to study the geologic history of the earth. Why? For about 12 million years the Colorado River has been cutting this gigantic gorge deeper and deeper. At the bottom of the canyon, scientists have found fossils of sea life and the first organisms that lived on the earth. Higher up, the multi-colored layers of stone reveal many changes in the earth since its beginning.

The Hualapai Indians have a tale that tells how the canyon came into being. They say that ages ago there was a flood that covered the earth. Water was everywhere, and there was no place for it to drain away. So Packithaawi, a legendary hero, "struck his knife deep into the water-covered ground, and there the great canyon was soon formed."

One of the greatest geological exhibits on Earth, the Grand Canyon is listed as one of the seven natural wonders of the world.

The Colorado River that flows through the Grand Canyon is red, or brick-colored, because of the heavy **silt** carried in the water. When the Spanish missionary Father Garcés saw the river, he called it the Río Colorado or Red River. It has been called the Colorado ever since.

Havasupai is the name of a small group of Native Americans who have made the canyon their home for more than 800 years. They take their name from the Havasu Creek. Havasu Creek is a beautiful turquoise color. It gets this color from limestone in the water.

Is it any wonder that Arizona is called the Grand Canyon State? The marvelous canyon is the landmark that helps the world remember the location of Arizona.

Meteor Crater

Ever wonder if a falling meteorite could bang into our planet? That's exactly what happened thousands of years ago. A giant meteorite crashed to Earth, creating a hole in solid rock almost a mile across.

Astronauts trained at Meteor Crater, as the hole was called, to prepare for walking on the moon in the 1960s. Meteor Crater is the best-preserved impact crater on Earth.

The Petrified Forest

The Petrified Forest east of Holbrook is a popular sight. The trees were hardened into stone millions of years ago when much of Arizona was under water. Uprooted trees were covered with silt before they could decay. Mineral water filled the tree cells and turned them into stone.

The plateau region has many natural phenomena that don't exist in very many other places in the world. Meteor Crater and the Petrified Forest are two fascinating places.

Recipe for Petrified Wood

"How can wood turn into stone?" If you have a pan big enough and lots of time, here is the formula of Reg Manning, Arizona's Pulitzer Prize-winning cartoonist:

Take a tree and immerse it in water. Stir gently till it becomes waterlogged and sinks to the bottom of the pan. Stir in generous quantities of silica, manganese, aluminum, copper, lithium, and carbon. And, for coloring, add iron as desired.

Now pour in a layer of sediment about 3,000 feet deep and allow the mixture to settle for a million years, drain off the water—you can't rush this.

Set out to dry in strong breezes. When the wind has blown away the 3,000 foot layer, you will find that the minerals have soaked into the tree, replacing the cell structure of wood with stone.

You'll be sure to get your money back if it doesn't work.

Petrified Forest National Park (Photo by Tom Till)

The Mountain Region

The Mountain Region has about thirty ranges separated by broad valleys. Called "sky islands," the highest peaks are covered with pine trees and other plants that thrive in a high, moist environment. Mount Graham is the highest peak in the Mountain Region. At 10,713 feet, this mountain towers above the town of Safford in the Gila Valley. Capped by a spruce-fir forest and Riggs Lake, Mount Graham is the home of endangered red squirrels. Two large telescopes are located on the mountain for astronomical research.

Mount Lemmon, close to Tucson, is a popular place to hike, fish, or just cool off in the summer. A snowy ski slope draws visitors to the mountain in the winter.

Mountain Region

The White Mountains are a great place to play in the snow.

The Gila River and its main branch, the Salt River, have cut deep channels through the mountains. The rivers roared out of the mountain canyons and fanned out over the desert plain. Today the water is stored in reservoirs and lakes behind dams on the Gila, Salt, and Verde Rivers.

Mining has provided many jobs for people in the Mountain Region. Bisbee, Clifton, Morenci, Globe, Miami, Jerome, and Bagdad are some of the towns that grew up near copper mines in the high country.

Ranching is also important. Arizona's best grazing lands are in the Mountain Region.

The Desert Region

The Desert Region has broad, level valleys bordered by mountains. The soil is deep and fertile. Only *irrigation* water is needed to convert the dry desert valleys into lush farms.

Mountains in the Desert Region are lower than in other parts of the state. They rise sharply above the desert floor and appear to be partially buried. In fact, they are. For millions of years, loose soil on the mountainsides has been washed down into the valleys. Picacho Peak, the main landmark between Phoenix and Tucson, is a good example.

The Tucson Mountains west of Tucson are famous for a dense forest of saguaro cacti. Tourists also visit two attractions located in these desert mountains. One is the Arizona-Sonora Desert Museum, which features living exhibits of desert wildlife and plants. The other is Old Tucson, where many western movies and television shows have been made.

The Desert Region bursts with color in the spring.
(Photo by Maryella Cundick)

The highest mountain in the Desert Region is Baboquivari Peak. The Tohono O'odham (Papago) people consider this peak the center of the world.

Desert Region

ARIZONA: A Journey of Discovery

Many Hispanic Americans live in the Southwest region. They find it easy to maintain close cultural ties with Mexico. After all, the "old country" is next door, not across the ocean. Most Hispanic immigrants came from Mexico in the twentieth century.

Arizona's largest cities are in the Desert Region. The flat land is easier to build cities and roads on. This is downtown Phoenix at night. (Photo by Bob Rink)

More Than Just Physical Regions

A region is a place where there are common characteristics. For example, the Navajo Reservation is a cultural region. The Navajos have their language, customs, and race in common. The reservation is mainly in Arizona but includes parts of New Mexico and Utah.

Regions are easier to understand when we see that most state lines are artificial boundaries designated by people. In fact, the Colorado River is Arizona's only natural boundary.

Arizona is part of a larger region known as the Southwest. A mixed population is a common characteristic of the Southwest region. American Indians, Hispanics, and Anglos have lived in most parts of this region since early pioneer days, but people from all over the world live here now.

Arizona is a Sunbelt state. The Sunbelt is a region that stretches from Florida to California. The warmest part of the United States, the Sunbelt is growing fast. Migration from other states is the reason for the population explosion in this region.

Navajo Reservation

Movement: Arizona People Interact with the World

Sonoran Trade Zone

What about the region we call the Sonoran trade zone? People on both sides of the Mexican border have much in common. Besides the desert and climate, they have trade. Tourists and shoppers of both countries cross the border.

Tucson is a major shopping center for people from northern Mexico. *"Se habla español"* (Spanish is spoken) is a sign seen in many Tucson stores. Trade is a two-way street. Mexican farmers raise vegetables for sale on the Arizona market. More and more items made in Mexican factories are sold in American stores.

PEOPLE TRAVEL FROM PLACE to place, sharing their knowledge and ideas and trading goods. Long before Arizona became a state, American Indians here had contact with other people. Hohokam farmers made pottery. They traded some of their pottery with natives of Mexico and other Indian groups. In return they got copper bells, seashells, exotic birds, and other items. The Hohokam also traded ideas. They learned how to build adobe houses and how to play new games.

Even during pioneer times, there was a lot of trading in and out of Arizona. Beginning in the 1850s, miners shipped silver ore from mines in the Tubac area. Some ore went by wagon to the seaports of Mexico, where it was loaded on ships bound for San Francisco. Traders hauled in supplies to sell to Arizona miners and soldiers. Cattlemen drove herds of longhorn cattle from Texas. Tucson, with its mixture of Mexican and Anglo cultures, became the center of trade and **commerce**. Butterfield stagecoaches bounced across Arizona, mainly with passengers going to or from California.

The arrival of railroads in the 1880s was a milestone in Arizona's growth and prosperity. New towns sprang up along the railroads. The steel rails opened up Arizona for commerce with the rest of the world. With good transportation, copper mining prospered. The cattle and lumber industries also benefited. They could ship their products to distant markets.

Modern Transportation, Tourism, and World Trade

Through the years, modern transportation, tourism, and world trade came to Arizona. Today we have an elaborate highway network. People depend on automobiles and trucks for transportation. Air travel is another important means of transportation in this state. Two of the country's busiest airports are located in Phoenix and Tucson.

Tourism is the unsung hero of Arizona's industries. It pumps billions of dollars into the state's economy. Tourism provides more jobs than any other industry. Many hotels, restaurants, gasoline stations, airlines, and other businesses depend on tourists. The millions of tourists who visit Arizona each year include people on short vacations, winter visitors, business people, shoppers from Mexico, delegates to conventions, and local sightseers.

The products of Arizona's factories, mines, and farms are sold in Mexico, Canada, Japan, South Korea, the United Kingdom, and other countries all over the world. Our state government maintains trade offices in several foreign countries to promote sales.

Scientists at the Kitt Peak National Observatory gather information from space.
The information is shared with other scientists in many places around the world.
Photo by Gil Kenny

Arizona is no longer a rural state. Though farming and ranching are still very important, the trend is the movement of people to the cities. This is called *urbanization*.

Rapid Growth

Arizona grows and grows. Since the end of World War II, swarms of people have moved to Arizona. People are coming from all parts of the country and world. Most of the newcomers settle in or near the big cities of Phoenix and Tucson.

What do you think?

According to the 1990 U.S. census, Arizona had 33 people per square mile. In China during the same year there were about 319 people per square mile.

- If this is the only statistic a student in China had about Arizona, what conclusions might he or she reach regarding the population here? Do you think the conclusions would be accurate for the whole state?
- Why is Arizona an urban state instead of a rural state?   Explain.

Human-Environmental Interaction: People Use and Modify the Environment

The red squirrel is an endangered species, in part because people use its native habitat for other purposes.

NO SPOT ON EARTH is a perfect place to live. Most places have both advantages and disadvantages. Our great state is no exception.

Throughout history, people have adapted to and changed the environment around them. People have always cut down trees and grasses, gathered rocks, and dug up earth to build shelters. From the first

The construction of Roosevelt Dam in 1911 was a milestone in taming the Salt River. The reservoir behind Roosevelt Dam assured a steady water supply for irrigation farming and the growing population of Phoenix.

Lining the huge canals with cement helps conserve water. The canal is part of the CAP.

American Indian shelters to modern cities, people have interacted with the land to meet their needs. In the dry Southwest, irrigation and air conditioning are two important ways in which people have modified their natural environment.

Finding Enough Water

Ever wonder why so many cities are built near rivers? In choosing a place to live, people first settled near water. Many of the small communities grew into larger cities. Phoenix, once a small farming community along the Salt River, is now the largest urban area between Chicago and Los Angeles.

The control of water in the Salt River Valley has been called "the Phoenix miracle." During the great flood of 1891, water spread out eight miles wide in places. It washed out small dams, a railroad bridge, and homes. Later in the decade, a long drought forced farmers out of business. Families packed up and left, expecting settlements like Phoenix to become ghost towns. Now, however, huge concrete dams control the river's flow.

Groundwater, pumped from deep in the ground, provides about two-thirds of Arizona's water. Tucson and other areas of the state depend almost entirely on groundwater. However, it is being pumped faster than it can be replaced by rainfall and snow. Wells are drilled deeper and deeper to find the water.

Managing the Water

To keep on growing, Arizona must:
- conserve water
- prevent waste
- find new sources of water

The Central Arizona Project (CAP) is now bringing water from the Colorado River to Maricopa, Pinal, and Pima Counties. The CAP water is taken from Lake Havasu above Parker Dam. The water is lifted by pumps to a mountain tunnel. From the tunnel it flows through an *aqueduct* to central Arizona. Another aqueduct takes part of the water to the Tucson metropolitan area. Arizona's growth and progress in the future depend on an ample supply of good water.

Cooling the Air

Refrigerated air conditioners and *evaporative* coolers give the desert region a livable year-round indoor climate. People no longer have to head for the mountains or seashore to escape the hot summer weather. Air conditioning was first used in Phoenix and Tucson in the early 1930s to cool theaters and other commercial buildings. Today, modern air conditioners cool homes, automobiles, and public buildings.

What do you think?

More water must be conserved or imported if Arizona is to continue growing at the present rate.

- Why is conserving water important in a desert?
- Decide which water needs you think are the most important—agriculture, industry, or home use?
- Predict some ways our water problems might be solved in the future. Consider de-salted ocean water, desert landscaping, and water-conserving devices.

Providing Energy

Using our natural resources such as water, coal, gas, and oil to provide energy is one way we interact with our environment. For many years most of the energy came from two sources: electricity generated by water power at dams and natural gas piped in from Texas.

Large thermal electric generating plants have been built to supply the growing demand for electricity. In these generators, natural gas is burned to heat the water that provides steam to move the generators. But oil and natural gas are becoming scarce and costly. In the future, industries and homes may have to replace natural gas with other sources of energy. Nuclear energy is a possibility, but many people wonder if it is safe. At present, the Palo Verde Nuclear Power Plant west of Buckeye is the only one in the state.

Coal is used to power steam generators, but coal pollutes the air more than other forms of energy. Black Mesa coal on the Navajo Reservation is being used at the huge Navajo Generating Station near Page and at the Mohave Power Plant across the river from Bullhead City.

Gifts from the Ground

Getting and using minerals from the earth is one important way people interact with their environment. Gold and silver used to be mined here in large quantities that made some miners rich fast. Today, many people still work in our copper mines, producing not only copper but smaller amounts of gold and molybdenum. Other people work in the *smelters,* where the pure metal is separated from the ore.

The Glen Canyon Dam on the Colorado River controls flooding, provides water to Arizona and California, and produces electricity. The water backed up behind the dam forms Lake Powell on the Arizona-Utah border.

Coal mining is big business on the Navajo Reservation.

Test yourself!

See how much you remember and then use the information to analyze situations and solve problems.

Location

1. Describe the relative location of Arizona.
2. Describe the relative location of places in your community, such as a park, cemetery, school, or business district.
3. What is the exact location of your home?
4. What are some ways your location has affected your life?

Place

1. Describe your town as if to a stranger, telling what kind of place it is. Include key factors such as the land, climate, natural resources, ways to make a living, nearby scenic attractions, entertainment, and education opportunities. Include the people and how they live.
2. Describe some geographic factors that help explain why a particular business developed in your town or county.

Plants and Animals

1. Agriculture includes raising both plants and animals for food and profit. Which animals produce income for Arizona farmers and ranchers?
2. What are some of Arizona's main plant crops?
3. Many wild animals are found in Arizona. How many can you name?
4. What Arizona animals and plants are important in your life?

Regions

1. Name Arizona's three main land regions.
2. Which region do you live in?
3. What caused the formation of the mountain ranges and the Colorado Plateau?
4. List three natural wonders found in the Plateau Region.
5. Why do mountains in the Desert Region appear to be buried?

Climate

1. Name two factors that affect the climate of a region.
2. What is the difference between Arizona's winter and summer rains?
3. How is climate important to your life?

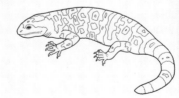

Movement

1. Name some things that move in and out of your town or your region.
2. Analyze how movement of things and ideas has affected your life.
3. Write a conclusion about how the movement of different kinds of people to and from your town has influenced the town.

Water, Minerals, and Energy

1. Name three sources of water the state uses.
2. What energy sources are used to produce electricity?
3. What minerals do we take from the ground?
4. What is copper used for?

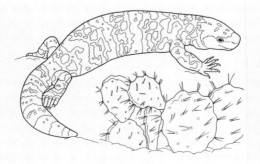

The Future

Try to imagine what Arizona or your town might be like in twenty years. Consider possible natural and human changes. Write a paragraph or be part of a discussion on "What would happen if . . . ?"

Physical and Political Arizona

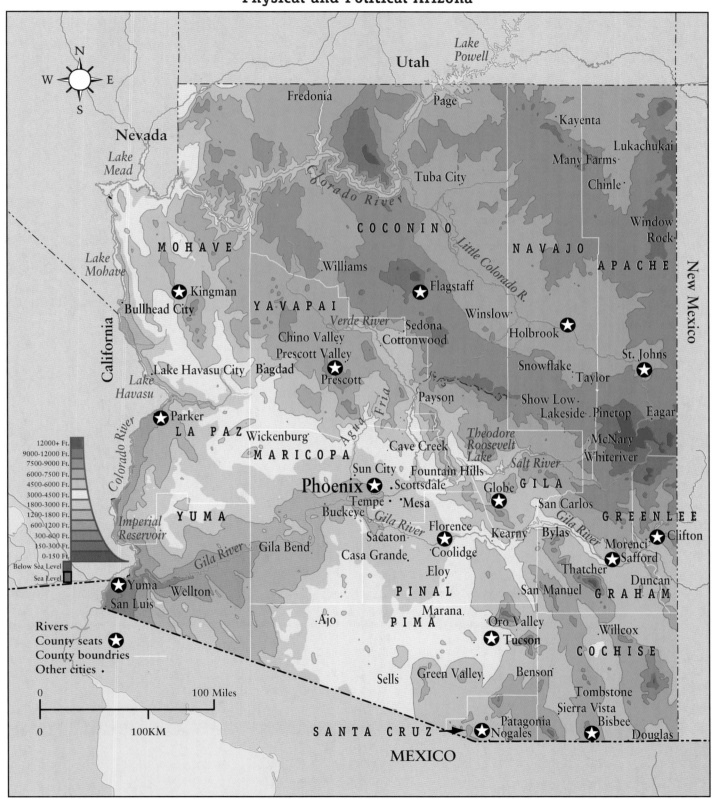

Utah

Lake Powell

Nevada

Lake Mead

Fredonia

Page

Kayenta

Lukachukai

Many Farms

Chinle

Tuba City

Colorado River

C O C O N I N O

N A V A J O

A P A C H E

Window Rock

California

Lake Mohave

M O H A V E

★ Kingman

Bullhead City

.Williams

Y A V A P A I

Verde River

Sedona

Cottonwood

★ Flagstaff

Little Colorado R.

Winslow

Holbrook

Snowflake

.Taylor

St. Johns ★

New Mexico

Chino Valley

Prescott Valley

Bagdad

★ Prescott

Payson

Agua Fria

Show Low

Lakeside .Pinetop

Eagar

Lake Havasu

Lake Havasu City

★ Parker

L A   P A Z

Wickenburg

Cave Creek

M A R I C O P A

Theodore Roosevelt Lake

Salt River

McNary

Whiteriver

Colorado River

Y U M A

Imperial Reservoir

Sun City

Fountain Hills

Phoenix ★ .Scottsdale

.Tempe . .Mesa

Buckeye

Gila River

Globe ★

G I L A

San Carlos

Gila River

G R E E N L E E

Morenci

Clifton ★

Sacaton

Florence

Casa Grande.

.Coolidge

Kearny

Bylas

★ Safford

Thatcher

Gila Bend

.Eloy

P I N A L

San Manuel

Duncan

G R A H A M

★ Yuma

San Luis

Wellton

.Ajo

Marana.

P I M A

Oro Valley

.Willcox

C O C H I S E

Rivers

County seats ★

County boundries

Other cities .

Sells

★ Tucson

Green Valley

Benson.

Tombstone

Sierra Vista

Bisbee

0 _____ 100 Miles

0 _____ 100KM

S A N T A   C R U Z →

Patagonia

.Nogales ★

Douglas

MEXICO

12000+ Ft.
9000-12000 Ft.
7500-9000 Ft.
6000-7500 Ft.
4500-6000 Ft.
3000-4500 Ft.
1800-3000 Ft.
1200-1800 Ft.
600-1200 Ft.
300-600 Ft.
150-300 Ft.
0-150 Ft.
Below Sea Level
Sea Level

THE TIME
12,000 B.C. – 2000 A.D.

PEOPLE TO KNOW
Archaic people
Hohokam
Anasazi
Mogollon
Sinagua
Patayan
Salado
Pima
Yuma
Hopi
Apache

PLACES TO LOCATE
Cochise County
Salt River Valley
Gila River Valley
Casa Grande ruins
Pueblo Grande ruins
Four Corners
Navajo National Monument
Point of Pines
Sunset Crater
Wupatki National Monument
Verde Valley
Montezuma Castle
Tuzigoot
Tonto National Monument
Oraibi

The First People

Prehistoric to Modern

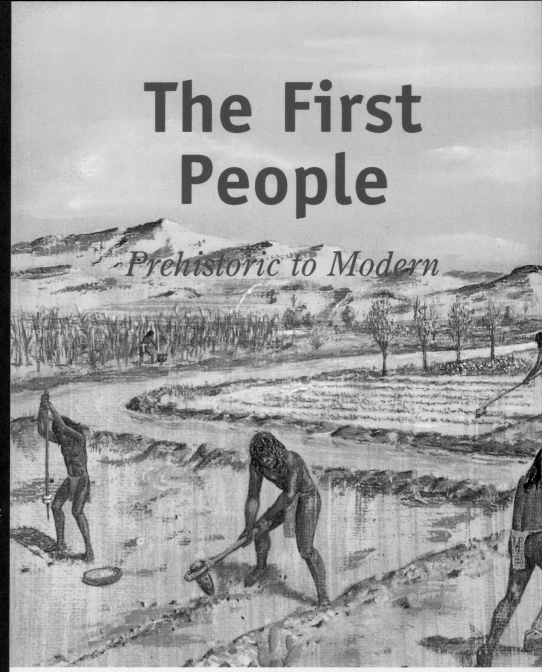

Prehistoric Hohokam canal builders are bringing water to their desert fields.

11,000 B.C.
Prehistoric people live all over
the American continent.

| 12,000 B.C. | 8000 B.C. | 4000 B.C. |

7000 B.C.
Archaic people live in
Arizona region.

chapter  2

TERMS TO UNDERSTAND
archaeologist
artifact
primary source
petroglyph
converge
vegetation
fluted
pit house
surveyor
terrace
etching
sentinel
excavate
domesticate
arable
communal
adobe
kiva
forage
firebrand

(Painting by Charles O. Kemper, Salt River Project)

A.D. **1065**
Volcano erupts (Sunset Crater)
and Sinagua people flee.

A.D. **1300**
Casa Grande is built by
the Hohokam. Anasazi
and Mogollon are gone.

| 0 | A.D. **500** | A.D. **1000** | A.D. **1500** | A.D. **2000** |

A.D. **1000** TO A.D. **1200**
Mogollon golden age of culture.

A.D. **1450**
Hohokam abandon Casa
Grande.

31

Archaeologists

SCIENTISTS WHO STUDY early people are called **archaeologists**. Archaeologists have learned much about the early people who lived in Arizona and surrounding regions. For example, we know that early American Indians ate animals because charred bones have been found at their campsites. Some left clay cooking pots as well as weapons and tools made of bone and stone. We know from burial sites how the groups buried their dead. These discoveries are **primary sources** of information.

Arizona's earliest inhabitants left numerous and interesting evidence of their existence—ruins, **artifacts**, and **petroglyphs**. Ruins are the remains of something destroyed or disintegrated. Artifacts are objects produced by humans, especially tools, weapons, pots, baskets, or ornaments. Petroglyphs are carvings or line drawings on rock made by prehistoric people.

Still, there are many things of which we have no evidence, or we don't know what the artifacts mean. For instance, archaeologists believe the earliest people did not have written languages because no books, newspapers, letters, or diaries have been found. We do, however, have beautiful rock art, but we don't know exactly what the paintings mean. A clay figurine or small twig deer, for example, could be a child's toy, a craft the people liked to make just for fun, or something much more important.

Archaeologists use the term "prehistoric" to refer to different groups of people who lived before any written records were made of them. We know of them only by the artifacts they left behind, and by oral legends. You can probably guess, then, that "historic" Indians are people about whom we do have written records. The records were written as diary accounts or reports by explorers or pioneers who observed the people, and, in later time periods, by the people themselves.

Early people made these deer out of twigs.

What do you think?

The first people in Arizona left no written records. How do we know about them? If studying artifacts is the only way to learn about the people, what information about their lives might we be missing? How important is being able to communicate by the written word?

An archaeologist carefully sweeps the dirt off an ancient pot at a Mogollon pueblo site in the Point of Pines area.

(Photo by Helga Teiwes)

Mammoth Hunt!

A T DAYBREAK A BAND of hunters discovers a small herd of mammoths on a sandbar in the river. Some of the animals are scooping up sand with their trunks and tossing it over their backs. The hunters slip quietly into the water and make their way to both ends of the sandbar. They begin yelling to frighten their prey. The mammoths, with trunks raised high in the air, squeal loudly. In panic, they head downstream, slipping and splashing until they see a place to scramble out of the water—all but one.

The hunters *converge* on the lone animal still lingering on the sandbar. They plunge at least eight stone-tipped spears into its right side and head. Other hunters cut the tendons in its hind legs. Wounded and unable to run, the mammoth topples with a heavy thump on the sand.

By this time the women, who were watching from the shore, arrive. They build a fire on the sandbar, anticipating a big feast of roasted meat.

A mammoth was trapped and killed by a group of hunters. (Art by Gary Rasmussen)

Linking the past and the present

Today it is against the law to take any artifacts from a site where ancient people once lived. It is also against the law to harm rock art or ruins.

Nomadic Hunters

NOMADIC HUNTERS WERE living in the Southwest at least 11,000 years ago, and probably much earlier. They were shorter than people today and had high cheekbones, straight black hair, and reddish-brown skin. The people were always on the move, searching for food. They ate what they found growing naturally and they also hunted large animals. They lived in temporary shelters or in caves and did not build permanent homes.

The first people found the Southwest region cooler and wetter than it is today. Land that is now desert was covered with dense *vegetation* and dotted with lakes and streams. Thick grass supported a variety of very large animals. The largest were the mammoths.

Mammoth hunters waited for the giant beast at a watering place. They worked together to kill it. Their wooden spears had a detachable *fluted* stone point. When the hunters removed the spears, the embedded points stayed in the body of the animal, mortally wounding it.

Mammoth hunters had to be brave and skilled. An enraged animal could pick a man up with its tusks and smash him against a rock or stomp him with its huge front legs.

Traces of ancient mammoth hunts are usually discovered accidentally. Two kill sites were revealed north of the Mexican border after floodwater eroded stream banks. At one of these sites, archaeologists from the University of Arizona unearthed bones from nine mammoths, a primitive horse, a bison, and a tapir (like a large pig with a pointed nose).

In a sandy bank near Naco, scientists uncovered the remains of a huge mammoth with eight stone spear points in its rib cage and head. The ashes from fires, probably built to roast the meat, enabled experts to date the killings at about 11,000 years ago.

> "To prehistoric people, a successful hunt meant food and survival. To a modern archaeologist, finding the same carcass provides fresh evidence and understanding of how people lived in this land long ago,"
>
> —Dr. Emil W. Haury,
> Archaeologist,
> University of Arizona

Mammoths were Ice Age animals. Many skeletons have been found in the Southwest.

Archaic People

The *metate* and *mano* were used for grinding seeds into flour.

THE ARCHAIC PERIOD is defined by archaeologists as the time between the disappearance of mammoth hunters and the emergence of the farming, pottery-making lifestyle. The climate gradually warmed as the Ice Age glaciers farther north melted. With less vegetation to browse, the mammoths disappeared from this area. People who came after the mammoth hunters had to adjust to an environment with fewer resources. They hunted smaller animals and gathered wild berries, grains, nuts, and roots.

The tools left by the people help us to understand their lifestyle. They made stones called *metates* and *manos* for grinding seeds into flour. They used stone scrapers for cleaning hides and shaping wood into spears. Their spear points were smaller than the ones used by the mammoth hunters. Many Archaic remains have been found along creek beds in Cochise County.

Recently, archaeologists uncovered seven Archaic villages along the Santa Cruz River in Tucson. The settlements had been buried by a blanket of sediment deposited by annual river floodwaters. From artifacts and plant remains uncovered at the villages, we know that the people planted and irrigated corn. Growing part of their food gave them more control over their food supply. They lived in **pit houses** near their crops, used the bow and arrow for hunting, and made pottery. Archaeologists now believe the Late Archaic Period should be called the Early Agricultural Period.

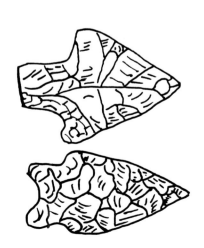

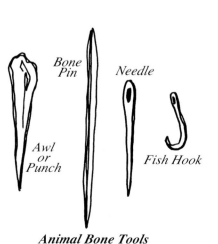

Bone Pin

Needle

Awl or Punch

Fish Hook

Animal Bone Tools

Later Prehistoric Groups

FOLLOWING THE ARCHAIC PEOPLE, three major Indian groups and other less famous cultures lived in the different land regions of what we now call Arizona. Exciting changes took place during the first 1400 years A.D. With improved varieties of corn from Mexico, Indian farmers produced a surplus of food. The people then had more leisure time to develop a more advanced lifestyle. Examples are permanent villages, the world's best canal irrigation system, spectacular cliff dwellings, and exquisite pottery.

Today, people in each of Arizona's geographic regions can be proud of at least one early Indian culture. The Hohokam occupied river valleys in the southern desert. The Anasazi settled on the high plateaus of the Four Corners region. The Mogollon lived in the mountains of eastern Arizona. Each group developed its own lifestyle and intermingled with the others.

Prehistoric Peoples

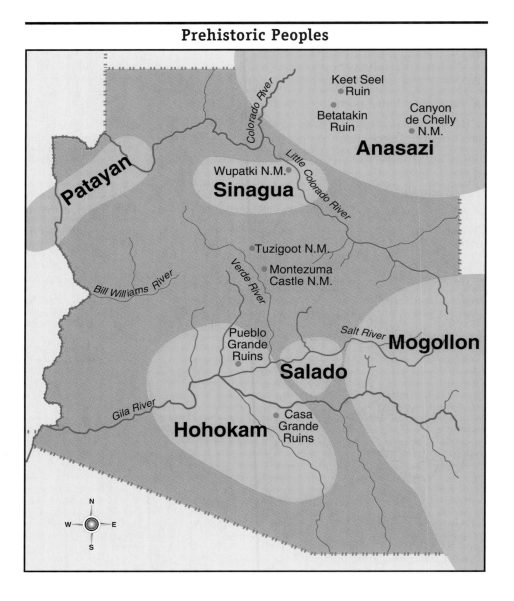

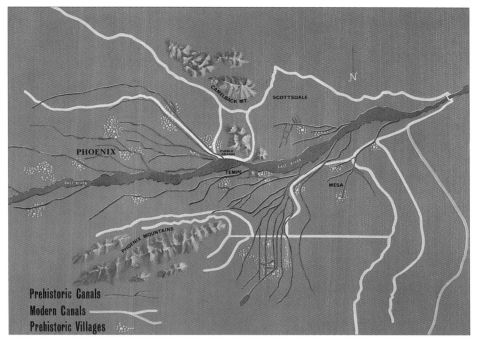

The map shows the location of ancient Hohokam canals and prehistoric villages, as well as modern Salt River Project canals in the Phoenix region. To water their fields, the Hohokam dug a system of canals on an incline so the water would run downhill. About 200 miles of these canals have been traced in the Phoenix area and nearly 100 miles around Florence. Some of the canals were fifteen feet deep.

The irrigation projects were a tremendous accomplishment for people who had no beasts of burden or machines. Modern engineers are amazed. When the present-day Grand Canal was built through Phoenix, the *surveyors* followed an old Hohokam ditch.

The Hohokam People

THE HOHOKAM PEOPLE BUILT a civilization in the desert that lasted many centuries. Scientists do not have the evidence yet to know where the Hohokam came from or where they went. Did they evolve from the Archaic people? Or did they come from Mexico, bringing their own tools, pottery, and skills with them? Are Hohokam people the ancestors of the modern Pimas and Tohono O'odham?

The Hohokam were a remarkable people. They were the first farmers to adapt successfully to life in the desert by using canal irrigation on a large scale. They also dammed *arroyos* (dry gullies) and spread rainwater over their fields. They **terraced** desert mountains near present-day Tucson so rainwater would go

The men dammed the canals when they wanted to flood farmland.

A Hohokam craft was **etching**. Designs, usually of an animal such as a toad, were etched on seashells. The technique was to make a design on a shell with pitch (gummy tar or sap from trees) and soak it in a weak acid solution. The unprotected part of the shell was eaten away by the acid, leaving the raised design. Then the pitch was removed.

Pottery from the Snaketown and Grewe sites shows the artistic skill of the people. (Photo by Helga Teiwes)

Potters made jars and bowls, some with a thirty-gallon capacity. Some experts consider Hohokam ceramic work the best in Arizona at that time.

Petroglyphs from the Hohokam people can be seen in the southern desert of Saguaro National Monument near Tucson. (Photo by Tom Till)

into the ground and not run off so quickly.

The Hohokam built irrigation projects in the Salt, Gila, and other river valleys. The water enabled them to grow corn to supplement a diet of mesquite beans, cactus fruit, deer, lizard, and rabbit meat. The Hohokam also cleared desert land to grow *agave* (a GAH vee) and other useful plants that don't require irrigation. They also grew cotton.

Permanent Villages

Irrigation farming made it possible for the Hohokam to have the food they needed without the constant travel of earlier groups. They built permanent villages.

In later centuries, the Hohokam built some multi-storied apartment houses. Snaketown was the largest Hohokam village. Ruins of the four-story Casa Grande (Big House), as well as the Pueblo Grande in east Phoenix, can be seen today.

Casa Grande's thick walls, made of cement-like desert soil, are forty feet high. Built about A.D. 1300, Casa Grande was America's first skyscraper. The top floors served as a watchtower. A *sentinel* there could see outsiders approaching and warn field workers by smoke signal. Casa Grande was occupied until A.D. 1450, when the Hohokam mysteriously abandoned it and the surrounding farmlands.

The Hohokam built pit houses by digging the shape of the home into the ground. Then they built a sturdy frame of logs and branches to form outside walls. Finally, the whole structure was covered with earth. The earth served as insulation from the outside temperatures. The pit homes were cool in summer and warm in winter. With no windows, however, the house was dark. Jobs such as pottery making, weaving, and corn grinding were done outdoors under a *ramada* (a pole-and-brush roof that gave shelter from the sun).

Where Did They Go?

Hohokam is a Pima word meaning "those who have vanished," and they did. Why did the Hohokam leave Casa Grande? No one knows, but there are many theories. The farmland may have eventually become waterlogged as constant irrigation caused the underground water table to rise. Centuries of cultivation probably resulted in poor soil. Maybe floods were the last straw. On occasion, flooded rivers washed out the brush, rock, and dirt dams, making farming impossible for several years. Maybe the Hohokam wanted to be forgotten. They cremated their dead and smashed their beautiful pottery, statues, and ornaments.

The Hohokam people played ball in a court *excavated* about five feet below ground level. The object of the game was to get a rubber ball through twisted grass rings fastened on the sides of the court. The large number of ball courts found throughout Hohokam villages indicate that the games were an important part of the people's social life.

Whatever the reasons for their departure from Casa Grande, the Hohokam likely remained in the desert country. Many archaeologists believe they are ancestors of the modern Pima and Tohono O'odham Indians.

Linking the past and the present

Is there a lesson in the Hohokam culture for our generation? They survived in a harsh desert environment for at least 1,200 years. Considering our current problems—water shortage, shrinking open spaces, city growth, and air pollution—will future generations be able to survive in the desert?

The Anasazi

THE ANASAZI CAME TO the Four Corners region about 2000 years ago. Thanks to archaeologists, we know about their lifestyle and even what they looked like. The Anasazi were short, slender, long-headed, and broad-nosed. The men often wore a bob of hair on each temple and a braid down the back. Sometimes the top of the head was shaved to give a bald or wide part effect. The women had a reason for wearing a shorter hairdo than the men. They cut their hair two or three inches from the scalp and used it to make ropes.

At one time the Anasazi started the practice of flattening the rear portion of the skull by strapping babies tightly against hard cradle boards. The baby's soft skull was flattened, which made the head broader.

The Anasazi excelled in arts and crafts, especially as basket makers. They used yucca fibers to make baskets for storage and other purposes. They also wove cloth from strips of fur or cotton.

Anasazi rock art and underground kiva murals tell us that religion was an important part of daily life.

Food and Homes

The Anasazi hunted, gathered wild foods, and farmed crops of corn, squash, and beans. They also *domesticated* (raised at home) turkeys. Before the bow and arrow came into use, hunters used an *atlatl*. This weapon was a notched stick with which a spear could be hurled with great force.

In earlier times, Anasazi homes were round pit houses, three-to-five feet deep with a cone-shaped roof. On one side of the one-room house there was always a small hole in the stone slab or dirt floor. This hole was a symbol for the mythical place where the first people emerged from the underground.

Anasazi culture flourished during a long period of peace and prosperity

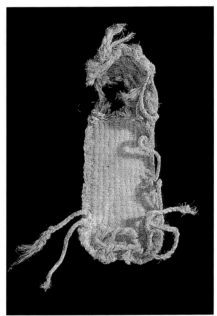

An Anasazi sandal was woven from yucca fibers.

Eventually the Anasazi learned to make pottery. Their style was usually a black design on a white or gray pot. The pots were used for storing and cooking food.

During the later periods, the people moved to higher, more protected ground. They built homes of stone and adobe in the openings of cliffs.

The remains of ancient shelters can still be seen on the shores of Lake Powell. (Photo by Tom Till)

prosperity (A.D. 700 to 1200). The population grew. Large families were an advantage because children could help tend the crops. The people traded pottery for turquoise, obsidian to make arrowheads, and even bracelets of shells made by the Hohokam. Villages were built wherever there was *arable* land and a water source nearby.

In the thirteenth century, drought and hard times led to wars with other groups. For protection against raids, the people moved higher up the valleys and canyons. They built large *communal* dwellings in caves high up from the valley floor. They collected ever-scarce water in hillside reservoirs. Farming was done on the top of the plateaus or down in the valleys below the cliffs. Despite the efforts to provide and store food, at one time there must have been an extended food shortage because skeletal remains show the results of malnutrition and early childhood deaths.

The impressive cliff pueblos of Betatakin and Keet Seel were built at that time. Occupied only briefly, they can be seen today at the Navajo National Monument. The cliff dwellings in Canyon de Chelly National Monument were also Anasazi defensive strongholds.

The Anasazi abandoned these great cliff pueblos in the last years of the thirteenth century. A severe twenty-three-year drought, worn-out soils, and wars probably caused their departure from northeastern Arizona. But later generations of Anasazi returned to this area. The Hopis can trace their ancestry back to the Anasazi.

Pueblos

Pueblos are communal dwellings. The small rooms are made of stone or *adobe*, with logs supporting the flat roofs. The apartments are built on top of each other several stories high, with ladders giving access to the top apartments. The flat roofs often provided gathering and working places for the people, somewhat like our patios today. Pueblos were built on flat ground or high up in the side of a cliff.

The Mogollon

THE MOGOLLON (muggy YONE) improved the culture of their Archaic ancestors. They lived in the mountains. To survive, the Mogollon hunted wild game and gathered berries, nuts, seeds, and roots in season. They did not rely on agriculture as much as the Hohokam and Anasazi. Yet the round-headed, medium-built Mogollon grew a good variety of corn which they got from Mexican Indians.

The Mogollon people lived in villages. A typical community had fewer than twenty pit houses. These houses, built on the side of a mountain that had the most rainfall, were entered down a ramp on the east side. A large ceremonial and religious *kiva* was in the central part of the village. All the people in a village belonged to a clan that consisted of families with a common ancestry.

A plate made by Mogollon people shows a man spearing a very large fish. The size of the fish may have been to emphasize its importance.

Archaeologists have dug up several Mogollon villages, including Point of Pines on the San Carlos Apache Reservation. The material goods uncovered at these sites were not very advanced. The Mogollon used *metates* to grind corn. They tilled the soil with thin slabs of rock. After the year 700 they wove cloth from cotton fiber supplied by the Hohokam. They learned to build stone and adobe houses from the Anasazi.

The Mogollon "golden age" of borrowed culture was from A.D. 1000 to A.D. 1200. During that time the people excelled at putting designs on their pottery. The pictures give us a glimpse of their lifestyle. The scenes show men picking bugs from corn plants, setting snares to catch birds, killing a deer with a bow and arrow, and dancing. The men were shown wearing a breechcloth. Women wore a fringed sash, sandals, and sometimes a blanket.

The practice of burying the dead under house floors began during this period. In some places the Mogollon left beautiful bowls and other pottery in the graves. Many of these objects had a hole punched in them to release either the spirit of the owner or of the potter who made it.

The Mogollon abandoned their mountain villages in Arizona and New Mexico around A.D. 1200. No one knows why they left, but archaeologists believe that they migrated to Chihuahua in present-day Mexico. Traces of Mogollon culture began appearing there about the time they left the mountain villages. No modern tribe in Arizona is descended from the Mogollon.

ARIZONA: A Journey of Discovery

A painting at the Wupatki National Monument shows how a Sinagua pueblo and nearby ball court might have looked.

The Sinagua, Patayan, and Salado

The Sinagua

IN 1065 A VOLCANO, now known as Sunset Crater, erupted near present-day Flagstaff. Streams of lava flowed down, leaving about 800 square miles covered with black ashes. The air filled with choking smoke and ash. The sky grew dark as the ashes and smoke blocked the sun. The Sinagua people were terrified and fled from their homes.

For 500 years the Sinagua had lived in the area in peace and prosperity. They were dry farmers who depended on rainfall, not irrigation, to water crops. Their homes were timber pit houses covered with grass or bark and banked over with dirt for protection against the cold winter weather.

The First People

Eventually the Sinagua drifted back. They were soon joined by other Indians bringing new skills. Visitors today can see the remains of Wupatki, a multi-room pueblo that shows Anasazi influence, and a Hohokam-type ball court nearby.

In the thirteenth century, the Sinagua deserted Wupatki and their other pueblos in the Flagstaff area. A long dry spell had turned their farms into a dust bowl. Many of the Sinagua moved south to the Verde Valley. There they adopted the Hohokam system of irrigation and built stone pueblos.

Tuzigoot, on a hilltop near present-day Clarkdale, was one population center. At one time, about fifty families of mixed cultures lived there. Montezuma Castle, another stone apartment house, was built in a cliff cave overlooking the Verde River. The Castle, misnamed centuries later by Anglo settlers who thought it was built by the Aztecs of Mexico, is still an imposing cliff house. Forty or fifty people lived there and worked in irrigated fields along the river. They also hunted, gathered wild foods, wove cloth, mined salt, and fired a finely-polished red pottery.

The Patayan

The Patayan farmed along the banks of the Colorado River. During flood season they went to the desert to hunt and to *forage* for edible plants. After the flood they returned to their fields and planted crops in the rich silt deposited by the river.

Most of the remains of the Patayan civilization were washed away or covered up by floodwaters. We do know that they made a simple gray-brown pottery. Shells for jewelry came from the Gulf of California. Patayan houses were usually made of tree trunks lashed together.

The Salado

The Salado people are remembered for their beautiful pottery and pueblos. Several of the Salado cliff houses can be seen at the Tonto National Monument near Roosevelt Dam. These pueblos were built for safety, not convenience. The nearest spring was half a mile away. Their cultivated fields on the Salt River flood plain were up to four miles from the cliffs. The Salado felt threatened by Anasazi invaders who were leaving their plateau homeland because of drought.

In one respect, the Salado were like the Hohokam, Anasazi, Mogollon, Sinagua, and Patayan. They all match the worldwide pattern of the rise and fall of ancient societies. Their achievements have been dimmed by time, but what we know about them has given drama to Arizona's past.

Modern tribes (Yuma, Cocopah, Maricopa, Mohave) and the three "pai" tribes (Walapai, Yavapai, and Havasupai) are descendants of the Patayan people.

Montezuma Castle National Monument in the Verde River Valley is a remnant of the Sinagua culture from the 1200s.
(Photo by Tom Till)

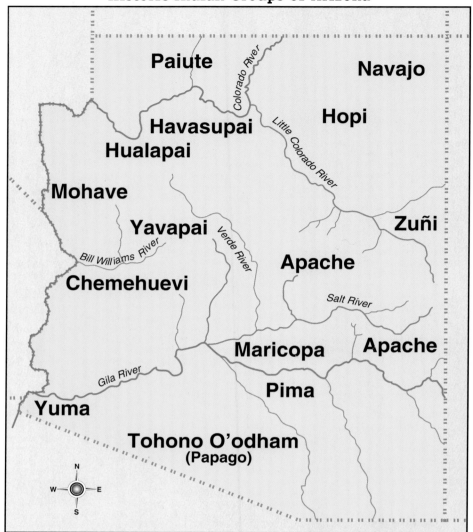

"The fields of wheat are so large one cannot see the ends because they are so long," wrote Colonel Anza after a visit to the Pima villages on the Gila River in 1776. What else happened in our country in 1776?

When Columbus landed in the Americas, he thought he was in a part of the world called East India. So he called the people he met "*los Indios*." Today, we call these people American Indians, or Native Americans, because they were here first. In their languages, they usually called themselves a name that meant "the people."

Historic Indian Groups of Arizona

The Pimas

TODAY, THE PIMA PEOPLE call themselves "O'odham" which simply means "people." The River Pimas were flood plain farmers. They relied on flooding river water to irrigate their crops. The Pimas also hunted and gathered wild plants.

Wheat, first brought to Arizona by Father Kino, was the principal crop harvested in the summer. But the Pimas also planted maize (corn), using only a pointed stick to make a hole in the ground for the seed. For cloth, the Indians planted cotton. They also raised sheep and sheared wool for spinning and weaving. Chickens, another Spanish contribution, were kept in the Pima villages.

Physically, the Pimas were described as dark, robust, and sometimes fat. The men wore cotton breeches and twisted their long hair into a crest-like crown held in place by a woolen cord. Pima women covered themselves with cloth or deer-skin. They wore their hair long in back, with bangs at eyebrow level in front.

The Tohono O'odham are Pima relatives. In winter they gathered wild foods and hunted. In summer they dammed *arroyos* to spread rainwater on crops of maize, beans, and squash.

The Yumas

Unlike the Pimas, the Yumas did not irrigate farmland. They waited for floods to recede each year. Then they planted crops of wheat, maize, beans, calabashes, and muskmelons in the rich soil deposited along the banks of a river. Ripe melons were buried in the sand for cooling and were available almost all year.

Yuma men daubed their bodies with red and black paint and kept warm in cool weather by carrying *firebrands*. The women wore skirts made of cottonwood or willows and went barefoot like the men.

The Spaniards sought the goodwill of the Yumas because they controlled a crossing place on the Colorado River.

The Hopis

Today's Hopis can trace their ancestry back to the Anasazi. For centuries they have lived on the same mesas of the Colorado Plateau. The name Hopi means "peaceful people" but the Hopis have not always been at peace. In fact, they built their villages high on the mesas for protection from other Indian peoples.

The Hopis did not like the Spanish explorers and missionaries. They tore down Spanish missions and drove out or killed the priests. One reason for the Hopi anger was smallpox—a white man's disease. The disease reduced the tribe's population from 14,000 to about 900 by the late 1700s.

The Hopis are united today by their cultural traditions. They have many spiritual ceremonies. Some parts of their ceremonies are held in underground kivas. Outsiders cannot go into the kivas, but some parts are done in the village plazas. Visitors can watch the ceremonial dances there.

The Snake Dance is popular with tourists. To the Hopis, however, it is a serious and sacred rain dance. They believe that the gods who make things grow live underground. Snakes are caught and brought to

A Pima village is shown in this drawing.
(Sketch by J. Ross Browne)

Hopi women of the twentieth century sell their pottery.

Oraibi, a Hopi pueblo, is the oldest continuously occupied settlement in the United States. This photo was taken in 1920.

the kiva. On the morning of the dance the snakes are sprinkled with sacred water. As each snake priest passes the kiva, he is given a snake. He holds the snake in his mouth and goes on dancing. The snakes are then put in a circle on the plaza. The women and girls put sacred meal on them. Then the snakes are turned loose. The priests talk to the snakes. "Go back to the gods," they say. "Tell them the Hopis are good and need rain."

The Apaches

The Spaniards classified the Apaches of Arizona and New Mexico into five principal tribes. Three of these were in Arizona—the Chiricahuas, Gileños, and Tontos. The tribes lived in bands of related families. Each band had a leader, or a chief. When the Spaniards came to the Southwest in the 1500s, the Apaches were living in the mountains.

The Apaches were physically healthy, strong, and untiring. They could walk for miles, day after day. They were constantly moving in search of deer, antelope, and smaller animals to hunt. They also collected wild foods and knew where the water holes were. The Apaches had a new source of food when the Spanish settlers brought in cattle, sheep, and horses. The Indians could then survive by hit-and-run raids; they drove off the livestock and plundered the settlements.

Like other native groups, the Apaches did not like outsiders coming onto their land. They fought the Spaniards, the Mexicans, and the settlers who later came from the United States. When chased, the Apaches sometimes lured their pursuers into ambush. More often, they fled swiftly across rugged mountains or deserts to a secluded camp.

You will read more about the Apaches in later chapters.

When the Apaches stayed in one place for a while, they lived in wickiups. The huts were made of strong branches covered with brush.

ARIZONA: A Journey of Discovery

1. How long have people been living in Arizona? Describe what this area was like when the first people arrived.

2. In what ways was the lifestyle of the Archaic people different from their mammoth-hunting ancestors?

3. List some ways the Hohokam used the scarce water supply.

4. The Hohokam may have been ancestors of which modern Indian tribes?

5. What kind of homes did the Hohokam build? What were the advantages of these homes?

6. Where did the Anasazi live? What kinds of crafts did they make?

7. Explain why the Anasazi built cliff houses and give two examples of these homes.

8. What modern tribe is descended from the Anasazi?

9. Who was in a Mogollon clan? List three things that Mogollon pottery designs tell us about their daily life.

10. Why did the Sinagua people move away from the Flagstaff region in the first place?

11. How did the Patayan make a living? Why don't we know more about them?

12. Where can Salado cliff houses be seen today?

13. How did the Pimas get food? What crops did they plant?

14. Where did the Yumas plant their crops? What important place did the Yumas control?

15. Which modern Indian group has a name that means "peaceful people?"

16. What is the oldest continuously occupied settlement in the United States? Which group lives there today?

17. Describe the lifestyle of the Apaches.

A Zuni village in the early 1900s shows interaction between the Zuni and white settlers.

chapter 3

THE TIME
1492–1821

PEOPLE TO KNOW
Cabeza de Vaca
Estevan
Fray Marcos de Niza
Francisco Coronado
Alarcón
Cárdenas
Espejo
Governor Oñate
Father Kino
Fray Garcés
Juan Bautista de Anza
Chief Palma
Captain Pedro de Allande

PLACES TO LOCATE
San Pedro Valley
Cíbola
Colorado River
Gulf of California
Zuñi villages
Hopi villages
Grand Canyon
Jerome
Pimería Alta
Oraibi
San Francisco, California
Bac
Tumacácori
Yuma Crossing

"The Anza colonizing expedition stopped at Tubac for a while in October, 1775."

1492
Columbus lands in the islands close to what is now Florida.

1536
Cabeza de Vaca arrives in Mexico.

1500   **1550**   **1600**

1540
The Coronado expedition gets underway.

chapter 3
Part of the Spanish Empire

Glory, Gold, and God

TERMS TO UNDERSTAND
empire
expedition
Moor
viceroy
reverence
martyr
convert
apostle
mission
presidio
ideal
musing
controversial
colonizing
pious
guerrilla
symbolic
foray
riotous

(Painting by Cal Peters at Tumacácori National Historical Monument)

1700
Padre Kino establishes mission of San Xavier del Bac.

1751
Pimas rebel against the Spaniards.

1781
Yumas rise in rebellion. The Yuma Massacre

1797
Mission San Xavier del Bac, the "White Dove of the Desert," is dedicated at San Xavier.

1650 — 1700 — 1750 — 1800 — 1850

1776
Fray Garcés is at the Hopi village of Oraibi.
Yuma Chief Palma is baptized in Mexico City.
Juan Bautista de Anza reaches San Francisco Bay.
Tucson is started as a fort.

1790 – 1821
Golden Age of Spanish Rule (Era of Peace)

Searching for Riches

SPAIN WAS THE FIRST European nation to send explorers to the Americas. Nearly thirty years after Columbus's first voyage in 1492, Hernán Cortés conquered the Aztec capital now known as Mexico City. Eventually, gold and silver from Mexico and Peru were shipped to Spain, making Spain the wealthiest nation in Europe.

During the 1500s, Spanish explorers laid claim to a vast *empire* called New Spain. The land we know as Arizona was part of that empire. The explorers who crisscrossed Arizona were looking for gold, but they found none. They did, however, partially map this region and keep written records about the geography and the native peoples, whom they called "Indians."

After the explorers, Catholic priests came as missionaries. For nearly 300 years, the missionaries were about the only contact the native people had with the Spanish culture.

Cabeza de Vaca

Cabeza de Vaca had a great influence on Arizona history even though he probably never came here. In 1536 he and three weary companions arrived in Mexico. They had just completed one of the most remarkable journeys in all of history—most of it through country never before seen by Europeans. De Vaca and his companions were survivors of a large Spanish *expedition* driven out of Florida by Indians eight years earlier.

> **"They stood staring at me . . . so confounded that they neither hailed me nor drew near to make an inquiry."**
>
> —Cabeza de Vaca, upon coming out of the wilderness into Mexico City. He eventually sailed back to Spain.

Cabeza de Vaca and three companions started out from Spain with five ships and 500 people, including Estevan. Eight years later they limped, almost starved, into Mexico City.

Only a few of the 242 men who left Florida in crude log boats survived a gulf storm, disease, and enslavement by other Indians on the coast of Texas. Cabeza de Vaca, one of the survivors, had won fame as a medicine man and was given freedom to visit other tribes.

Eventually, de Vaca met three other survivors, including a *Moor* named Estevan. Followed for a while by crowds of natives wanting medical care, the ragged, long-haired, half-starved men slowly made their way from Texas to Mexico City. They came close enough to New Mexico and Arizona to hear rumors of rich cities to the north.

The Adventures of Estevan

In Mexico City, a government official, Viceroy Mendoza, interviewed Cabeza de Vaca and his companions and was impressed by their fantastic stories of the Seven Cities of Cíbola, which were supposed to be cities of gold. The *viceroy* decided to check out the rumors with a small scouting party. Fray Marcos de Niza, a Catholic priest, was selected to head the group, with Estevan as his guide.

Estevan, probably the first non-Indian to touch Arizona soil, scouted ahead of Fray Marcos. He couldn't read or write, so a simple system of communication was devised. The plan was to send an Indian messenger back with a cross—the larger the cross, the more important the land.

Estevan was a tall man, and made quite a showman. In some Indian villages he acted the part of a medicine man—a role that Cabeza de Vaca had taught him. He shook a gourd filled with pebbles and adorned himself with red and white feathers. Bells jangled on his ankles and elbows. The native people treated Estevan with awe and respect.

When Estevan got to a Zuñi village, however, things changed. The Zuñis were not impressed by Estevan's claims to be a man who could perform magical cures. Normally peaceful, the angry Zuñis filled Estevan's body with arrows and sent his escorts hurrying to tell Fray Marcos that Estevan had been killed.

In spite of the tragedy, Fray Marcos later claimed that he went ahead to view the village from a safe distance and erected a wooden cross on a hill. He took for granted that the Zuñi pueblo was one of the Seven Cities of Cíbola. After a hasty retreat to Mexico City, he reported to Viceroy Mendoza.

Stretching his imagination, Fray Marcos told the viceroy about a city larger than Mexico City, with buildings ten stories high. He said the Indians decorated their doors with turquoise, used much gold and silver, and wore giant pearls, gold beads, and emeralds. Strangely enough, Fray Marcos actually may have believed that these fantastic stories were true.

Estevan walked into a Zuñi village of present-day New Mexico with two greyhounds.

"Fray" is another word for a Catholic "father," or priest.

Defenders of a Zuñi village lost the battle with Coronado's army. The survivors abandoned their pueblo.

Coronado traveled from Mexico,
searching for gold.
(from a mural by Charles B. Wilson)

Francisco Coronado

Francisco Coronado was a typical Spanish adventurer. A younger son in a family of nobles, Coronado came to Mexico at age twenty-five. Within a few years he married a wealthy heiress, rose fast in the viceroy's favor, and was chosen to head an expedition to Cíbola.

Coronado easily recruited men to go with him. Lured by possible riches and glory, men of all walks of life clamored to join. Some 225 young *caballeros* (horsemen) were selected. That day in 1540 must have been a glorious time for them. They assembled at the coastal town of Compostela and paraded before Viceroy Mendoza. The next day they moved out, followed by sixty foot soldiers carrying swords, long pikes, and shields. A thousand Indian allies armed with native weapons were next in line of march. Then came herdsmen with thousands of cattle, sheep, and goats that would insure a food supply on the journey. Fray Marcos de Niza reluctantly agreed to go along as the guide.

Coronado, with 100 men, traveled ahead through heat and dust to a pueblo ruin in present-day Graham County. Fray Marcos had been wrong in his praises of the pueblo and was now questioned on another point. He had reported that a sea could be seen from there. Actually, the Gulf of California was ten days away. Coronado was disappointed. He had planned on getting supplies from three ships sent up the gulf by Viceroy Mendoza.

The commander of the ships, Captain Hernando de Alarcón, had anchored them at the mouth of the Colorado River and gone upstream with twenty men in small boats. There he talked to Yuma Indians, with help from an interpreter, and presented them with gifts. Failing to make contact with Coronado, Alarcón returned to Mexico. He had made history as the first European to sail the Colorado River and to see the native people near present-day Yuma.

Meanwhile, Coronado, short of supplies, led his army into the rugged mountains of eastern Arizona. After about five months of travel through the desert lands of the Southwest, the exhausted and half-starved treasure-seekers arrived at the mud-and-stone pueblo of Hawikuh. What a shock it was! They were at the end of the rainbow and there was no gold.

To make matters worse, several hundred Zuñi warriors met the Spaniards at the edge of town. They drew lines on the ground with sacred cornmeal and ordered the Spaniards not to cross. The warriors also made threatening gestures with their war clubs and bows and arrows. They showed no fear of the weary armored soldiers and strange horses. The situation was tense. When the Zuñis tried to kill Coronado's interpreter, peace was out of the question.

With swords flashing in the sunlight, the Spaniards attacked. Hunger drove them on. During the battle, Coronado, in gilded armor, was a special target. Twice he was knocked off his horse by rocks hurled from atop the pueblo. He also received an arrow wound in the leg.

In less than an hour the Zuñis were forced to abandon the pueblo, leaving their food supplies. The famished soldiers gorged themselves—it was their first good meal in weeks. Even the long-sought gold and silver would have been less welcome at that moment.

Coronado discovered no gold, no silver, and no jewels. But he continued to search, not catching on to an Indian trick. The Indians had gotten rid of the Spaniards by telling them of riches to be found somewhere else.

He didn't find gold, but from Coronado's expeditions later generations gained a knowledge of southwestern geography and a description of the native peoples.

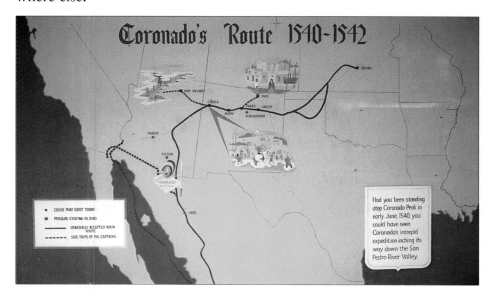

The Great River and the Grand Canyon

Two side expeditions were important in the history of Arizona. First, Coronado sent a small company of soldiers to the Hopi mesa-top villages. The Hopis gave the men cotton cloth, cornmeal, and pine nuts. The Hopis also told about a great river and people farther west who had great wealth.

Coronado was excited. He was curious to find out if the "great river" was the mythical Strait of Anian—a waterway that was supposed to connect the Atlantic and Pacific Oceans. To find out, Coronado sent his toughest officer, Captain López de Cárdenas, with twenty-five horsemen. The Hopis furnished them with guides and provisions.

Traveling over the plateau of northern Arizona, the Hopi guides led Cárdenas to the rim of the Grand Canyon. To the Spaniards, the stream at the bottom looked no more than six feet wide. They were surprised when the guides said it was a wide river. Cárdenas and his escort were the first Europeans to see the canyon. Unable to get to the bottom, they returned to the Hopi village.

After one more unsuccessful trek all the way to present-day Kansas, Coronado led his tattered army back to Mexico City. Coronado was denounced as a failure. He had found no golden cities. He had given up much of his fortune, two years of his young life, and his health. His report was so discouraging that forty years passed before another white man entered Arizona.

Captain Cárdenas was led by Hopi guides to the Grand Canyon. He was not interested in natural wonders, however. He was after gold.
(Painting by Maynard Dixon)

Espejo discovered silver in Arizona thirty-seven years before the Pilgrims landed at Plymouth Rock. Some modern geologists think that Espejo stumbled on the site of the modern-day United Verde copper mine near Jerome. Hundreds of years later, the mine eventually produced a billion dollars worth of copper, silver, and gold—enough for the king of Spain to have conquered the world.

Antonio de Espejo

De Espejo was the first Spanish explorer to enter Arizona by way of the Rio Grande. Espejo, a well-to-do man from Mexico, took the risk of leading a small expedition on horseback in search of precious metals. With only four soldiers and some Indian guides, he reached the Verde Valley and discovered rich silver ore in the vicinity of present-day Jerome.

"Eureka! It is a mine of great richness. We will take possession," Espejo shouted in Spanish. "In the name of God and King, make ready. Fire!" Flame and smoke belched from their guns. The hostile Indians who had followed the Spaniards scattered like quail.

Espejo was enthusiastic about his discovery and took ore specimens back to Mexico. But he realized the impossibility of cashing in on ore that was still in the ground in such a remote location.

Juan de Oñate

Governor Juan de Oñate of New Mexico traveled more within the present boundaries of Arizona than any previous explorer. A wealthy man, Oñate established the New Mexico colony in 1598 at his own expense. He then turned to exploration, making two treks into Arizona. He was accompanied by soldiers and a Catholic priest, who kept a diary of the trip.

One attraction was Espejo's mines. Oñate led an exploring party as far as the Hopi villages. Because of severe winter weather, he stopped and made camp, but sent a group of men ahead to look for the mines. They located some rich silver ore near present-day Prescott. But Oñate never got around to developing any of the mines.

Later, Oñate crossed northern Arizona and followed the Colorado River to the Gulf of California and back. His goal was to find the Pacific Ocean so traders could use the closest water route to China.

With Oñate's return to New Mexico, the first period of Arizona's exploration came to a close. Nothing was found to attract colonists. No gold. No pearls. No ocean. The explorers succeeded only in making the region known to Europeans.

The written records of Oñate's trip have some interesting tales. The Mohave described a tribe of one-legged people, other people who slept in trees, and people who slept under water. Supposedly, there were Indians along the Colorado River who lived only on the odor of food. No one believed the stories, of course.

Catholic Missionaries

GOLD-SEEKING EXPLORERS HURRIED through Arizona, claiming a vast area for the Spanish king. Well-educated Catholic priests traveled with them to map the new lands and to describe the native peoples in their diaries. In the 1600s the churchmen took on a bigger role as missionaries. The first religious *martyrs* to die on Arizona soil were Franciscans, who tried in vain to *convert* the Hopis to Christianity.

The Franciscans were one of two European missionary groups that sent priests to present-day Arizona. The black-robed Jesuits (Society of Jesus) worked mainly with the Pima Indians. In 1767, when the missions were in bad shape, the Spanish king expelled the Jesuits from "New Spain." Then the grey-robed Franciscans took over.

Father Kino

Father Eusebio Kino, the "*Apostle* to the Pimas," was Arizona's first successful missionary. By any comparison, Father Kino was one of the most important people in Arizona history. Priest, explorer, rancher, astronomer, map maker, and defender of the frontier—he was all of these.

The region in which Father Kino lived and worked was called Pimería Alta, or "land of the Upper Pimas." There was no United States at that time and no Arizona.

Father Kino realized that the Pimas would be more receptive to the Christian gospel if they were assured a regular food supply. He believed in the "Give us this day our daily bread" part of the Lord's Prayer. For that reason, he made each mission a complete community, teaching his

The Indian people had their own sacred rites, time-honored ways of obtaining food and shelter, and *reverence* for nature. The Spanish padres, with the best intentions, worked diligently to change the native lifestyle and ways of thinking.

Father Kino
1645–1711

Born in Italy, Father Kino was well educated. He was especially good at math and astronomy. As a young man he became a Jesuit priest and was sent to Mexico, then to the Sonora-Arizona region. He loved the Indian people and tried to understand their customs and ways. He wanted to make life better for them and brought them seeds and plants for new crops such as wheat and fruit trees. He brought in horses and thousands of cattle and taught the Indian people to rope and ride. Often called "The Padre on Horseback," for twenty-four years Father Kino rode thousands of miles, visiting different missions he had established.

A fellow padre described him: "If anyone showed him disrespect, he controlled his temper. . . . He prayed much . . . He neither smoked . . . nor took wine except to celebrate mass . . . He never had more than two coarse shirts because he gave everything to the Indians." After his death, Father Kino was buried in a church in the town of Magdalena south of Nogales.

Christian Indian converts the best methods of crop production. He brought in horses, mules, sheep, and cattle and started the stock-raising industry in Arizona.

Kino's Arizona *missions* were in the Santa Cruz Valley. He established the first at the Indian village of Bac, near present-day Tucson, and named it San Xavier del Bac. Farther south, he started Guevavi with a *visita* (a place where a visiting priest could stop and baptize converts) at Tumacácori.

Always on the go, Kino crossed the Colorado River to explore the Gulf Coast. He proved his theory that the blue abalone shells (used by the Yumas for cups and decoration) were brought overland from the Pacific Coast and that Lower California is a peninsula, not an island. His accurate map of Baja California and Pimería Alta was published in 1710.

One story shows the devotion of Father Kino to the Indian people he served. He was at Tumacácori mission saying Mass at sunrise when a messenger arrived to inform him that an Indian man had been sentenced to death by flogging for a minor crime. By nightfall, Father Kino had ridden sixty-two miles across the country. Early the next morning he rode the last eight miles. In his diary he wrote, "I arrived in time to say mass at San Ignacio, and we succeeded in rescuing the prisoner from death."

Father Kino was Arizona's first cattleman. He brought livestock to the Pimas.

Pimería Alta and the Early Missions

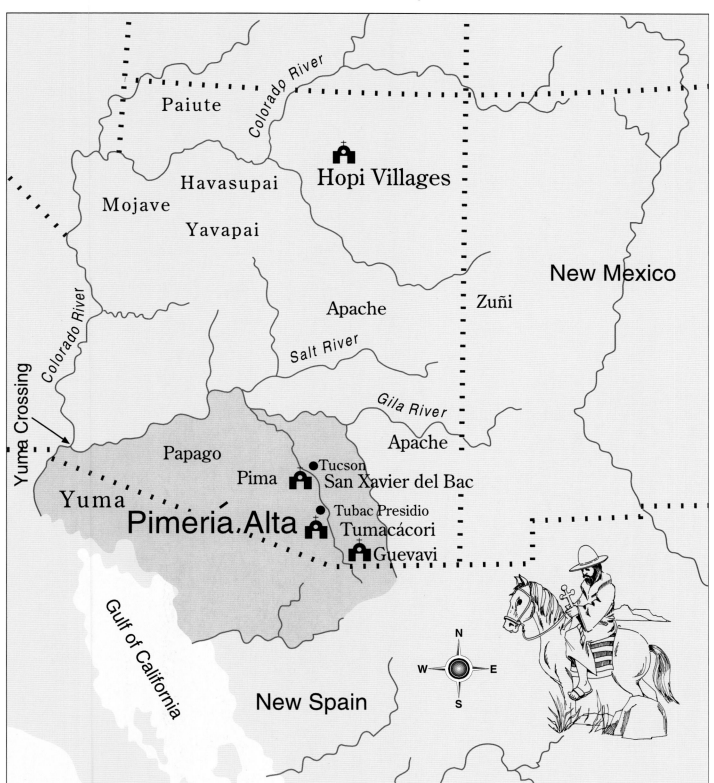

Paiute

Colorado River

Havasupai

Mojave

Yavapai

Hopi Villages

New Mexico

Apache

Zuñi

Salt River

Gila River

Colorado River

Yuma Crossing

Apache

Papago

Tucson

Pima

San Xavier del Bac

Yuma

Tubac Presidio

Pimería Alta

Tumacácori

Guevavi

Gulf of California

New Spain

N

W E

S

The Pima Rebellion, 1751

After the discovery of silver at Arissona, rough-and-ready Spanish miners continued to search the hills of Pimería Alta for gold and silver. Their activity created a threat to the slow-paced lifestyle of the Pimas. An ambitious Pima leader named Luis took advantage of this unrest. He circulated stories about missionaries who used the whip or other cruel punishments. Luis was eager to drive out the Spaniards and to loot their missions, mines, and ranches.

The usually peaceful Pimas rebelled against Spanish rule. The rebellion started south of the present Arizona-Mexican border. Within a few days, two priests and more than a hundred miners, herdsmen, and farmers were killed. The rebels destroyed Kino's missions in Arizona and murdered Spaniards. Spanish soldiers finally captured Luis in the Santa Catalina Mountains.

Tubac

A *presidio* (fort) was built to prevent further Pima uprisings and to protect Spaniards from the Apaches. Fifty soldiers were assigned there. The commander of the presidio was twenty-five-year-old Juan Bautista de Anza.

At that time the growing town around the fort consisted of single-family adobe units. Then settlers, both Spanish and *mestizos* (people of mixed European and Indian blood), began moving to Tubac. Feeling safe near the presidio, the first white women to touch Arizona soil came in 1752. In five years, Tubac had a population of 400 people.

Tubac was a fort, or presidio, built in 1752 to protect Spanish missionaries and settlers from hostile Indians. (Drawing by Don Bufkin)

Fray Garcés, A Franciscan Missionary

Fray Garcés was an *ideal* missionary and a remarkable explorer. He arrived at San Xavier in 1768. Rapidly he became the idol of the Pima Indians, who affectionately called him "Old Man," though he was not even thirty.

Garcés learned to speak the Pima language fluently. During a measles epidemic in Indian villages on the Gila River, Garcés cared for the sick and baptized many Pimas.

A fellow priest, Fray Pedro Font, said of Garcés:

> [Garcés] appears to be but an Indian himself. . . . He sits with them in the circle, or at night around the fire, with his legs crossed, and there he will sit *musing* two or three hours or more . . . talking with much serenity. . . . And although the foods of the Indians are coarse . . . the father eats them with great gusto, and says they are good for the stomach, and very fine.

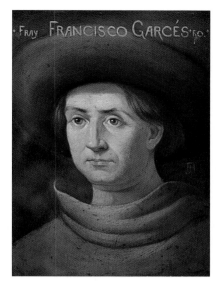

Fray Garcés

Things didn't always go smoothly for Garcés, however. On July 4, 1776, he was in the Hopi village of Oraibi. The Hopis feared that the Spaniards wished to conquer them. After only two days at Oraibi, Garcés was packing his mule and preparing to leave town. As he adjusted the load, he was thinking about how the Hopis would not invite him into their homes or accept his gifts of tobacco and shells. He thought about the night before, when he had huddled in a dark corner of the village. Garcés wrote in his diary for July 4:

> As soon as day broke I heard singing and dancing in the streets . . . only then did I see that some of them were painted red, with feathers and other decorations on the head, beating the sound of the dance on a kind of drum . . . I saw coming nigh unto me a great multitude of people, the sight of which caused me some fear of losing my life. There came forward four Indians who appeared to be leaders. The tallest of them asked me with a grimace. "For what hast thou come here? Get thee gone without delay back to thy land!"

Realizing that he had failed as a missionary to the Hopis, Garcés could at least take satisfaction in other things. As he rode out of town on his mule he passed a peach orchard and saw flocks of sheep—examples of European culture which the Hopis had accepted.

Garcés finally arrived back at San Xavier del Bac. In the wilderness for eleven months, he had traveled more than 2,000 miles.

Juan Bautista de Anza

The Last Years of Spanish Rule

Juan Bautista de Anza

The commander of the presidio at Tubac, Juan Bautista de Anza, made friends with the Yumas, opened an overland route to California with Fray Garcés, and founded San Francisco.

Anza wanted to colonize California. He needed to find a land route to the Pacific Ocean. His first expedition got underway from Tubac in 1774. After reaching the Yuma Crossing, he lingered a while to win the friendship of Yuma Chief Palma. The Yumas cheered as Anza strung a silver medal on a red ribbon and placed it around Palma's neck. The Yumas treated their guests with watermelon and helped them across the river. Fray Garcés guided the expedition to the coast and then returned to Yuma. Anza went north to present-day Monterey, California, and back. By this time, the Colorado River was flooding. The Yumas built rafts to help Anza's caravan cross the river.

Anza reported to the viceroy of Mexico and got permission to lead a *colonizing* expedition to the San Francisco Bay area. He recruited settlers in Mexico and Tubac. He took seventeen soldiers from the Tubac fort and replaced some of his lame horses there. With a caravan of 240 potential settlers, more than half of them women and children, Anza moved to the Gila River and down that valley to the Colorado River. Babies were born and baptized. Cattle wandered into the brush and became wild. Horses died from drinking salty water. Saddles grew hard and feet grew heavy. The desert alkali dust caused eyes to sting and throats to burn. But no one turned back.

The colonists reached the Bay Area in June, 1776. Anza picked a site for the presidio of San Francisco before returning to Tubac.

On July 4, 1776, Anza and his friend Chief Palma were en route to Mexico City. Anza received a hero's welcome there. He pleaded for a presidio and missions at the Yuma Crossing. The Indian leader Palma was baptized in the Cathedral of Mexico. Anza was made governor of New Mexico and Palma returned to his people near the Colorado River.

"In all my life," Anza wrote in his diary, "I have never crossed another river with greater confidence. . . . Even though the craft might have capsized, I had close to me more than 500 persons ready to rescue me."

The Yuma Rebellion

The Spanish military commander decided to establish two settlements in the Yuma country. Each would have two missionaries, about ten soldiers, ten families of colonists, and a half dozen laborers. The two settlements got underway in the fall of 1780. Garcés was one of the missionaries.

Not all the Spanish soldiers and settlers were kind to the native people. They made fun of the Yumas for their method of planting—punching a hole in the soil with a stick for the seeds. Settlers crowded the Indians out of the missions and took the best farmland. The soldiers overused the whipping post and the stocks. Worst of all, the Spaniards grazed their horses and livestock on wild mesquite beans—a valuable food source that the Yumas ground into flour. The Yumas became more and more hostile.

In 1781 the Yumas rebelled. They murdered about fifty Spanish men, including Fray Garcés and three other priests. Spanish troops came from Sonora to trade blankets, beads, and tobacco for the release of captives, who were mainly women and children. The Yumas remained hostile and would not let the Spanish use the important Yuma crossing on the Colorado River. The Yuma massacre forced the Spanish to abandon the overland route to California.

A bronze marker in Yuma honors Fray Garcés.

The Death of Fray Garcés

Three days after the Yuma rebellion started, rebels found Garcés and another priest drinking chocolate at the home of a friendly Indian, whose wife was a Christian convert. The rebel leader shouted, "Stop drinking that and come outside. We're going to kill you!"

"We'd like to finish our chocolate first," Father Garcés replied.

"Just leave it!" the leader shouted. The two fathers obediently stood up and followed him, and were murdered.

"The Yumas did not want to see the fathers killed," a survivor said later. "Nevertheless, their blood was spilled. The husband of the *pious* woman recovered their lifeless bodies and buried them."

—Letter of Maria Ana Montiel, a survivor of the Yuma massacre

Tucson and a New Indian Policy

After the Yuma massacre the Spaniards adopted a new Indian policy. They gave top priority to the conquest of Apaches. All contact with the Yumas ceased.

Meanwhile, the headquarters for protection of the Santa Cruz Valley was moved from Tubac to what is now Tucson. In 1776, Captain Pedro de Allande built a temporary fort of logs and started what became first the fort, and eventually the city, of Tucson.

Allande led several *campaigns* against the Apaches in the Gila River country. He cooperated with troops from other pueblos in a mass invasion. The Apaches were impressed by the presence of Spanish troops, but did not stop raiding settlements. They used *guerrilla* tactics, wisely refusing to fight the Spaniards in open battle.

There was no peace on the frontier until a new Indian policy was adopted in 1796. Offered gifts to surrender, the Apaches were encouraged to live near the presidios. They were given free food, alcohol, and firearms of inferior quality. This peace-at-a-price policy seemed to work. But an outspoken Franciscan priest, Fray Diego Bringas, said the free handouts made the Apaches weak and dependent. He argued that the money should be spent for farm tools and instruction to the Indians on how to support themselves.

In 1777, Tucson's soldiers and settlers donated money to help the thirteen colonies in the East fight the Revolutionary War. They sent a large sum—459 pesos. At the time, 4 pesos would buy a cow. An excellent riding horse could be bought for 7 pesos.

What do you think?

Was it wise to give the Apaches alcohol and guns in exchange for peace? Was bargaining for peace with food a good idea? Would there have been a better way? Discuss the situation from the point of view of the Apaches. Then discuss it from the point of view of the Spanish. How does that time in history relate to our welfare system today?

The Golden Age of Spanish Rule

During the era of peace, 1790 to 1821, settlements in southern Arizona began to prosper. More gold and silver mines were opened than in all the previous years of Spanish rule. Ranchers brought in large herds of cattle, mainly in the Santa Cruz Valley.

Tucson was the center of population of northern Sonora. More than 1,000 Spanish settlers, soldiers, and Indians lived there. Most of the people were engaged in farming and the livestock industry. Wheat, corn, beans, and vegetables were the main crops. The Pimas also raised cotton to weave into cloth for their own use.

A herd of nearly 4,000 cattle helped provide food for Apache families. Surplus hides were sold in Arispe, the state capital. Government leaders called for more growth. They said that Tucson could support woolen and cotton weavers, a leather tanner, a shoemaker, and a saddle maker.

For the Spaniards, new churches were *symbolic* of the peace and prosperity of the Golden Age. At Tumacácori, the Franciscans built a large church with a domed roof. And, in 1797, they dedicated the beautiful "White Dove of the Desert" at San Xavier. This church still stands as one of the best-preserved Spanish missions in North America.

Early Tucson, as it looked about 1790. Adobe living quarters surrounded an open square and were backed against the outside wall for protection from Indians. A church is on the far side. The people farmed on the land outside the fort.

Life at an Arizona Mission

"Guevavi probably never had more than two or three hundred families living there. Unlike the California mission Indians, the Pima retained much of their independence, moved with the seasons to hunt and gather food, and went on **forays** against the Apache. They retained many of their own religious customs and shocked the fathers by holding their **riotous** cactus wine festival on a Catholic holiday. Priests, many of them Swiss and German after 1732, came and went. . . . Some of the less popular priests were poisoned by the Indians . . ."

"While the Indians benefitted from the Spanish herds, fruit trees, new foods, and better farming methods, the very presence of cattle and horses attracted Apache raiders, who harassed the mission and their enemies, the Pima, continually."

—Howard R. Lamar, historian, Yale University

Father Kino founded the Guevavi Mission in 1701. Thirty years later, another priest and Indian laborers built a permanent church. Only traces of the building remain near Nogales.
(Painting by Lola Dunaway)

Tumacácori was a Pima village of forty families when Kino first arrived in 1691. The Pimas built brush shelters where visiting priests could baptize converts. In the 1770s the Franciscans made Tumacácori a head mission. But Apaches soon drove away 2,000 cattle and most of the population. The adobe church pictured here was started about 1800 and later abandoned. Today, Tumacácori is preserved as a national monument.
(Photo by Gill Kenny)

The "White Dove of the Desert"

Father Kino, the popular Jesuit "padre on horseback," started the San Xavier mission at the Indian village of Bac in 1700. In the late 1770s, Franciscan missionaries began building the present church there, borrowing money from a local rancher. Artists from the Mexico City region worked with local Indian laborers to sculpt and paint the beautiful interior. They created thirty-eight life-size statues.

"The reason for this ornate church out here on the farthest frontier is to attract by loveliness the unconverted Papagos and Pimas," wrote the commander of Spanish soldiers at the Tucson presidio, ten miles to the north.

In 1997, San Xavier's bicentennial was celebrated. Every square inch of the interior had been tediously cleaned by experts from the United States, Italy, and Turkey.

A fine example of Spanish architecture, San Xavier is one of the few colonial missions in the U.S. still serving the native peoples it was designed for. Today the mission is on the San Xavier Indian Reservation, Tucson. (Photo by Gill Kenny)

activity

Make a Chart

Make a chart of Spanish place names in Arizona. You could use these headings for columns: Rivers, Towns & Cities, Streets, Parks, etc. A highway map, the yellow pages, and a street map might help you fill in your chart.

activity

Search It Out

The year 1776 is famous for both an important document in the history of the United States and the founding of a city that you read about in this chapter. Research the lifestyle of the people in the Southwest and the people in the thirteen American colonies of the East during 1776. How were they different? How were they the same?

This statue of Father Kino stands in front of the Arizona Historical Society in Tucson.
Another similar statue is in the nation's capitol in Washington, D.C.

1. Why is Cabeza de Vaca important in Arizona history, even though he likely never set foot here?

2. How did Estevan happen to cross the area that is now Arizona? What happened to him?

3. For what is Alarcón remembered in Arizona history?

4. What did the Spaniards do when the Zuñi Indians refused to let them enter the village?

5. Why did Coronado send Captain Cárdenas to the Grand Canyon?

6. In what way was Coronado a failure? How might he be considered a success?

7. What did Espejo do?

8. Why did Oñate cross Arizona and go as far west as the Colorado River?

9. What were three accomplishments of Father Kino?

10. What is the origin of the name "Arizona?"

11. Why did the Pima leader Luis want to drive out the Spaniards?

12. When and why was the presidio at Tubac established?

13. Who was the most famous Franciscan missionary in Arizona?

14. How did the Apaches benefit by the presence of Spaniards in Arizona? How were they harmed?

15. Why did Anza want to find a land route to California?

16. Give two reasons why the Yumas rebelled against the Spaniards in 1781.

17. What were the changes in Spanish policies as a result of the Yuma Rebellion?

18. Explain why a Catholic priest objected to the Spanish policy of giving free rations to the Apaches.

19. Why are the years 1790 to 1821 called the "Golden Age of Spanish Rule?"

20. What is the "White Dove of the Desert?"

chapter 4

THE TIME
1810 – 1854

PEOPLE TO KNOW
Ignacio Pacheco
Miguel Hidalgo
José Romero
José Leon
Thomás and Ignacio Ortiz
Elías Gonzalez family
William Becknell
James Ohio Pattie
"Old Bill" Williams
Pauline Weaver
Kit Carson
Hilario Gallego
Teodoro Ramirez
U.S. President James K. Polk
General Stephen W. Kearny
Mormon Battalion
Captain Philip St. George
    Cooke
U.S. President Franklin Pierce
Mexican President Santa Anna
James Gadsden

PLACES TO LOCATE
State of Sonora, Mexico
Santa Cruz River/Valley
San Pedro River/Valley
Santa Fe Trail
Santa Fe, New Mexico
Taos, New Mexico
Gila River
Salt River
Verde River
Colorado River
Gulf of California
San Diego, California
Pima Villages
Prescott
Yuma Crossing
Texas
Guadalupe Hidalgo, Mexico

1810 SEPTEMBER 16
Mexico declares independence
from Spain.

1821
Mexico wins independence
from Spain. Huge Arizona
land grants are given to
Mexican citizens.

1821
William Becknell
drives a wagon
train from Missouri
to Santa Fe.

1805   1810   1815   1820   1825

1826
First Anglo fur trappers
come into Arizona.

chapter 4

Mexican Arizona

Mexican Rule, Mountain Men, and the Mexican War

School children of Mexican descent dress up in traditional style.

TERMS TO UNDERSTAND
land deed
republic
grant
self-sufficient
barracks
stockmen
pelt
flint
cured
inoculate
amateur
niche
apprentice
menial
bounty
renegade
Manifest Destiny
dispatch
battalion
Mexican Cession
territorial legislature
ratify

1833
Santa Anna becomes
president of Mexico.

1846
Kearny's army and the Mormon
Battalion pass through Arizona.

1854
Gadsden Purchase makes
southern Arizona and
southern New Mexico
part of the U.S.

1830   1835   1840   1845   1850   1855

1846 - 1848 Mexican War is
fought between Mexico and
the U.S.
1848 Treaty of Guadalupe Hidalgo
ends the Mexican War.

1850
Compromise of 1850 gives new
territories a choice in slavery
issues.

1830
Pauline Weaver
comes to Arizona

1836
Texas revolts against
Mexican rule.

A New Government for Mexico

SEPTEMBER 16 is celebrated in Mexico and Arizona as Mexican Independence Day. On that day in 1810, Father Miguel Hidalgo called upon the Mexican people to revolt against Spanish rule. Hidalgo was killed and the rebellion failed.

In 1821, after many more years of conflict between the Mexican leaders and their Spanish rulers, Mexico succeeded in winning independence from Spain. This meant that the land we know as Arizona was under Mexican rule.

In Mexico City, leaders of the new nation drew up a constitution and organized a *republic*. The government was very unstable, however. As a result, the frontier regions far from Mexico City, including Arizona, were neglected.

In Tucson, Captain José Romero raised the Mexican flag over the presidio and took an oath of allegiance to the new government of Mexico. During the time that the Mexican flag flew over Tucson, the small settlement was part of Sonora, a Mexican state.

José Leon was sworn in as the first constitutional mayor of Tucson. The Mexican constitution limited mayors to a one-year term, so Leon was soon replaced by Ignacio Pacheco.

Descendants of Ignacio Pacheco, the Mexican mayor of Tucson, still live in Arizona. They have Mexican *land deeds* and cattle brands dating back to the early 1800s.

Mexican citizens bought large land **grants** and moved to the Arizona region.
Dancing the fandango was a way to bring the traditional culture to their new home.

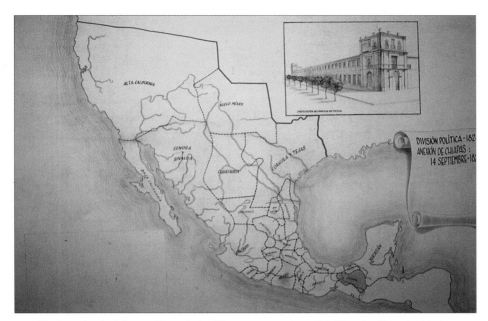

Mexican land claims, 1821–1848. The current states of California, Nevada, Utah, New Mexico, and Arizona were part of Mexico.

Aguirre

Amado

Otero

Robles

Aguirre

Aros

Pacheco

Samaniego

Ainsa

Elías

Robledo

Villa

Life in Mexican Tucson

Under Mexican rule, Tucson was an isolated, *self-sufficient* community of rancher-farmers. They supported themselves, as well as soldiers at the presidio. *Vecinos* (Mexican residents) lived in one-room adobe houses. They channeled scarce water from the Santa Cruz River through *acequias* (canals) to fields of wheat and other crops. Several hundred friendly Apaches worked for the Mexican farmers and also tilled their own fields. All the residents of Tucson supplemented their crops with desert foods, especially mesquite pods, which they ground into flour, and the juicy red fruit of the saguaro.

All the water users met once a year to elect a *zanjero* (water judge) who made sure each farmer got his fair share of water. The women washed family clothes in the canals. They got drinking water from a protected well inside the presidio.

Missions Were Closed

The Mexican Congress forced all Spanish priests to take an oath of loyalty to the new republic or leave Mexico. Foreign missionaries were sent back to their homelands. The missions all but disappeared. San Xavier had no priest for years. Soldiers used the chapel and mission buildings as barns, stables, and *barracks*. Tumacácori was abandoned when its priest was sent back to his native Spain. The mission farmland and the adjacent stock ranch were sold at auction. The new owner converted an old church into a ranch house and hired herdsmen to tend his sheep and goats on the old mission lands.

Mexican Land Grants

The cattle industry got a good start during the last years of Spanish rule. After Mexico won independence, Mexican **stockmen** applied for huge land grants and drove their herds northward.

The phrase *el rancho grande* well describes the Mexican ranches in the 1820s. A typical government land grant consisted of about twenty-seven square miles. In addition, a *ranchero* (rancher) could occupy and buy surrounding lands.

Most of the land grants were in the valleys of the Santa Cruz and San Pedro Rivers. The biggest operators in the Santa Cruz Valley were two brothers, Tomás and Ignacio Ortiz. They selected the Canoa Ranch south of Tucson and paid about nine dollars per square mile for it. The brothers also inherited a large ranch from their father.

The large Elías González family settled at least five land grants in southern Arizona. The family produced a line of famous people—including four governors of Sonora, a president of Mexico, presidio commanders, mine developers, and big landowners. Ignacio Elías González paid only $380 for the huge Babocomari grant (west of present-day Tombstone). Visitors at the Elías ranch house fished in the nearby stream and sometimes rode out with the *vaqueros* to round up wild horses. For nearly twenty years, huge herds of Mexican cattle roamed the valley.

The Mexican owners of the land grants were Arizona's first big cattlemen. By the 1840s, however, Apache raids forced nearly all the ranchers to leave. Some ranchers moved into town for safety. Their cattle became wild.

> **"As soon as a child was old enough to toddle he was thrown on a pony's back, to be held there by a grown person. Among his earliest recollections was the rhythm of a horse in motion."**
>
> —Jo Moro

Catching Wild Horses
(Drawing by Jo Moro)

Santa Fe: A Port of Entry

After Mexico won independence from Spain, *Americanos* were welcomed in Santa Fe, the closest Mexican town to the United States. Merchants in Santa Fe were eager to exchange their silver, gold, mules, beaver furs, and Indian blankets for American manufactured goods.

Before long, heavy white-topped wagons loaded with trade goods were grinding deep ruts across the plains from towns in Missouri. In 1821 William Becknell put together a pack train in Missouri and led it 800 miles through Indian country to Santa Fe. The goods were sold to Mexicans for a handsome profit. Becknell went back home and organized the first great wagon caravan. A party of eighty-one adventurous men transported $30,000 worth of merchandise in twenty-five wooden wagons. They sold the goods for $180,000 in gold and silver and $10,000 in furs.

Becknell did more than bring back bags of money. He opened up the Santa Fe Trail for all who followed. It was the trail used by thousands of immigrants to the Southwest. Many of the early arrivals were fur trappers, better known as mountain men.

There is much noise and color as the last boxes and barrels are placed in the wagons. The drivers pop their whips and the wagon train begins the two-month journey to Santa Fe. There was danger of storms and Indian attack, but traders came to love life on the trail. The land stretched as far as a person could see. Fresh buffalo meat was roasted over campfires. At the end of the trail, the traders put on clean shirts and washed their faces so they would look their best when they arrived in town. The people of Santa Fe waved and called out, "Los Americanos!" The Americans had many good things to sell.

—from the writings of an early newspaper reporter

Mexican Ranching Language Heritage

Most of the American cowboy's language, equipment, and methods are of Spanish-Mexican origin. From the Mexican cowboy, called a *vaquero*, came the horned saddle, roping techniques, and branding. Even the term "ten-gallon hat" comes from a mistranslation of "*su sombrero galoneado*," which means a "fancy, braided hat."

The very language of the range is Spanish: bronco, lasso from *lazo*, lariat from *la reata*, rodeo, corral, remuda, stampede from *estampida*, and rancho. The Mexican expression "dale vuelta," meaning "to twist a rope about the horn of a saddle," became "dolly welter" or simply "dolly."

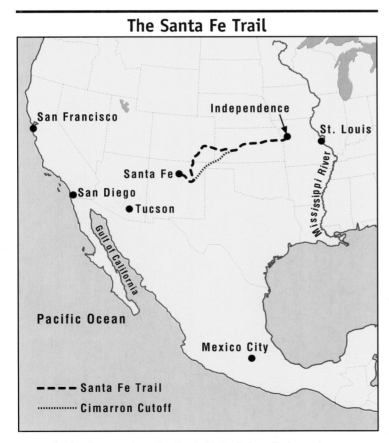

The Santa Fe Trail

Becknell opened up the Santa Fe trail from Independence, Missouri, to Santa Fe, New Mexico.

Trapping Beaver

IT WAS THE LOWLY SONORAN BEAVER—not gold or silver—that lured the first Americans to the Arizona region. The furs were in demand to make high-crowned beaver hats, then the fashion craze in the East and in Europe. In their search for beaver, the trappers explored nearly every river valley in present-day Arizona. The most valuable skins were taken during the winter, when they were the thickest.

Taos and Santa Fe, New Mexico, became head-quarters for American as well as Mexican and Indian fur trappers in the Southwest. The trappers sold their *pelts* and bought supplies in these towns.

Contrary to common opinion, many of the desert or semi-desert rivers of the Southwest were major trapping fields. For the beaver was—and still is—at home . . . in the deep chasms of the San Juan and Colorado Rivers, where the summer heat becomes almost unbearable for human beings; in the warm, sluggish waters of the lower Gila; and along the winding channels of the Colorado delta.
—Robert Glass Cleland

A Mountain Man's Life

A tough, self-reliant fur trapper is ready to explore the mountains and streams of Arizona in search of beavers. Mounted on a lean horse, he wears buckskin clothes that are shiny and greasy from many hand-wipings. A fur cap covers his shaggy hair.

The trapper carries his flintlock rifle, ready to shoot a deer or other animal for food. He carries *flints*, a hickory ramrod, a powder horn, and a bullet pouch. The rest of his equipment consists of a short-handled axe or tomahawk, a skinning knife, a few blankets, and cooking gear. He relies on horses and pack mules for transportation.

Like most of the trappers, he lacks formal education but is well-trained for survival in the wilderness. He stays alive by adopting Indian ways and using Indian skills. He wears his hair like the native Indian people and may have an Indian woman for his wife.

After a season of hunting, trapping, and skinning animals, the mountain man emerges at the trading post. There he sells a load of dried beaver pelts and probably uses his profits to celebrate, gamble, and buy new supplies. Itching to move on, he loads his pack horse with traps, gunpowder, and lead. He adds sacks of flour, salt, coffee, tobacco, and sugar and rides out into the wilderness once again.

(Art by Frederick Remington)

Deer, elk, antelope, and bear were favorite food animals with the mountain men. Beaver tail was a great delicacy, but the rest of the beaver was eaten only when other meat was scarce. According to many reports, a true mountain man preferred lynx meat to any other delicacy. French dumplings, a very special treat, were made of minced meat rolled in balls of dough and fried in marrow [fat].

—Robert Glass Cleland

Men in the East and in Europe wore tall felt hats made from beaver fur.

Arizona's Pathfinders

Mountain men—following their urge to explore and trap beavers—made known the mountains, rivers, and deserts of Arizona. The colorful James Ohio Pattie was the first American from the States to describe Arizona and his trapping days for a book—and maybe the first to step foot in Arizona. His popular *Personal Narrative* is basically a true account of what he saw and did here. It also contains many exaggerated hair-raising adventure tales. Yes, Pattie saw grizzly bears—but more than 200 in one day? Other trappers, especially Kit Carson and Pauline Weaver, later provided valuable service as guides for U.S. soldiers and pioneers who began entering this region during the Mexican War.

How to Catch a Beaver

To catch beavers, mountain men used a strong steel trap with a five-foot chain. They staked the trap in three or four inches of water close to the bank. The bait, a sweet-smelling secretion from the musk gland of the beaver, was dropped on a twig above the trap. After the beaver was trapped and drowned, the skin was carefully removed and dried on a willow hoop. The *cured* pelts were packed in bundles. Bundles were tied with green buckskin thongs; they shrank while drying and tightened around the bundle like an iron band.

Photo by Lynn Chamberlain

James Ohio Pattie

James Ohio Pattie was only twenty years old when he arrived in Santa Fe with his father, Sylvester, and a caravan of other traders and trappers. While in Santa Fe, the younger Pattie had an exciting experience. He joined a rescue party and helped to free captives who had been carried away by Comanche raiders. For his personal bravery in rescuing the daughter of a former Mexican governor, James won both the affection of the girl and a Mexican trapping license.

In the winter of 1825–26, the Patties joined a party of trappers—the first known citizens of the United States to enter present-day Arizona. They trapped the Gila River in New Mexico to where it joined the Salt River, southwest of modern-day Phoenix. Pattie described the Gila as "a beautiful river running between banks covered with cottonwoods and willows."

On the return trip, the men were caught off guard when Indians crept into their camp at night and drove away the horses. The stranded trappers hid their heavy bundles of beaver pelts and went on foot to New Mexico to get pack horses. By the time they returned to the hiding place, their furs were gone. The trappers had nothing to show for months in the wilderness.

The next winter the younger Pattie joined a group of French trappers. This group was attacked by shrieking Indians with war clubs near the fork of the Salt and Gila Rivers. Luckily, Pattie and two other

Pattie wrote that he *inoculated* people in California for smallpox. Actually, the Mexican people were suffering from an epidemic of measles, according to documents recently examined.

An old-time trapper

survivors soon stumbled into Ewing Young's camp, which was not far away. Young led his party downstream. He was pleased to find a great number of beavers along the Colorado River. In the spring, the men returned to New Mexico, only to have the Mexican governor seize all their furs. He charged the Americans with trapping without a license.

After recovering from that experience, James and his father joined another company for their last trapping journey across Arizona. Once again their horses were stolen, this time by Indians on the Colorado River. The trappers improvised by hollowing out cottonwood trees to make boats. Then they floated their furs downstream to the Gulf of California. After hiding the furs, the men struck out across the desert to San Diego, California. There the whole party was put in jail, where Sylvester died.

James got the other men released as a reward for his services as an *amateur* doctor. The Mexican governor sent him around California to vaccinate people against smallpox and granted him a passport to the United States. He returned to Kentucky. In six action-packed years, James Ohio Pattie had carved out a permanent *niche* for himself in the history of Arizona and the United States.

"Old Bill" Williams

William Shirley "Old Bill" Williams has a mountain, stream, and a city in Arizona named after him. Raised a Methodist in Missouri, Williams became a missionary and trader to the Osage Indians. He married a young Osage woman and developed an admiration for Indian culture and ceremonies. After the death of his wife, the restless Williams went west over the Santa Fe Trail to hunt and trap.

Williams was with a party of trappers at a Pima village on the Gila River. The Pima chief didn't know what to make of the mountain men. He reported news of "sixteen foreigners bearing arms along the river" to the highest Mexican official available, Mayor Ignacio Pacheco in Tucson. Actually, the American trappers were no threat to the Pimas or the Mexican people. They just wanted to buy horses and get information about other rivers that might have a lot of beavers.

Williams usually preferred to travel alone. He was as solitary as "the eagle in the heavens or the panther in the mountains," said a Ute Indian who knew him. Tall, lean, and tough, the red-haired Williams could run along streams all day with a bunch of five-pound beaver traps on his back.

A good trapper, Williams would show up at Taos, New Mexico, with big bundles of well-prepared beaver skins from his secret trapping grounds. Then he let loose, drinking and gambling away his profits. One observer said Old Bill lost $1,000 in one game of cards. An expert rifleman, he did better in shooting matches. He sometimes won as much as $100 a shot with his gun—"Kicking Betsy."

"He is a man about six feet one inch in height, gaunt, red-headed with a weather-beaten face deeply marked by smallpox . . . tireless hunter and trapper . . . a shrewd, original man, and far from illiterate . . . signs his name 'Bill Williams, Master Trapper'. . . dirty and greasy appearance . . . joins other trappers to steal herds of horses from big Mexican ranches in California . . . Indian fighter with scars from arrows and rifle balls . . . like the Indian he doesn't cook his meat and believes in dreams to foretell the future . . . the bravest and most fearless mountaineer of all. . . ."
—Albert Pike, who traveled with Williams for two months, and other acquaintances

Pauline Weaver

A large granite rock marks Weaver's grave at the old log Governor's Mansion in Prescott. Arizona school children collected pennies to pay the cost of bringing his body back from the military cemetery in San Francisco. The inscription on the monument reads:
"He was born and died on the frontier of this country, always in the ever advancing westward move of civilization and was the first settler on the site of Prescott. He was descended from the best blood of the white man and the Native American, and his greatest achievement was as peacemaker between the races, understanding as few ever did the true hearts of the two peoples."

Weaver, on horseback, waits for a fish supper.
(Mural by Paul Coze, Prescott City Hall)

Pauline Weaver

Like Williams, Pauline Weaver (sometimes called Paulino) was a "lone wolf" mountain man. He came to northern Arizona about 1830 when this area was an unsettled part of Mexico.

Weaver, born in Tennessee, was half Indian. His mother was the daughter of a prosperous Cherokee chief. At an early age, Weaver went to the Northwest and trapped for the big Hudson's Bay Company. But he grew tired of the cold winters and worked his way to Arizona.

The unsettled land north of the Gila was only a place on the map. Weaver found plenty of beavers, though the pelts were not always of good quality. In time he learned the geography of Arizona. With this knowledge he was later able to guide the Mormon Battalion during the Mexican War and, a few years later, an army of California soldiers during the Civil War.

Weaver, the peacemaker, picked up a smattering of several native languages and moved among the Indians without fear. He taught them to say "Paulino-Tobacco" when approaching white people. This password would indicate they were friendly.

In Prescott, Weaver worked for several years as a government scout. After his death in 1867 he was called "the first citizen of Prescott."

Christopher "Kit" Carson

At age sixteen, Kit Carson was an *apprentice* in a saddle and harness shop in the town of Franklin, Kentucky. He was supposed to work for free for many years in exchange for learning a trade. Carson didn't like the work or the man he worked for. After about a year he ran away to lead a more exciting life in the West. While Carson was en route to Santa Fe, his ex-employer ran an insulting advertisement in the newspaper. A reward of one cent was offered for the boy's return. The idea was to show what a worthless apprentice Kit was.

Physically small and too poor to provide his own trapping equipment, Carson spent three years in Mexico doing *menial* jobs. During that time he became an expert rifleman. He also learned enough Spanish to serve as an interpreter.

Then came Carson's big opportunity. He joined a party of forty trappers organized by Ewing Young for an expedition into Arizona. After the company trapped along the Salt and Verde Rivers, about half the group was sent back to New Mexico with the furs. The rest, including Carson, set out for the West Coast. By the time the men returned and stopped at the Santa Rita copper mines, they were packing 10,000 pounds of beaver pelts. Carson returned from his first trapping expedition a full-fledged mountain man. He had experienced near-starvation and fought with unfriendly Indians.

Kit Carson trapped beaver throughout the Rocky Mountains and guided expeditions for government explorer and mapmaker John C. Fremont. It was Fremont who made Carson a famous figure in American history.

Kit Carson became the most famous trapper, guide, and scout in America.

What do you think?

There are many examples of children and teenagers who don't fit into the "norm" of expected behavior. They often have trouble in school, and people think they won't amount to anything. Later they become very successful. Thomas Edison, Albert Einstein, and Winston Churchill are a few famous examples of people who started slowly.

- Does changing from failure to success in school and life just happen accidentally? What ideas and actions might help make the change?

- Do you agree that schools and society should be glad that some people are different? Despite differences, do you think people should show respect for others?

Kit Carson's firsthand knowledge of geography of the Southwest served him well as a guide during the Mexican War.

Apache Raids

Apache boys trained for raiding and warfare. They practiced with the bow and arrow, ran long distances, and swam in the cold mountain streams. "I was born at Canyon Day [1837]. . . . In those days there were no white people here. The trails in these mountains were well-traveled. . . . Our people used to go on raids down into Mexico to bring back horses, mules, burros, and cattle. . . . I can remember the first time I ever went on a raid. I was only a boy and not very big."

—Palmer Valor, Apache
Interview by
Grenville Goodwin, 1932

FOR YEARS THE APACHES had tried to keep strangers off their lands. In the 1830s they took to the warpath again. Going into Sonora, Mexico, they stole livestock, burned and looted buildings, carried off women and children, and left a trail of blood. Most ranches and settlements on the frontier were abandoned.

Governors and presidio commanders pleaded with Mexico's President Santa Anna for help. They asked for a well-equipped army to stop the Apache raids. But little help was given. Santa Anna regarded the Sonora frontier as a kind of wasteland not worthy of the army's time.

In desperation, the Mexican governors of Sonora offered *bounties* for Apache scalps. The bounty system attracted some of the worst Mexican and American *renegades*. To collect bounties, ranging up to $100 per head of hair, the scalpers brought in hundreds of scalps—some of them belonging to innocent Mexicans and peaceful Indians. The only result of this system was to increase the hatred of the Apaches for both Mexicans and Americans. The Apache raids continued throughout the period of Mexican rule and after in Arizona.

Apache warriors survey a Mexican ranch for a possible raid on the horse corral.

The Mexican War

Hilario Gallego is talking about old times:

> I was born inside the walled city of Tucson on January 14, 1850. Our house was a little one and stood about where the city hall now stands. My father was Isidor Gallego. He had some land west of here. He was a farmer and had a few cows. Two little Apache boys worked for him. There was a peaceful tribe that had a camp right out here a little way. Then there were the wild Apaches who stole a lot of cattle. The adobe wall around the presidio was about six feet high and two feet thick. As far back as I can remember, Teodoro Ramirez had a store inside the wall.

Hilario amused people with this riddle: "I was born in Mexico in 1850, never moved, and lived most of my life in the United States. How could that be?" The answer to Hilario's riddle is revealed in two big events in our history—Mexican independence and the Gadsden Purchase.

Manifest Destiny

By the 1840s, many Americans believed it was the destiny of the United States to extend its western boundary all the way to the Pacific Ocean. This idea was called *"Manifest Destiny"* and it finally came about as a result of a war with Mexico.

A Texas boundary dispute was the spark that set off the war. Both Mexico and the U.S. claimed parts of Texas. U.S. President James Polk asked Congress to declare war after Mexican troops crossed the Rio Grande. "Mexico . . . has shed American blood on American soil," said Polk.

The Army of the West

Arizona got involved in the war when General Stephen W. Kearny, leading U.S. troops, got orders to occupy New Mexico and help conquer California. Traveling over Arizona land was part of the journey.

General Kearny put together his "Army of the West" at Fort Leavenworth (now in Kansas). The men were sent ahead in small groups. They followed a branch of the Santa Fe Trail to Bent's Fort (now in Colorado). When Kearny arrived, he found that his army had a large group of traders under its protection. Their merchandise, packed in 400 wagons, was worth a million dollars.

Kearny paved the way for an easy conquest of New Mexico, which at that time included Arizona. He sent a message to the governor of Santa Fe, promising safety and religious liberties to the Mexican

What do you think?

The earliest known use of the term "manifest destiny" was by John O'Sullivan, a New York editor, in 1845. He said: ". . . Our manifest destiny [is] to overspread the continent allotted by Providence for the free development of our yearly multiplying millions."

• What did O'Sullivan mean by "overspread the continent?"
• "Allotted by Providence" meant the eastern settlers' "God Given" right to the land. Would the American Indians have agreed with O'Sullivan's statement?
• What did O'Sullivan see for the future of America's growing population? Was he right?

General Stephen W. Kearny led the Army of the West to take Sante Fe from the Mexican government. The army later moved through Arizona and into California.

Kearny, Arizona, is named after the commander of the Army of the West. The town was started on the Gila River by the Kennecott Copper Company.

Philip St. George Cooke led the Mormon Battalion across Arizona.

people. Before Kearny's army arrived, however, the governor deserted his people and rode south. The weary troops entered the old mud village of Santa Fe without firing a shot. Kearny claimed the whole region for the United States.

Kearny and his mounted soldiers later left Santa Fe. South of Albuquerque they met Kit Carson, who was carrying *dispatches* to inform President Polk that the war was over. Carson reluctantly turned his messages over to another courier and agreed to guide Kearny through Arizona to the California coast. Heeding Carson's advice about the rugged Gila River route ahead, Kearny sent 200 men and the heavy wagons back to Santa Fe. He moved on with only 100 men and pack mules carrying supplies.

Along the way Kearny traded with the Pimas for cornmeal, flour, beans, pumpkins, and melons. He was also able to get cattle from the Maricopas. The Army of the West did not lack for food in its winding journey down the Gila River.

A surprise awaited Kearny in California. The war was not over! He had arrived just in time for some action. About a third of his small force was killed or wounded in a battle with Mexican lancers. The remaining men were saved by the timely arrival of an American force from San Diego.

The Mormon Battalion

The Mormon Battalion was the second major military group to travel across Arizona during the Mexican War. President Polk had requested a *battalion* of members of The Church of Jesus Christ of Latter-day Saints to help fight the war. Nicknamed "Mormons," thousands of the religious group were traveling in covered wagons to the Rocky Mountains. When the request for soldiers came, the people agonized about leaving women and children to continue their trip without the men. Even though they were leaving the boundaries of the United States, however, the Mormons wanted to demonstrate their patriotism. They also needed the money the government offered to pay the soldiers. A large group of men joined the army, some bringing wives and children along. They left the pioneer trail and traveled south.

Captain Philip St. George Cooke, one of Kearny's officers, took command of the battalion in Santa Fe. Cooke trimmed the group to 340 men and five women before hitting the trail in October, 1846. He had a wagon train and could not follow the dangerous Gila route taken by Kearny.

The only "battle" the group experienced was with a herd of wild bulls near present-day Benson. The animals gored mules, damaged wagons, and injured some of the men. The bulls were hard to kill. Private Henry Standage wrote in his diary that "they would run off with a half dozen balls [shots] in them unless they were shot in the heart."

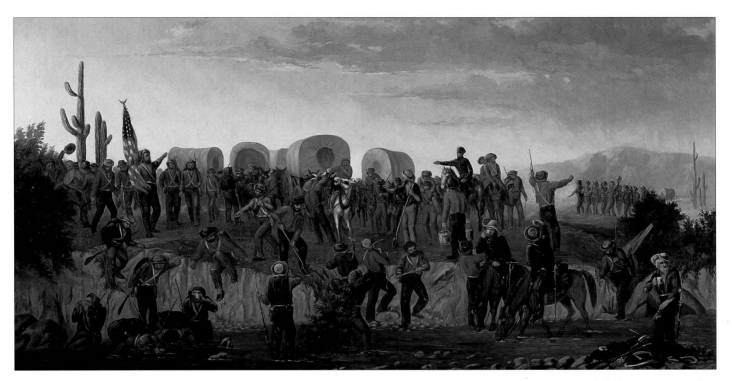

The Mormon Battalion built a wagon road from Santa Fe to San Diego. Known as Cooke's Wagon Road, it extended the Santa Fe Trail by a thousand miles. The route was used by pioneer wagon trains, including forty-niners headed for the California gold fields. This painting shows the battalion building a section of the road along the Gila River. (Painting by George Ottinger)

When news reached Tucson that Cooke's soldiers were coming, the presidio commander chose not to defend the town. He led his small army and most of the Mexican residents south to the San Xavier mission. The Mormon Battalion took Tucson without firing a shot and raised the American flag over an Arizona city for the first time. The men also bought supplies and enjoyed tortillas with the friendly Mexicans who had not fled.

From Tucson the battalion went north to the Gila River, where hundreds of friendly Pimas welcomed them. Downstream, the Maricopas turned over some badly needed mules that Kearny had abandoned on his earlier trip. By the time the battalion reached the Yuma Crossing with the rickety wagons, the men were exhausted and hungry. A sergeant wrote in his diary, "We had a weighing frolic. I weighed 128; weight when I enlisted, 198." Three weeks later the weary battalion was in San Diego. The war was over.

Mexican War, 1846–1848

Treaty of Guadalupe Hidalgo, 1848

After American troops entered Mexico City as conquerors, peace terms were signed in Guadalupe Hidalgo, a small town outside the Mexican capital. The terms were severe. Mexico was forced to give up two-fifths of its land. The enormous region was called the *Mexican Cession.* Included was the wilderness part of Arizona north of the Gila River. Mexico had claimed that region but never explored or settled it. The rest of the cession gave the United States most of New Mexico and all of present-day California, Nevada, and Utah, in addition to parts of Wyoming and Colorado.

In return for the land, the United States paid Mexico $15 million. The U.S. also agreed to pay Mexico's debts to American citizens. The amount was over $3 million.

The peaceful entry of the Mormon Battalion into Tucson is commemorated in this bronze sculpture by Clyde Ross Morgan. Teodoro Ramirez (on the left) was a leading merchant in Tucson. He is trading wheat and beans with Captain Jefferson Hunt. Private Christopher Layton (standing) raised the first American flag in Tucson.

Treaty of Guadalupe Hidalgo

At the end of the Mexican War, the treaty gave to the United States:
- a huge amount of land called the Mexican Cession.

The treaty awarded Mexico:
- $15 million for the land.
- payment of Mexico's debts to Americans of over $3 million.

People living in the Mexican Cession could choose either Mexican or U.S. citizenship.

The Compromise of 1850

At the end of the Mexican War the burning issue of slavery split the states, half slave and half free. The nation's attention focused on the Mexican Cession. Would slavery be permitted in the new region?

The Compromise of 1850 settled the question of slavery in the new territories, but only after a bitter debate in Congress. After the compromise, California was a free state. The new territories of New Mexico (which included Arizona) and Utah could let their *territorial legislatures* decide whether or not they wanted to allow slavery. Utah chose to allow slavery, though it wasn't practiced much there. New Mexico voted to be a free territory.

ARIZONA: A Journey of Discovery

The Gadsden Purchase, 1854

United States

Utah Territory

California

New Mexico Territory

Gadsden Purchase 1854

Mexico

Gulf of California

A SECOND MEXICAN WAR nearly erupted in the early 1850s over a strip of land 35 miles wide and 175 miles long.

This land was in dispute because an inaccurate map was used for the Treaty of Guadalupe Hidalgo. The line was surveyed too far north. Both Mexico and the United States claimed ownership of the strip. Troops from both sides were sent there to protect the claim. Any little incident could have started a new war.

United States President Franklin Pierce naturally wanted the boundary errors corrected. He was also persuaded to buy more land from Mexico to build a southern railroad route to California. Pierce sent James Gadsden, a railroad promoter, to Mexico City with five different offers. The first offer was $50 million for a huge stretch of Mexican land that included all of Baja (Lower California). The smallest offer was $15 million for a railroad route and an outlet on the Gulf of California.

Mexican dictator Santa Anna needed money, but he refused to give up the land. He wanted to keep Mexico's land bridge to Lower California. After a long debate, a compromise was reached. The amount of territory was reduced and the southern boundary of Arizona and New Mexico was set as it is today. Mexico kept its land route to Lower California. The purchase price was cut to $10 million.

The Gadsden Purchase Treaty was *ratified* by both nations in the summer of 1854 (not in 1853 as usually stated in history books). The United States had made a good bargain.

Linking the past and the present

In what ways would Arizona be different today if the Gadsden Purchase had included land next to the Gulf of California?

What do you think?

Slavery was very much a part of the culture of the Southern States. In a Senate debate, the Southern States wanted to buy as much Mexican land as possible. The Northern States opposed buying any land. Why do you think the two sides disagreed so much?

Long after Arizona was part of the United States, people in Arizona lived a Mexican lifestyle. Nearly every Tucson home had a "corn-cracker." That was the name a member of the Mormon Battalion gave to a burro mill called a *molino*. A blindfolded burro went round and round, turning a rough stone that ground wheat or other grains—including corn—into meal or flour.

The United States in 1854

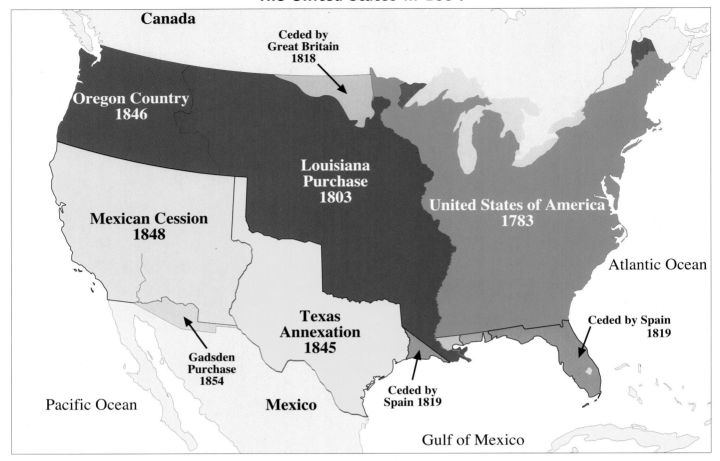

Canada

Ceded by
Great Britain
1818

Oregon Country
1846

Louisiana
Purchase
1803

United States of America
1783

Mexican Cession
1848

Atlantic Ocean

Gadsden
Purchase
1854

Texas
Annexation
1845

Ceded by Spain
1819

Pacific Ocean

Mexico

Ceded by
Spain 1819

Gulf of Mexico

activity

A Giant Puzzle

Think of this map as a giant puzzle.

1. Which two pieces are most important to Arizona?
2. Which piece was most involved in events that led up to the Mexican War?
3. Which present state did Spain give to the United States in 1819?
4. What did the historian mean when he said: "The Gadsden Purchase was the piece of the puzzle that fills in the now-familiar profile of the United States?"
5. What are the two newest states that don't fit into this puzzle?

activity

Working with Maps

Locate Arizona in an atlas. Locate the Gila River. Then make a list of five Arizona cities or towns located on land that was part of the Mexican Cession. Make another list of five cities or towns that were part of the Gadsden Purchase.

Flags Over Arizona

The first flags over Arizona (left to right) are:

1. The 1846 flag with thirty-one stars, carried by Kearny's army and by the Mormon Battalion.
2. The Mexican flag.
3. The flag of Spain.
4. The Confederate flag raised over Tucson in 1862 (Civil War).

The flags are displayed at the Arizona Historical Society in Tucson.

These flags are not displayed in chronological order. On a piece of paper, list the flags in the order they were actually used.

1.   2.   3.   4.

Chapter 4 Review

1. Briefly describe what happened to Arizona's missions after Mexico got its independence from Spain.

2. Where were most of the Mexican land grants located?

3. List four words that we got from the *vaqueros*.

4. What was the scalp bounty system?

5. Why was William Becknell important in the history of the Southwest?

6. How were the mountain men able to stay alive?

7. Who were the first known Anglo-Americans to touch Arizona soil? When did they arrive?

8. List two hardships experienced by the Patties in Arizona.

9. Briefly describe "Old Bill" Williams.

10. How did Pauline Weaver put his knowledge of Arizona geography to good use?

11. What did Stephen Kearny do? Why did he stop at the Pima villages?

12. Why is the Mormon Battalion important in Arizona history?

13. What did the Treaty of Guadalupe Hidalgo accomplish?

14. What dispute almost caused a second Mexican War?

15. How did the Gadsden Purchase affect Arizona?

chapter 5

THE TIME
1850–1870

PEOPLE TO KNOW
Charles D. Poston
Santiago Hubbell
Sylvester Mowry
Mark Aldrich
Solomon Warner
J. Ross Brown
Sam Heintzelman
Sarah Bowman
Jacob Snively
Captain Lorenzo Sitgreaves
Lt. Amiel Whipple
Lt. Edward Beale
Hadji Ali
Captain Richard Ewell
Captain Sherod Hunter
Estevan Ochoa
General James H. Carleton
Ammi M. White
Cochise
Henry Wickenburg
U.S. President Abraham
   Lincoln

PLACES TO LOCATE
Tubac
Tucson
Yuma Crossing
Colorado City (Yuma)
Rio Grande
La Paz
Wickenburg

This diorama shows the Butterfield Overland Mail stage, 1858. The Concord coaches were used

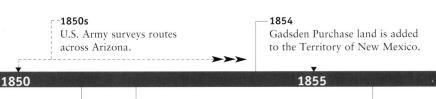

1850s
U.S. Army surveys routes across Arizona.

1854
Gadsden Purchase land is added to the Territory of New Mexico.

1850

1855

1851
Fort Defiance is built in northern Arizona.

1852
Fort Yuma is built. The first steamboat goes up the Colorado River.

1856
Tucson leaders petition Congress to make Arizona a separate territory.

Arizona under U.S. Rule

Silver, Forts, Transportation, and the Civil War

TERMS TO UNDERSTAND
sanction
engraver
venture
constable
desolation
navigate
prospector
arid
morale
secede
Union
Confederate
Yankee
Rebel
skirmish
artillery
martial law
reservation
ultimatum
overgraze
ingot
annex

to carry mail and passengers from Missouri to California and back.

1858
The first southern Arizona wagon road is built. The Butterfield stage and mail line goes into business. Jacob Snively discovers gold up the Gila River.

1862 Civil War skirmishes occur in Arizona.

1863
Territory of Arizona is created. Wickenburg discovers Vulture Mine.

1866
Arizona Territory's northwest corner (Las Vegas) becomes part of Nevada.

1860

1865

1870

1856
The first stagecoach line runs across Arizona. The first road across northern Arizona is begun. Camels are brought to Arizona.

1859
The *Weekly Arizonian*, Arizona's first newspaper, is printed in Tubac. Fort Mojave is established.

1868
Navajos walk to new Arizona reservation.

Settling the "Paradise for Devils"

THE FIRST ANGLO-AMERICAN PIONEERS, like the Spaniards and Mexicans before them, were attracted to the area south of the Gila River. They started calling the region "Arizona" in the 1850s. Another name was "Paradise for Devils."

The people had almost no law to keep outlaws in check. The United States government had sent few soldiers to hold off raiding Apaches. Every man had to carry a gun for protection. Considering the obstacles, the work done by pioneers during this time seems amazing. Miners, ranchers, merchants, freighters, stagecoach drivers, surveyors, and road builders—all these pioneers made progress in the 1850s.

Tubac Mining Boom

AFTER THE UNITED STATES TOOK OVER, Arizona's first mining boom exploded. Eastern businessmen eagerly invested in Arizona silver-mining companies. The biggest company, organized in Cincinnati, Ohio, was managed by Charles D. Poston, who went by the title of "Colonel." Poston established his headquarters at the old Tubac presidio. The town grew fast. Mexicans came in great numbers. Some were skilled miners. Others came to cultivate farms. Traders arrived with goods from Sonora and other places. By 1860, a thousand miners and farmers were living along the Santa Cruz River near Tubac.

Santiago Hubbell, a trader, hauled the first mining machinery in heavy wagons from Kansas City to Tubac. His twelve large wagons were each pulled by twelve mules. On the return trip he transported smelted silver ore packed in rawhide bags. Most of the ore from Tubac mines, however, was sent to Mexico, where ships took it to San Francisco.

Poston acted as the government at Tubac. He even performed wedding ceremonies for young Mexican couples from Sonora. He gave them a certificate stamped with a seal made from a Mexican *peso* and threw in a free wedding feast. Poston also arranged for a Catholic priest "to give the *sanction* of the church to the marriages."

Poston had paper bills, known as *boletas*, printed in New York. The *boletas* were paid to the company's miners on Saturday. Not many of the miners could read, so the value of the bills was indicated by pictures of animals:

pig	12.5¢	one bit
calf	25¢	two bits
rooster	50¢	
horse	$1	
bull	$5	
lion	$10	

Charles D. Poston

"Everybody holding boletas was interested in the success of the mines. When a run of silver was made, the boletas could be redeemed for silver bars. They were all redeemed."
—Charles D. Poston diary

The Civil War ended the Tubac silver boom. Troops were withdrawn from Arizona forts when they were needed to fight in the war. With the soldiers gone, Apaches stepped up their raids. By the end of 1861, most miners, afraid of Indian attack, had left. Tubac was a ghost town.

Arizona's First Newspaper

Arizona's first newspaper began publication in Tubac in 1859. The *Weekly Arizonian*, edited by Edward Cross, was a neat four-page journal. It was full of advertisements for eastern goods, local gossip, and articles on Indian raids and mining activities.

Cross did not want Arizona separated from the Territory of New Mexico. Sylvester Mowry, an army officer, strongly disagreed and challenged Cross to a duel. The contest was bloodless—both men missed.

THE WEEKLY ARIZONIAN.

VOL. 1. TUBAC, ARIZONA MARCH 3, 1859. No. 1.

THE ARIZONIAN,
A WEEKLY PAPER.
DEVOTED TO THE GENERAL INTERESTS OF ARIZONA.

— TERMS —

Single copies, per annum, - - $3 00

RATES OF ADVERTISING:

One Square, of 10 lines, or less, one insertion,		$2 00
" " " " "	three "	4 00
" " " " "	one quarter,	10 00
" " " " "	one year,	30 00

All communications and business letters must be addressed to THE ARIZONIAN, Tubac, Arizona.

Mexican Politics.

There are in Mexico three great leading parties, answering to the type of party wherever that product of imperfect civilization exists. The first, because the eldest, is the CONSERVATIVE, with principles cognate with its name; strenuously adhering to ancient realism as distinguished from modern speculation; anxious to concentrate power in individual hands, and therefore to weaken the authority of popular constitutions and popular legislation; dependent upon the sympathy of the Church and the onfort who only abandoned power to place all its resources at the command of the enemies of popular rights; and, to whose weakness more than to any other cause, Mexico is this day indebted for the lamentable confusion into which its affairs have fallen. If the events of the past year have proved anything, it is that the Liberal cause is predominant everywhere outside of the capital; and that the Constitution which Comonfort betrayed met, in a general sense, the wants and wishes of the people. The only point unattainable to the popular party is the City of Mexico, which it was in the power of Comonfort to have secured to them. He gave it to their adversaries, and hence this protracted series of woes.

Since the departure of Comonfort to the United States, there has been a constant state of warfare between the opposing factions, with varied success, until very lately, when the Conservatives are reported to have triumphed, and elected General Miramon President. We may, however, still look for a continuance of this strife between the various parties.

Condition of Mexico.

The London Times uses strong language in its articles on Mexico. In an article written

Leech's Wagon Road.

Before Congress grants further appropriations for "wagon roads" we venture the suggestion that some official investigation be instituted as to the expenditures made and the work done by late expeditions. If no more good was accomplished by the north n wagon road companies than was effected by Colonel Leech and his corps on the Southern line, the money might as well be kept in the Treasury.

From El Paso, along the old road to Tucson, to the point where Leech's road strikes off to the Gila, the amount of labor performed was very trifling. As to the road along the Gila, we doubt very much if it has ever been traveled by a wagon since the expedition left, and the faint tracks made by the expedition wagons are rapidly growing up to grass. Col. Leech's ox train, under the superintendence of a sea captain, was eleven months making the distance from Fort Belknap to La Mesilla and arrived just in time to be sold out, not having been of the least benefit. There are circumstances

getic individuals may have made "four" dollars per day, which is a very fine average yield of the diggings, but the "hundred-and-fifty-dollars-per-day"-men it would puzzle even a "Washington correspondent" to discover.

We are next enlightened to the effect that:

A new silver "lead" had been discovered on land belonging to Lieut. Mowry, which pays as richly as, if not richer, than the celebrated Heintzleman silver mine. These more recent discoveries had produced an excited mining fever throughout the country.

In view of the fact that silver mining is receiving considerable attention in this section of Arizona, we should really be glad to know by whom that identical "lead" (on land belonging to Lieut Mowry,) was discovered, when, and where? We feel confident that such information will be "new" to our readers, and no doubt highly gratifying. We shall also be equally gratified if the New York Times will designate some particular locality in this Territory where a few cases of the above mentioned "mining fever" may be found!

Tucson, A Growing Town

IN THE 1850s TUCSON was a one-story Mexican farming village. On holidays the Mexican citizens celebrated with dances and lively parties. Occasionally, traveling entertainers drifted into town with the popular *titeres* (puppet shows) or a circus of acrobats and clowns.

A classic description of Tucson is found in the diary of an *engraver* who worked for Charles Poston:

"Arrived in Tucson last evening by stage. . . . There is no tavern or other accommodation here for travelers. The corral is where I slept comfortably as the ground was made soft by manure. Yesterday a dispute occurred between two men . . . one shot the other dead on the spot . . . and no particular notice is taken of it. . . . There is no law here, or if there is it is not enforced. Might makes right."

—Phocion R. Way diary, 1857

Mark Aldrich was the first American to open a store in Tucson.

Solomon Warner opened Warner's General Store.

Butterfield Overland Mail Company

THIS COMPANY HAD THE FIRST dependable, well-organized stage line across Arizona. The line ran from the railroad terminal at St. Louis, Missouri, to San Francisco, California. Passenger and mail service was provided twice weekly in each direction.

Stagecoach stations were stocked with fresh horses or mules, extra coaches, hay and corn for the animals, and food for passengers. Most of the Arizona stations were built of adobe and surrounded by a wall for protection against Indian attack.

The trip was supposed to be made in twenty-five days. John Butterfield's instructions to his drivers were "Remember, boys, nothing on God's earth can stop the U.S. mail!" During the line's existence, the mail was late only three times at the terminals—a remarkable record.

After a few years the Butterfield route was shifted north through Utah. Residents of southern Arizona regretted the loss of regular mail and passenger service. But, for a brief time, the region had been an important link in the greatest overland stage *venture* ever undertaken.

What do you think? What characteristics of a good businessman did John Butterfield need to start and operate a 2,651-mile-long stage line?

The Butterfield Stage Route

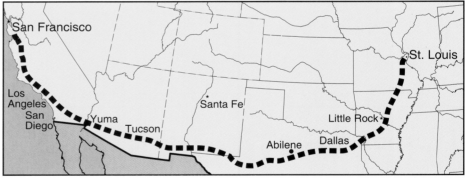

Stage Lines Help Merchants

The stage lines and the mining activity in southern Arizona brought prosperity to Tucson merchants. The clank and clatter of wagons on village streets meant business for storekeepers and freighters.

Mark Aldrich from Illinois was the first American to open a store in Tucson. He was also the town's first postmaster. Aldrich became the first American *alcalde*, or mayor, and was also elected as a judge. Since there was no jail, he sentenced a few horse thieves to be flogged at a whipping post in the public plaza. His *constable*, a muscular Mexican, administered half the lashes. "Now," Aldrich would then say to the culprit, "come back tomorrow for the other half." Before the appointed time, the man was far away, as it was intended he would be.

Solomon Warner arrived from Fort Yuma with merchandise packed on the backs of mules. Before long, Warner's General Store was the shopping center for southern Arizona.

This Concord coach was used on the Butterfield stage line. The purpose of the stagecoach companies was to carry mail and passengers more quickly than ever before over the new roads. The roads, however, were only dirt, and were often muddy and rocky, making the ride very uncomfortable for passengers.

Yuma Crossing

TRAVELERS CROSSED the Colorado River at Yuma, which became a beehive of activity. Thousands of California-bound gold seekers used the crossing. U.S. soldiers camped on the California side of the crossing "to aid the worn-out gold seekers and boundary surveyors." The soldiers lived in brush huts that sheltered them from the hot sun and allowed a free circulation of air.

Two of the gold seekers deserve special mention. The wife of Elias Howard gave birth in a wagon to "Gila," one of the first children born of Anglo-American parents in what is now Arizona. Howard sold his wagon to an army lieutenant, who used it as a boat to pull travelers across the river. Abel Lincoln, another gold rusher, operated the first regular ferryboat at the Yuma crossing. He grossed $60,000 in three months.

A band of murdering scalp hunters, led by the infamous John Glanton, saw how well Lincoln was doing and forced him to join them in a partnership. Then Glanton's gang began mistreating the Yumas, who were running a competing boat. Glanton set the Indian boat adrift and beat up the chief. At the first chance, the Yumas got revenge. They killed all the white men except three who were away cutting willow poles.

ARIZONA PORTRAIT

J. Ross Browne
1821–1875

As a boy in Dublin, John Ross Browne had two ambitions: to see the world and to become a writer. These goals began to take shape after his family sailed from Ireland to live in the United States. As a teenager, Browne floated down the Mississippi on a flatboat. Later he worked on a whaler in the Indian Ocean and wrote a book about his experiences. During his lifetime, he traveled to nearly every part of the world.

In 1864, Browne toured the new Territory of Arizona. Escorted by Charles Poston, he mingled with some of the Indian tribes and observed the *desolation* of mines, ranches, forts, and towns. Browne wrote six entertaining articles, which he illustrated with sketches for *Harper's Weekly*. These articles were published later in a book called *A Tour of Arizona and Sonora (1864): Adventures in Apache Country.*

Yuma

Samuel P. Heintzelman directed the building of Fort Yuma. He was also involved in silver mining at Tubac. He worked to get Arizona created as a separate territory.

Colorado City (Yuma)

The Yuma region was part of Mexico until the Gadsden Purchase in 1854. In that year the townsite of Colorado City was surveyed. Later called Arizona City, then Yuma, this settlement was described as "a flourishing little town with a few adobe houses, two stores, two saloons, and a post office."

Sarah Bowman's Inn, two blacksmith shops, a stage depot, and boat docks were located downstream. Bowman is sometimes called "the first citizen of Yuma." She first came to this area as a cook for soldiers at Fort Yuma.

This drawing of Yuma Indians was made by an artist who accompanied a military expedition to explore the Colorado River by steamboat. The Yumas traded at the crossing of the Colorado River for clothes and other items. They also ran a ferry across the river for travelers.

Gila City's Gold Boom

Gila City was Arizona's first wild and wicked gold rush town. Jacob Snively discovered gold about twenty miles up the Gila River from Arizona City. He swished a little water over the sand in his pan and saw gold glistening in the sun. Within a year, about a thousand people rushed to pan the coarse gold found in sand and gravel near the stream.

Gila City became a village of tents and brush shanties. Merchants rushed there with barrels of whiskey and ready-made clothing. Traders crowded in with high-priced food. Gambling and drinking occupied the miners after dark. Gila City had everything except a church and a jail.

An estimated $2 million in gold was found. The bonanza, however, was soon over.

Steamboats on the Colorado River

The arrival of steam-powered boats was a great event. Steamboats solved the problem of getting food and equipment to Fort Yuma. Before the steamboats, men unloaded supplies from ships at the mouth of the Colorado River. Other men then took the cargo upstream on flatboats, using long poles to push the boats up the river.

The *Uncle Sam* became the first of many steamboats to **navigate** the Colorado River. These steamers carried freight and passengers to Fort Mojave and beyond.

Cargo was unloaded from steamboats at "ports" that sprang up along the Colorado River. The freight was then hauled overland in wagons to mines, forts, ranches, and settlements. The steamboat-wagon combo helped conquer the Arizona wilderness in three decades—something the Spanish empire didn't do in three centuries.

Steam navigation on the Colorado River was difficult, however. The channel changed constantly because of shifting sand. Fifteen miles a day was the most a steamboat could make going upstream. Yet, land transportation along the river was even slower.

People at Yuma sometimes took a steamboat ride just for fun.

Northern Arizona and the U.S. Army

WHEN THE UNITED STATES TOOK OVER in 1848, northern Arizona was *tierra incognito*, known only to the native people and a few mountain men. No Spanish or Mexican settlements had sprung up there. In the 1850s, however, army engineers began to explore, survey, and map the region.

In 1851 the army built Fort Defiance to protect new settlements from raiding Navajos. That same year, Captain Lorenzo Sitgreaves led surveyors and a military escort along a route where Holbrook, Flagstaff, and Kingman would later be built. At the Colorado River they turned south to Fort Yuma. His men, exhausted and short on food, survived by butchering pack mules along the way. Sitgreaves and Lt. Amiel Whipple, who did a second survey along the same route, proved that a railroad could be built over northern Arizona's rough terrain. Whipple was also the first to report that settlers could do well in the region.

As a young lieutenant, General Amiel W. Whipple surveyed a railroad route in northern Arizona. He was later killed in a Civil War battle. Fort Whipple is named for him.

Edward Beale and his crew built the first wagon road across northern Arizona. He was also responsible for Arizona's first camel caravan.

Beale's camel camp in northern Arizona is shown in this diorama at the Arizona Historical Society.

What Happened to the Camels?

Some of the camels that were brought to the territory were auctioned to circuses. Others were used to transport ore at Nevada mines. Eventually, some camels ran loose in the Arizona desert. Fascinating camel tales were told over and over. One story said that a huge red camel, known as the Red Ghost, ran wild with a human skeleton strapped on its back. It was spotted occasionally by ranchers and *prospectors*.

Nobody would believe their stories until hoofprints were seen and red hair was found on bushes. Finally, the Red Ghost was killed. When the camel was examined, its back was still covered with knotted rawhide straps, but no skeleton.

Beale's Wagon Road and Camels from Africa

In 1857 Lieutenant Edward F. Beale was selected to build the first wagon road across northern Arizona. Beale had the challenge of combining road building with a camel experiment. The federal government hoped that camels might solve the army's transportation problems in the *arid* West.

Beale's caravan was a strange-looking procession: mule-drawn wagons, horses, 350 sheep for food, and 25 exotic camels imported from North Africa. Each camel wore a large jingle bell around its neck. Hadji Ali, better known as Hi Jolly, and other brightly-costumed camel drivers were quite a contrast to the army men and mule skinners who wore flannel shirts and buckskin clothing. Hi Jolly's crew knew how to handle the camels. They sang cheery Arabian songs to soothe the animals and never used a whip or spur while riding them.

As the survey for a wagon road moved through the vicinity of present-day Flagstaff and on to the Colorado River, Beale praised the camels. "The camels pack water for others under the hot sun and never get a drop," he said. "They subsist [live] on bitter greasewood but keep fat. I look forward to the day when every mail route across the continent will be worked by this economical and noble brute."

There were problems, of course. The camels frightened the pack mules and wagon teams, causing them to panic. Some of the soldiers got "seasick" riding the so-called "ships of the desert." Camels roll from side to side, like a ship on the ocean waves, because, unlike horses, the two left feet move forward at the same time and then the two right feet.

Nothing ever came of "Operation Camel." Beale's work crew, however, had smoothed out a wagon road, built some temporary bridges, and located water sources along the way. The road was used by many pioneers going to California.

ARIZONA: A Journey of Discovery

Apache Raids

MEANWHILE, WAY DOWN SOUTH, the Apaches continued to raid ranches, wagon trains, and settlements.

> "We were passing the usual quiet Sunday in Tubac when a Mexican *vaquero* came galloping furiously into the plaza crying out "Apaches! Apaches! Apaches!" The Apaches had made an attack on Canoa [a big ranch south of Tucson] and killed the settlers."
>
> —Charles D. Poston diary

> "At the break of day, the Apaches gave a whoop and disappeared with the entire herd—146 horses and mules—before the astonished gaze of five watchmen, who were sleeping under a porch within thirty yards."
>
> —Charles D. Poston diary

The pioneers had little protection from these raids, even after the Army built Fort Buchanan in a valley east of Tubac. Experience with summer heat at Fort Yuma no doubt had influenced the selection of a higher, cooler site for the new fort. Unfortunately, malaria-spreading mosquitos were bad during the rainy season. The buildings had no ventilation and the mud roofs leaked during wet weather. This made for low *morale* at Fort Buchanan.

Captain Richard Ewell and his men pursued Apaches who were threatening settlers.

Richard S. Ewell was an officer at Fort Buchanan and became a famous general in the Confederate Army during the Civil War.

While Fort Buchanan was being built, Captain Richard S. Ewell led troops into Apache country. The soldiers destroyed some Indian crops and killed a few men. The Apaches were not crushed, so Ewell tried the treaty approach. He met with Pinal Apaches in Cañon del Oro, near Tucson, and gave them corn and beef for signing a peace treaty. But Apache raids continued. They drove away horses, mules, and cattle from ranches, mines, and even the forts.

After the Civil War erupted in the Southeastern United States, the army closed Arizona's military posts. The soldiers left and bands of Apaches increased their raids. They forced nearly every rancher and miner to leave. Charles Poston, whose brother had been killed at a mine near Tubac, fled to California. Other pioneers moved to Tucson for safety.

Civil War, 1861–1865

ELEVEN SOUTHERN STATES *seceded* from the Union over the issue of state's rights and slavery. They formed their own country and called it the **Confederate** States of America. War broke out when Confederate soldiers fired on Fort Sumter in South Carolina.

Far away in the West, the Territory of New Mexico, which included Arizona, got involved in the war because it was the connecting link between Texas (a Confederate state) and California (a Union state). During the war, both the Confederacy and the **Union** formed a Territory of Arizona, but the boundaries were very different from each other.

A Divided Nation
North: Union (Yankees)
South: Confederacy (Rebels)

Confederate Territory of Arizona

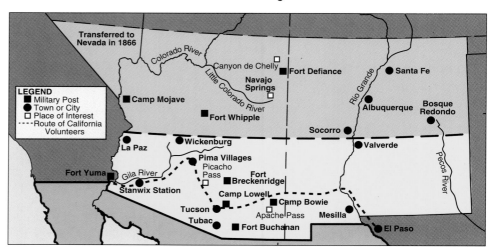

The proposed territory (in yellow) stretched from Texas to California. The capital was at Mesilla. The South wanted an outlet on the Pacific Ocean as well as the gold and silver from Arizona mines. Confederate soldiers occupied only a small part of the territory and only for a short time.

Union Territory of Arizona

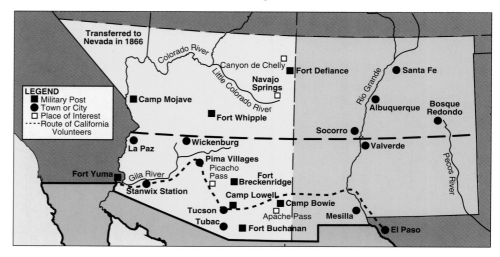

The territory (in yellow) is now the state of Arizona, though that didn't happen for a long time.

Captain Sherod Hunter

A large number of pro-South residents in Tucson eagerly awaited the arrival of Confederate troops in their town. They warmly greeted Captain Sherod Hunter and his rough, unmilitary-looking company of volunteers from Texas and the Rio Grande region. The citizens cheered as the Stars and Bars flag was raised at the town plaza. One happy merchant even danced the jig. During Hunter's short stay in Tucson, he outfitted his men with new clothes from local stores. None of the men had a Confederate gray uniform while in Arizona.

The captain then talked to Union supporters, including Estevan Ochoa, a prominent merchant and wagon freighter.

"Mr. Ochoa, I trust you will take an oath of allegiance to support the Confederacy and relieve me of the necessity to take your property."

Politely but firmly, Ochoa replied, "Captain Hunter, that is out of the question. I owe all my prosperity and happiness to the U. S. government. When, sir, do you want me to leave?"

"Immediately," was the answer. "You may take your favorite horse, together with arms, ammunition, and such provisions as you can quickly collect."

Only a small number of Tucson residents remained loyal to the Union and left. Why did so many people side with the South? One reason is that a lot of them came from the Southern States. They also resented the way Union troops had been assigned elsewhere, leaving Arizona pioneers at the mercy of Apaches and outlaws. Finally, the people needed protection and didn't care which side provided it.

The Confederate Captain Hunter did not linger long in Tucson. His next objective was to scout the Gila trail where a large Union army—the California Volunteers, also called the California Column—would appear sooner or later. At the Pima villages Hunter arrested Ammi White, a miller and storekeeper who was buying supplies for the Californians. Captain Hunter seized the loot, including 1,500 sacks of wheat. He divided the grain among the Pimas since he had no wagons to haul it away.

Hunter had a second unexpected bit of luck. Union Captain William H. McCleave rode in with nine Union scouts. Captain Hunter, posing as the miller, was able to get the Yankees inside and take them prisoners. After this success, Hunter returned to Tucson.

> "... a ragged, undisciplined, poorly-armed, and badly-equipped company that lived off the country."
> —J. Ross Browne, writing about Hunter's soldiers in *Harper's Magazine*, 1864.

> "I do solemnly swear that I will be a true and loyal citizen . . . of the Confederate States of America."
> —Captain Sherod Hunter's loyalty oath

Estevan Ochoa remained loyal to the Union.

Skirmish at Stanwix Station

At Stanwix Station, only eighty miles from Yuma, a Rebel patrol stumbled upon a large Union camp. After exchanging shots and wounding a soldier, the Confederates retreated. They outran the Union cavalry who pursued them. While not a battle, the fight at Stanwix Station can be called the westernmost *skirmish* between soldiers during the entire Civil War.

Sylvester Mowry

Trial of Sylvester Mowry

Carleton went after every suspected Confederate sympathizer he could catch. The most notable was Sylvester Mowry, who had worked hard to get Arizona created as a separate territory. It was decided that Mowry had helped Hunter's troops and corresponded with Confederate leaders. His rich Patagonia silver mine was taken and auctioned for a mere $2,000.

"I am innocent," Mowry insisted. "All I wanted was protection from the Apaches. I petitioned both sides for help." Mowry was confined to Fort Yuma until Carleton's superior officer investigated the case and found no grounds for holding him.

After the war, a federal court awarded Mowry $40,000 for damages. But his reputation was never completely restored.

James H. Carleton

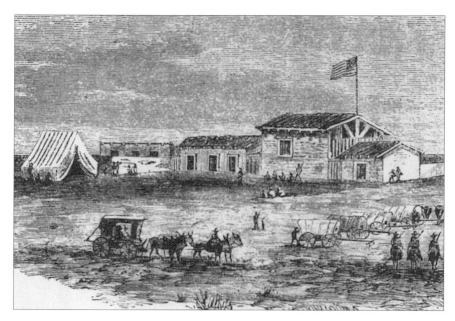
Ammi White's mill at the Pima Villages was sketched by J. Ross Browne in 1864.

Battle of Picacho Pass

Scouts of the California Volunteers caught up with one of Hunter's patrols near Picacho Peak, forty miles north of Tucson. The small squad charged head-on into the brush without dismounting. The Rebels emptied their rifles, killing the leader and two other soldiers, and wounding three others. After some fierce fighting, both sides withdrew. Called the "Battle of Picacho Pass," this skirmish dashed any hope the South had of opening a "lifeline" to the Pacific Ocean.

General Carleton and the California Volunteers Occupy Tucson

In Tucson, Captain Hunter realized that his small force would be no match for the 1,800-man California Volunteers and left for New Mexico. Colonel Carleton, the leader of the Union group, arrived in style, saluted by four *artillery* pieces which his men had dragged across the desert. A short time later, he was promoted to brigadier general.

General Carleton brought law and order to Arizona, making life almost as hard for his friends as his enemies. He appointed himself as the military governor and declared *martial law*. All citizens were required to take an oath of allegiance to the United States. They also had to have a job. Since there were no civil courts, a military commission conducted trials. Carleton ordered the arrest of nine Tucson outlaws and had them imprisoned at Fort Yuma. He taxed gambling houses and saloons, using the money for the care of sick and wounded soldiers. He later moved most of his army to New Mexico.

This sketch shows the headquarters of Mowry's silver and lead mine.
(Sketch by J. Ross Browne, 1864)

Battle of Apache Pass

The largest battle of the Civil War was in Arizona between the California Volunteers and a band of Apaches. As Carleton's soldiers reached Apache Pass, the Indians, led by Mangas Coloradas and Cochise, fired on them from behind rocks.

After stubborn resistance, the Apaches were finally dislodged by bursting shells. The Battle of Apache Pass was a victory for the troops. Two soldiers had been killed and three were wounded. The Apaches lost sixty-six men and a large number were wounded. Cochise later told an officer who had been at the battle, "You never would have whipped us if you had not used the wagons that shoot." Cochise was referring to cannons on wheels.

Mangas Coloradas (Red Sleeves) and his son-in-law, Cochise, were two of the most feared Chiricahua Apache chiefs. The great Mangas stood six-and-a-half feet tall. Cochise was "built as perfect as any man could be," said an Anglo man who knew him.

Carleton built Fort Bowie at Apache Pass. For many years this fort protected travelers, wagon trains, stagecoaches, and cattle herders passing through the Apache danger zone.

Arizona under U.S. Rule

The Long Walk

BY THE TIME GENERAL CARLETON got to Santa Fe, the Confederates were already beaten and headed back to Texas. With the Rebels gone, Carleton began rounding up Navajos in Arizona and Mescalero Apaches in New Mexico. He forced them to live at Bosque Redondo, a *reservation* "far down the Pecos River on the open plain." His *ultimatum* to the Indians was, "surrender and go to the reservation or every male capable of bearing arms will be killed."

Carleton chose a not-very-willing Colonel Kit Carson to bring the Indians in. Carson's soldiers tried to track down every Navajo who didn't surrender. They slaughtered sheep, burned corn crops, and cut down peach trees. The last Navajos to give up were hiding in the beautiful Canyon de Chelly.

By 1865, more than 8,000 Navajos surrendered and began the painful "Long Walk" of 400 miles to Bosque Redondo. At this "concentration camp" they suffered. They were weakened by a smallpox epidemic that took hundreds of lives, by hunger when crops failed due to cutworms and bad irrigation practices, and by longing for their plateau homeland. The Navajos became wards of the federal government, depending on rations to survive. They were no longer proud, self-supporting people.

After several years of dismal failure, the Bosque Redondo Reservation was investigated by the Department of War. In 1868 the Navajos agreed to a peace treaty and were permitted to return to their former lands.

Manuelito, the leader of a small Navajo warrior band, did not surrender until 1866.
(Photo by Charles Bell)

Posing in front of the family hogan, this Navajo girl and her dog will drive the sheep to pasture.

Navajos: The Rest of the Story

Home at last! The Diñeh, as Navajos call themselves, left captivity at Bosque Redondo, New Mexico, and walked the long journey to their new reservation in Arizona. They soon began raising sheep for food, wool, and trade. The women spun wool into yarn and wove brightly-colored rugs and blankets with intricate designs. Some of the men made beautiful jewelry from turquoise and silver. The Navajos sold most of their excellent handicraft products at nearby trading posts.

Elle, the most famous Navajo weaver, lived at Ganado on the reservation. After the Santa Fe Railroad laid a track across Arizona, she enjoyed working for the Fred Harvey Company at Santa Fe and other places. Thousands of tourists photographed Elle weaving rugs or making natural dyes from native plants for her colored yarns. Her husband Tom, a silversmith, was usually working nearby. Tom spoke four languages (Navajo, Hopi, English, and Spanish) and interpreted for Elle.

This postcard shows Elle of Ganado weaving a blanket for U.S. President William Howard Taft.

For a long time, the Navajo economy depended on sheep. A large flock became the symbol of a family's wealth and prosperity. A mother at at public dance, for example, might push her daughter toward a "good catch" and say something like, "Go ask that boy for a dance. His mother has 2,000 sheep."

Eventually, however, the Navajos owned too many sheep. Their flocks **overgrazed** the fragile desert vegetation. By the 1930s, soil from the reservation was eroding into the lake behind Boulder (Hoover) Dam. The federal government then ordered nearly half of the sheep destroyed. This order naturally angered many people on the reservation, even though they were paid for the slaughtered sheep.

Today, the Navajo tribe officially calls itself the Navajo Nation. Leaders are earning more income for the tribe from oil, gas, coal, uranium, and timber resources on the 15-million-acre reservation. Factories and a coal-burning power plant also provide jobs.

Education is another key to Navajo progress. More Navajo teachers are taking jobs in community-controlled schools. The people are proud of an academy for gifted high school students and the Navajo Community College. At the college, Navajo students take classes to learn about their native culture, including the art of rug weaving. Navajo plans for the future include a medical school for the reservation.

With better jobs, education, and health care, Navajo people are moving with the rest of Arizona citizens into the twenty-first century.

Peshlakai, a famous Navajo silversmith, shows his work in 1885.

Michael Goldwater
1821–1903

A federal census in 1864 listed seventeen merchants in La Paz. One of the leaders, Michael Goldwater, was a Jewish immigrant who left Russian-occupied Poland to escape persecution. "Big Mike," as he was called, and his brother Joe began hauling freight to Prescott and started a chain of mercantile stores in Arizona.

Mike's grandson, Barry Goldwater, became a U.S. senator.

Gold Rush to Central Arizona

PAULINE WEAVER FOUND GOLD along the Colorado River north of Yuma. After he took a small amount of gold dust to the Yuma area, his discovery was not a secret very long. Hundreds of gold seekers, many of them Mexicans from Sonora, rushed to the new town of La Paz. The boom lasted two years. Miners collected gold worth several million dollars.

At the height of La Paz's prosperity, it was Arizona's largest city. The people lived in tents or adobe houses. La Paz had a good steamboat landing and prospered for a while as the supply center for mines in the Prescott area.

The people moved to nearby Ehrenberg when the Colorado River changed course, leaving La Paz landlocked and a "vanished city."

Walker and Weaver Mining Districts

The area south of soon-to-be Prescott bustled with mining activity. Joseph Reddeford Walker led thirty hardy frontiersmen from New Mexico. This group panned gold along Lynx Creek and dug out gold ore in the mountains.

Pauline Weaver guided the Abraham Peeples party, a California group, to the Prescott region. They struck gold in Weaver's Gulch. Then a Mexican man in this party accidentally discovered nuggets on what came to be called Rich Hill. He rushed back with samples in his hand, shouting, "Eureka!" Before breakfast the prospectors forced out gold worth thousands of dollars, using only knives. Rich Hill became the richest "placer" discovery ever made in Arizona.

Prospectors worked along Lynx Creek.

(From a mural by Paul Coze in the Prescott City Hall)

Linking the past and the present

Thousands of people rushed to places where gold was discovered. Can you think of things people do today to "get rich quick?"

Wickenburg's Vulture Mine

"Gold!" shouted the lonely prospector to a vulture hovering overhead. Henry Wickenburg examined the outcroppings of metal glittering in the sun. He was standing on a gold mine.

Late in 1863 Henry Wickenburg discovered Arizona's largest and richest gold deposit about fifteen miles south of the Hassayampa River. The rich ore on the surface of the land was easy to chip out. After several years, Wickenburg decided he was a prospector, not a businessman. He knew that more heavy machinery and a big crew of miners would be needed to blast out the wide vein of gold under the ground. He sold out to an investor who formed the Vulture Mining Company.

Meanwhile, the town of Wickenburg sprang to life. The J. Goldwater and other stores sold high-priced goods and food freighted in by wagon. Saloons stayed open at night, offering billiard tables, gambling, and beer from the local Magnolia Brewery. Wickenburg became one of the largest towns in the territory.

A Wells Fargo guard protects a pile of gold *ingots* smelted at Wickenburg.

The Territory of Arizona

ARIZONA'S GOLD AND SILVER WEALTH was the main reason Congress finally made Arizona a territory separate from New Mexico. During the debate, however, opponents of the bill argued that Arizona didn't have enough people to justify a territorial government. The federal census takers counted fewer than 2,500 non-Indians living in the region. (People in the various Indian groups were not counted.)

"The Arizona Stage Company soon provided service between Wickenburg, La Paz, Tucson, and Prescott."

—The *Weekly Arizona Miner*

John S. Watts, a delegate from Santa Fe, saved the day. During a debate in Congress, he held up a large chunk of silver ore for all to see. Watts said that millions of dollars worth of Arizona silver could be put in circulation. "All the miners need to develop the mines is protection, [from Indians]" he explained. A local territorial government could provide that protection.

Congress passed a territorial bill, and President Abraham Lincoln signed it on February 24, 1863. The law set the present boundaries of Arizona, except for the loss of the northwest corner to Nevada in 1866.

What do you think?

What did John Watts mean by this statement to Congress? "Let it not be said of us that we have the power to conquer and *annex* provinces [Mexican Cession and Gadsden Purchase] but not to protect or defend them."

The Tardy Inkstand

Charles Poston wanted to dramatize President Lincoln's signing of the bill that made Arizona a separate territory. He designed a silver inkstand. In the center of the stand was a miniature capitol dome that covered the inkwell itself. On one end was an Indian woman and on the other a frontiersman with his rifle. The name "'Abraham Lincoln" was inscribed on one side of the base. The other side read, "From Charles D. Poston, Arizona—1865."

As the date indicates, the gift was two years late for the signing ceremony. Lincoln had the privilege of using the massive stand only a month before he was assassinated.

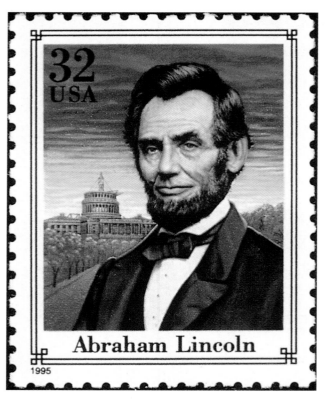

United States President Abraham Lincoln signed the bill that made Arizona a separate territory.

Good transportation is needed for economic growth.

1. List the forms of transportation used in Arizona during the 1850s and 1860s.
2. Why did the U.S. Army do surveys in Arizona in the 1850s?
3. What are the main ways people travel and haul goods in Arizona today?
4. The popular song "Route 66" reminds us not to forget Winona, Arizona. On an Arizona Highways map, trace Route 66 and locate Winona.

The plaque on this monument at Quartzsite reads, "Hi Jolly, born somewhere in Syria about 1828. Came to this country February 10, 1856. Camel driver–Packer Scout. Faithful to the U.S. Government for over 30 years."

Chapter 5 Review

1. For what reasons did the population of Arizona increase slowly in the 1850s?

2. How did travelers in the 1850s describe Tucson?

3. What was unusual about the early settlement of Yuma on the Colorado River?

4. Explain why you think the Gila gold discovery was reported in every major newspaper from San Francisco to New York.

5. Briefly describe what was happening in northern Arizona during the 1850s.

6. Why was Fort Buchanan built where it was?

7. How would you describe relations between Apaches and the pioneers before the Civil War?

8. Where was the "Confederate Territory of Arizona?"

9. In what places in Arizona were skirmishes fought between Confederate and Union troops?

10. Why did General Carleton have Sylvester Mowry arrested? What punishments did Mowry suffer?

11. What was the biggest battle of the Civil War in Arizona? Which fort was later built there?

12. Give two reasons why life was difficult for Navajos on the Bosque Redondo Reservation.

13. For what economic reason was the Territory of Arizona created in 1863?

14. What part did President Abraham Lincoln play in the history of Arizona?

THE TIME
1863 – 1912

PEOPLE TO KNOW
Governor John Goodwin
Judge William T. Howell
Charles D. Poston
Francisco S. Léon
Jesús M. Elias
José M. Redondo
Moses Sherman
Richard C. McCormick
Governor Anson P. K.
   Safford
John Spring
Josephine Brawley Hughes
Mary Elizabeth Post
Governor Frederick A. Tritle
Estevan Ochoa
Carlos Velasco
Mariano Samaniego
James Addison Reavis
Governor Myron H.
   McCord
"Buckey" O'Neill

PLACES TO LOCATE
Prescott
Ehrenberg
Lake Mead
Arizona City (Yuma)
Phoenix
Florence
Tempe
Mesa
Globe
Safford
Maricopa
San Pedro River
Santa Cruz River
Nogales
Santiago, Cuba

1864
Prescott is built as the
territorial capital.

1871
A law provides for taxes to
support public schools.

1860   1865   1870   1875

1867 – 1877
Tucson is the
territorial capital.

1875
Territorial prison
is built at Yuma.

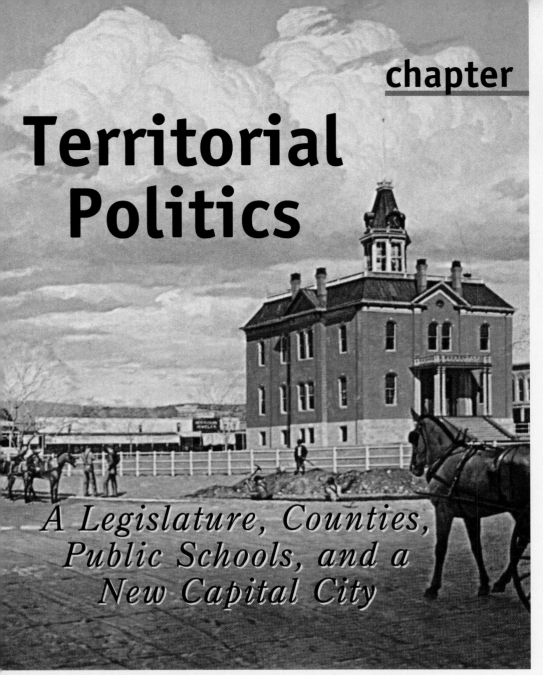

Territorial Politics

A Legislature, Counties, Public Schools, and a New Capital City

This painting shows Prescott, Arizona's first territorial capital city, in the early days. (Mural by Charles E. Kemp)

TERMS TO UNDERSTAND
delegate
rostrum
Howell Code
poll tax
convene
legislator
"thieving thirteenth"
exceed
politicking
levee
suffragette
junket
discrimination
absentee owner
speculator
title
defraud
rustler
posse
cavalry
Rough Riders

1863 – 1912 Territory of Arizona

1877 – 1889 Prescott is again the capital.

1889 Phoenix becomes the capital.

1912 → Arizona becomes a state.

| 1880 | 1885 | 1890 | 1895 | 1900 | 1905 |

1885 Thirteenth legislature creates schools of higher learning.

1898 Spanish-American War

1901 Territorial capitol building is completed in Phoenix.

111

Organizing a Territory

The first territorial governor was John N. Goodwin.

The first territorial delegate to Congress was Charles Poston.

The first territorial capitol building was destroyed in the great Prescott fire in 1900.

Judge William T. Howell

ARIZONA WAS A TERRITORY from 1863 to 1912. During that time it was governed by sixteen different governors who were appointed by the president of the United States. A two-house legislature, called the Assembly, was elected every two years by the people. The voters also elected a *delegate* to the U.S. Congress in Washington, D.C., who could speak there in the House but not vote. County officers were also elected. Only men could vote in these elections. Women and American Indians could not vote.

Governor John Goodwin was appointed by President Abraham Lincoln. Goodwin was eager to get the territorial government underway. With a military escort, Goodwin and others made a tour of the territory. He considered several locations for a permanent capital. Tucson was the logical choice. Nearly half of the territory's non-Indian population lived in that region. But the governor decided on a new town. Why? In 1864 the nation was still fighting the Civil War, and a number of Tucson leaders had Confederate sympathies. He picked a mile-high spot in the pines and named it after William H. Prescott, the historian.

In the new town of Prescott, two territorial buildings were constructed out of rough-hewn logs. One of the buildings was an eleven-room Governor's Mansion. A two-room capitol was not completed when the first elected legislature assembled. The walls were not chinked with mud, so cool autumn breezes whistled through the cracks. Tallow candles lit the rooms. There were no windows, just wooden shutters. The seats and tables were made of rough boards. There were no spittoons, usually found in legislative halls in those days, but that didn't matter. The floors were dirt.

One of Governor Goodwin's first actions was to divide the territory into three judicial districts. Each judge, appointed by the president, was assigned a town—Tucson, La Paz, or Prescott—where he presided over trials.

The courtrooms were not elegant. Judge William T. Howell, who presided at Tucson, left Arizona before a year was out. He told Governor Goodwin that he would not serve as judge in a district where two out of three people were barefooted. Court was held in an adobe shack with a dirt floor, and a dry goods box was used as the judge's *rostrum*.

Linking the past and the present
The first six delegates to Congress from Arizona ran and were elected as Independents. This means that they were not a member of any political party. Is that possible today? Would it be a good idea? Explain the pros and cons.

The First Territorial Legislature

The first legislature had a head start. Judge Howell had compiled a code of laws before the members came together. The Howell Code, with some amendments and changes, was adopted by the first legislature. The code protected mining claims and dealt with such things as water rights, property ownership, crime, jury trials, gambling licenses, and a *poll tax*. Howell was paid $2,500 in addition to his salary as a judge. By contrast, the legislators received only $3 a day for the forty-day session.

The legislature had no money to build needed roads, so it authorized six toll roads. One of them, the Santa Maria Toll Road, ran from Prescott to steamboat landings on the Colorado River. The toll charge was four cents a mile for a wagon and two and a half cents a mile for a rider on horseback.

People in the territory wanted weekly mail service between all the major towns, so the legislature asked the U.S. Congress for federal aid. Charles D. Poston, the delegate to Congress, succeeded in getting mail routes that connected Prescott to Tubac, Los Angeles, and Santa Fe.

The Congress in Washington also set aside 75,000 acres for the Colorado River Indian Reservation. No money was voted, however, until 1867 to settle Yumas, Yavapais, Mohaves, and Hualapais there.

Some of the first officers of the Territory of Arizona were Governor John N. Goodwin (front center) and secretary and future governor Richard C. McCormick (to his left).

Frontier Legislature

Arizona's first legislature *convened* at Prescott in September, 1864. The Assembly consisted of a Council and a House of Representatives. Nearly half the members were either miners or mining engineers. One of the miners was Jackson McCrackin from Lynx Creek. The story is told that his friends thought he should go to Prescott looking like a *legislator*. They escorted him to the creek and scrubbed him with soap, water, and a horse brush. A hand-me-down suit and a trip to the barber shop gave him all the dignity he needed in frontier Arizona.

Only two members of the legislature, Francisco S. León and Jesús M. Elías, were born in the territory. They spoke only Spanish. Another Mexican American, José M. Redondo, was informed after reaching the capital at Prescott that members had to be citizens of the United States. Redondo, a prominent pioneer of irrigation and cattle raising in Yuma County, returned home to complete the citizenship process he had already begun. He served several times in the legislature.

Two Tucson lawyers were put in leadership positions. Coles Bashford, a former governor of Wisconsin, was president of the Council. W. Claude Jones was Speaker of the House.

A Territorial Governor

President Lincoln appointed the territorial officers. The first man he appointed as governor became ill and never made it to Arizona. He was replaced by John N. Goodwin from Maine.

Goodwin and other officers traveled to Santa Fe, where they stopped to visit with General Carleton. The general suggested that the territorial capital be located near the gold mines. "Goldstruck" by what Carleton told them, Goodwin's party quickly agreed that Fort Whipple, near the mines, would be a good temporary capital for Arizona. Early in 1864 their creaky, heavily loaded wagons pulled into the fort. Arizona was a territory at last!

A Capital on Wheels

The log buildings in Prescott were used by the territorial government until 1867. Then the legislature moved the capital to Tucson. After ten years, the legislature moved the "capital on wheels" back to Prescott. By that time the town was growing rapidly.

Arizona Portrait

Richard C. McCormick
1832–1901

Before coming to Arizona, McCormick had been an editor of a New York City newspaper and a war correspondent during the Civil War. He brought a printing press to Arizona and started a newspaper, the *Journal-Miner*. After he became governor in 1865, he published another paper, the *Arizona Citizen*, in Tucson.

As the territory's second governor, McCormick and his young wife Margaret made an extended horseback trip through the western and southern parts of the territory. After weeks in the saddle, Margaret died during childbirth in Prescott. So did the baby girl she was carrying.

Arizona voters elected McCormick a delegate to Congress three times. While in Washington, D.C., he married Rachel "Lizzie" Thurman.

The short, red-haired McCormick is remembered as one of the territory's most popular, distinguished, and intelligent governors. A good speaker and smart politician, he worked hard for efficient government, economic progress, better transportation, and law enforcement in the new Territory of Arizona.

Territorial Counties

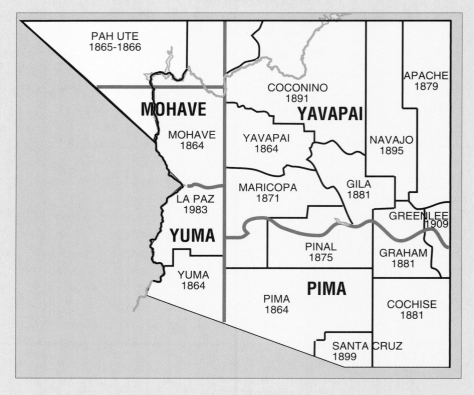

⎯⎯⎯ Boundaries of the four original counties

───── Present county boundaries and the years they were organized

☐ Congress gave this section of the territory to Nevada in 1866.

Counties and County Seats

In 1864, the first legislature divided the territory into four counties, each named after an Indian tribe. The next year, the legislature created Pah Ute County from the northern part of Mohave County. Farmers were rapidly settling there along the Little Colorado River. Today, the sites of the two small Mormon towns are submerged under Lake Mead behind Hoover Dam. Congress gave the portion west of the Colorado River to the State of Nevada in 1866. The "lost county" is now famous for the gambling city of Las Vegas.

Occasionally, a county seat was changed. In 1871 the legislature decided La Paz, the county seat of Yuma County, was becoming a ghost town, and it made Arizona City (now Yuma) the county seat. The sheriff put the county records and property on a steamboat and transported them downstream—an unusual way of moving a desert county seat.

The "Thieving Thirteenth"

OF ALL THE TWENTY-FIVE territorial legislatures, none was more colorful than the thirteenth, which convened in Prescott in 1885. This group is sometimes called the "bloody thirteenth" because of several fights in the legislative halls and in local saloons. But the legislature is usually labeled the "thieving thirteenth" because of the extravagant way it spent money. Its operating expenses greatly *exceeded* the legal limit set by federal law.

Some clerks later testified before a grand jury that their only duty was to sign the payroll. The lawmakers requested more in travel allowances than they were entitled to have. The biggest requests came from five Pima County legislators who claimed fifteen cents a mile for 2,200 miles of travel to and from Prescott. Ordinarily, the legislators would ride the stagecoach to Prescott. But the Salt River was flooding. So they took a train to Los Angeles and returned on another train line to Ash Fork. From that junction they reached Prescott by stage.

With all its faults, the Thirteenth Legislative Assembly accomplished much. The larger towns all wanted large expensive government institutions. At the time, the two big prizes seemed to be the capital or an insane asylum. Cities also wanted a university or a teachers' college.

When the *politicking* was over, the capital was still at Prescott and the prison at Yuma. Phoenix got the desired asylum. Tempe was given the Normal School for Teachers (now Arizona State University). Tucson wanted the capital but had to settle for the university.

Yuma was also promised a new *levee* along the Colorado River. Florence received a bridge over the Gila River. The bridge turned out to be a complete waste of money. It was left "high and dry" in the desert when flood waters cut a new channel.

Prisoners build a new wall at the territorial prison, established at Yuma in 1875.

The thirteenth territorial legislature established Arizona's two largest schools of higher learning. Tempe was pleased to get the teacher's college, which was called Tempe Normal School. The college later became Arizona State University, or ASU, as it is fondly called today.

Tucson got the University of Arizona, but many Tucson residents were disappointed in not getting the state capital. C.C. Stephens, a Council member, came home to an angry crowd. He was greeted with "a shower of ripe eggs, rotting vegetables, and, reportedly, a dead cat." On the other hand, the *Arizona Daily Star* expressed the viewpoint of the town's more enlightened citizens. "It will not only add to the importance of the city," the *Star* reported, "but bring hither several hundred students from abroad who would live here at least ten months of the year."

Territorial Schools

A PUBLIC SCHOOL SYSTEM developed slowly. When Anson P. K. Safford became governor, there were no public schools operating in Arizona. He persuaded the legislature to pass the School Law of 1871. It provided for taxes to support schools. The law required schools to remain open for at least three months each year and teach arithmetic, geography, grammar, physiology, reading, and spelling.

Two schools were opened in Tucson under this law. John Spring, a well-educated Swiss immigrant, taught boys in a one-room adobe building. The crude furniture and equipment included splintery desks and benches, two brooms, and a sprinkling pot for the dirt floor. The parents brought in some ash whipping sticks and urged Mr. Spring to use them liberally. The first public school for girls opened in an old brewery. The teacher was Mrs. Josephine Brawley Hughes. She was the wife of Louis C. Hughes, who later became a territorial governor. Mrs. Hughes was well known as a reformer and *suffragette*. Years later, she was the first woman honored with a plaque in the halls of the Arizona State Capitol.

Safford's enthusiasm for education resulted in new schools all over the territory. Some of the buildings were not planned as schools but served the purpose. In Ehrenberg an abandoned saloon was the school where Mary Elizabeth Post taught for five months. Sometimes prospectors, who used to visit the saloon, would wander in, only to be embarrassed to see the "school marm." Miss Post came to Arizona from San Diego. "I rode a stagecoach as far as Yuma and went upstream by steamboat to Ehrenberg," she said. Ms. Post later taught for nearly forty years in Yuma.

The class of 1898 poses at Tempe Normal School (Now Arizona State University).

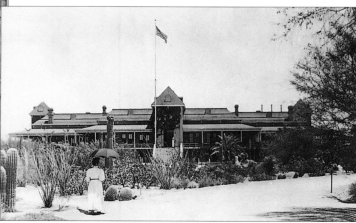

Old Main was the first building on the campus of the University of Arizona.

ARIZONA: A Journey of Discovery

The first real schoolhouse in Phoenix was built in 1873 of adobe.

"At the close of each school year, until the railroad came to Yuma in 1877, all the children were taken on a steamboat excursion and picnic. This was a gala day . . . dancing, and all sorts of games were in order."
—Mary Elizabeth Post

The first school in Phoenix was held in the courthouse. Twenty-two students attended. The boys wore jackets and ties. The girls dressed in long skirts and tight-collared blouses.

The pride of Prescott was a two-story brick schoolhouse. It was the first graded school in the territory, and the best-equipped.

Governor Safford worked for good tax-supported schools throughout his administration. In his last message to the legislature in 1877, Safford reported progress. "About half of nearly 3,000 children of school age in Arizona have learned to read and write," he said.

John Spring, shown here in his Union Army uniform, taught at a school for boys in Tucson.

Josephine Brawley Hughes was Arizona's first female public school teacher.

Governor Anson. P. K. Safford was called the "Father of Education."

Railroads to Phoenix and Prescott

THE THIRTEENTH LEGISLATIVE ASSEMBLY authorized the building of two branch railroads. Phoenix was connected to the Southern Pacific at Maricopa. The last spike on this branch was driven in Phoenix on July 4, 1887. For the first time, Phoenix was free from dependence on animal-drawn stagecoaches and wagons for transportation.

Governor Frederick Tritle took the lead in organizing the Prescott and Arizona Central Railroad. He wanted cheaper transportation for the United Verde Copper Company. For years the copper ore had been hauled in freight wagons to the Santa Fe main line. The branch was completed to Prescott in 1887. Two locomotives puffed into town with whistles blowing. Soldiers at nearby Fort Whipple fired a 100-gun salute.

The first train to come into Prescott was named the "Governor Frederick A. Tritle," 1887.

Phoenix Becomes the New Capital

IN 1889, after the legislators voted to move the capital from Prescott to Phoenix, they boarded a train for a joyous *junket*. They used their free railroad passes and traveled in royal style via Los Angeles. At Maricopa, their two Pullman cars were switched to the new Maricopa and Phoenix Railroad. The mayor of Phoenix happily picked up the entertainment tab for the entire trip and presented each official with a shining silk hat.

The legislature reconvened in Phoenix's brand-new City Hall. The contractor had worked his crew day and night for six weeks to finish the second floor before the lawmakers and officers arrived. The territorial government used the Phoenix City Hall for twelve years. The permanent capitol was completed in 1901.

Arizona's capitol building was completed in 1901. It was made of gray granite and volcanic tufa.

This drawing shows Phoenix in 1885. The population grew to 3,152 in 1890.
(Painting by C. J. Dyer)

Hispanic Americans

MEXICAN AMERICANS were a majority in Arizona until the 1870s, but they did not hold political power. While Arizona was a territory, only seven Hispanic men were elected to the legislature. Five of them were well-to-do Tucson businessmen—Jesus M. Elías, Francisco S. León, Juan Elías, Estevan Ochoa, and Mariano Samaniego. Add the names of José M. Redondo, a Yuma rancher, and Ramón Romano of Tubac and the short list is complete.

Until the 1880s, the Anglo and Mexican American upper classes enjoyed social equality. A shortage of Anglo women was one reason for harmony. Prominent merchants married into Mexican families. Before the railroad arrived, trade was mainly with Mexican Sonora. Tucson businessmen had good relations with Mexican merchants and freighters. The *peso* was the most-circulated type of money.

The railroad ended the days of mutual interests, bringing both merchandise and Anglos into the territory. By the 1890s, Hispanic American leaders were forming organizations to fight *discrimination*.

Mr. Hiram Stevens was a prosperous merchant in Tucson. He married Petra Santa Cruz.

The Alianza Hispano Americana

The *Alianza Hispano Americana* (Spanish American Alliance) was organized in 1894. Carlos Velasco and Mariano Samaniego were leaders in the *Alianza*. Velasco had a law degree from the University of Sonora. He published an outstanding Spanish language newspaper, *El Fronterizo*, in Tucson. Samaniego was born in a socially prominent family in Sonora. After coming to Tucson, he ran a stage line and served in the legislature.

The *Alianza* had some political success. By the time of statehood, however, the *Alianza* had declined.

> **What do you think?**
>
> Estevan Ochoa was a strong legislator even though he was a Republican in Democratic territory. Do you think Hispanic Americans today should put all their power behind one party or try to influence both major parties?

Californians William Randolph Hearst and his mother Phoebe Hearst were the most famous *absentee owners* of an Arizona land grant. The Hearsts owned a large chain of newspapers. Their claim along the San Pedro River west of Tombstone was confirmed in 1899.

Land Grants

CLAIMS TO SPANISH AND MEXICAN land grants held back development. When pioneers began moving into the Santa Cruz, San Pedro, and other valleys, they found the choice sites in the hands of absentee owners. *Speculators*—people who wanted to get rich by buying and reselling land—had sought out heirs to huge Spanish and Mexican land grants. They bought the titles for a song.

The United States government had agreed, by the Gadsden Treaty, to recognize all valid Mexican *titles* to land grants. No time limit was set. Land surveys, title searches, and court hearings went on for fifty years.

The Court of Private Land Claims

Created by U.S. Congress in 1891, this court was unusual—all decisions had to be based on Spanish or Mexican laws. When disputes over land arose, the court had to decide who owned the land. About 180 square miles of claimed land were confirmed in Arizona by the court. This was in addition to two 100,000-acre Baca Float grants, one north of Nogales and one near Prescott.

A Giant Land Swindle

James Addison Reavis claimed a huge rectangle of land that included present-day Phoenix, Tempe, Mesa, Globe, Safford, Clifton, Florence, and Casa Grande. With this claim, Reavis almost pulled off the most gigantic swindle of all time. What he did was invent a Spanish aristocrat named Baron Peralta and forge documents to show that the king of

Spain had given Peralta a land grant in 1748. First there was a forged deed to the Peralta land grant. Reavis explained how he got this document from a mine developer, who supposedly purchased the deed from a descendant of Peralta. The miner could not contradict Reavis's big lie. He died the day after he recorded the deed.

There was another real character in the plot—a Cinderella–like creation of Reavis's imagination. He found a Mexican orphan girl and had her educated. He even altered her California church birth records to show that she was the last surviving descendant of the Peralta family. He eventually married the girl, giving her the title of "Baroness of Arizona."

Even though the claim had not been validated in any court, people were frightened that Reavis could charge them a lot of money for the property they thought was already theirs. Dozens of ordinary people began to pay varying amounts for deeds to their homes, farms, mines, businesses, and even schools. With his big income, Reavis and his baroness were able to live in courtly style. They had homes in St. Louis, Washington, D.C., Spain, and Mexico.

Meanwhile, the territorial surveyor carefully investigated the claim and was able to prove it false. Six years later, the Court of Private Land Claims declared that Reavis had secretly planted forged documents in Spain, Mexico, and California. Reavis was arrested and charged with conspiracy to *defraud* the government. He was fined $5,000 and sentenced to two years in prison.

Linking the past and the present

There have always been crooks who cheat their fellow citizens, though few scams have been on the scale of the Reavis fraud. Can you think of some recent ways the public has been defrauded? What happened? Was justice done?

James Addison Reavis, the "Baron of Arizona," almost pulled off a huge land grant swindle.

The "Baroness of Arizona" was supposedly the only heir to the Peralta family's huge land grant.

William "Buckey" O'Neill

Buckey O'Neill was one of the most colorful pioneers in Arizona history. Only nineteen when he rode into Phoenix on a burro, O'Neill worked as a typesetter and deputy sheriff. He then joined the silver rush to Tombstone and became a newspaper reporter at the time Wyatt Earp and his brothers were policing the town. Later, O'Neill started his own newspaper in Prescott. He offered a $100 reward for the capture of any *rustler* who stole cattle with a brand advertised in his paper.

O'Neill was elected sheriff of Yavapai County in 1888. In that job he gained fame by tracking down four train robbers. O'Neill and a small *posse* trailed the outlaws into Utah and captured them after a gun battle.

When the Spanish-American War started, O'Neill was mayor of Prescott and captain of the militia unit. He was killed fighting in Cuba.

The Spanish-American War

When the United States declared war on Spain in 1898, Arizona's young men were eager to volunteer. Governor Myron H. McCord easily raised two companies of cavalry troops and placed Major Alexander O. Brodie in command. The flag for the Arizona troops was homemade by women in Phoenix. Today, it is displayed in the capitol building tattered, weather-beaten, and bullet-ridden.

The Arizona recruits trained at San Antonio, Texas. They were part of a *cavalry* unit known as the Rough Riders, organized by Theodore Roosevelt. Led by Colonel Leonard Wood, the Rough Riders went into action near Santiago, Cuba, without their horses. The horses were left behind because of a lack of ships. The cavalry became known as "Wood's Weary Walkers." They fought through the thick of the campaign. Brodie, though wounded in battle, served as Roosevelt's second in command. After the war, when Roosevelt became president, he appointed Brodie to be governor of the Territory of Arizona.

Captain Buckey O'Neill was killed in the Cuban campaign. Instead of hugging the ground, he carelessly stood up as Spanish soldiers fired. Just before a sniper shot him, O'Neill supposedly told his sergeant, who had pleaded with him to lie down, "The Spanish bullet isn't molded that will kill me." Colonel Roosevelt said that O'Neill was a serious loss to the Rough Riders since he was the idol of the Arizona troops.

The Spanish Army and Navy were no match for the Americans. The "splendid little war," as one official called it, was quickly finished. The Spanish-American War showed that Arizonans were ready to participate in the affairs of the nation.

Charge of the Rough Riders at San Juan Hill
(Painting by Frederic Remington)

1. How did Governor Goodwin choose a capital city for the new Territory of Arizona?

2. What two government buildings were constructed in Prescott, the new capital?

3. How were territorial governors chosen? List the territorial offices that were filled by election.

4. Identify William T. Howell and Charles D. Poston.

5. How did the first territorial legislature help to solve the need for roads?

6. List the cities that were Arizona's capital during the territorial period.

7. Name Arizona's original four counties.

8. Why is Pah Ute County now known as the "lost county?"

9. Why was the School Law of 1871 important?

10. What did each of the following have to do with Arizona's pioneer schools: Anson P. K. Safford, Josephine Brawley Hughes, and Mary Elizabeth Post?

11. List two ways that the thirteenth territorial legislature overspent.

12. What were some important accomplishments of the thirteenth legislature?

13. When did Phoenix become the capital? In what unusual way did the legislators move to the new capital?

14. What event contributed to the decline of Hispanic-Anglo equality in the territory?

15. What land problems delayed settlement in some parts of southern Arizona?

16. How did James Addison Reavis try to claim 10 million acres in Arizona?

17. Who were the Rough Riders and where did they fight?

18. Why was a statue of "Buckey" O'Neill placed in front of the courthouse in Prescott?

Students and parents pose in front of Scottsdale's first school, 1896. Winfield Scott was on the school board. The city is named after him.

THE TIME
1870–1910

PEOPLE TO KNOW
Geronimo
General George Stoneman
William S. Oury
Jesus Maria Elias
Sidney DeLong
Vincent Colyer
General O. O. Howard
Tom Jeffords
Cochise
General George Crook
John P. Clum
Nock-ay-del-klinne
General Nelson Miles
Martha Summerhayes

PLACES TO LOCATE
Fort Bowie
Santa Cruz Valley
 Camp Grant
Aravaipa Canyon
Chiricahua Reservation
White Mountain
   Reservation
Fort Apache
San Carlos
Camp Verde
Tonto Basin
Fort McDowell

Hostile Rancheria, a painting by Francis H. Beaugureau, shows the antagonism

1870
Military Department of Arizona is organized.

1873
General Crook defeats Apaches at Turret Peak.

1874
John P. Clum is appointed Indian agent at San Carlos.

1882
Battle at Big Dry Wash

1870

1875

1880

1871
Camp Grant Massacre

1872
Cochise meets with General O.O. Howard. Crook fights the Battle of Skull Cave.

1875
General Crook leaves Arizona.
The Camp Verde and most of the Fort Apache Indians are moved to San Carlos.

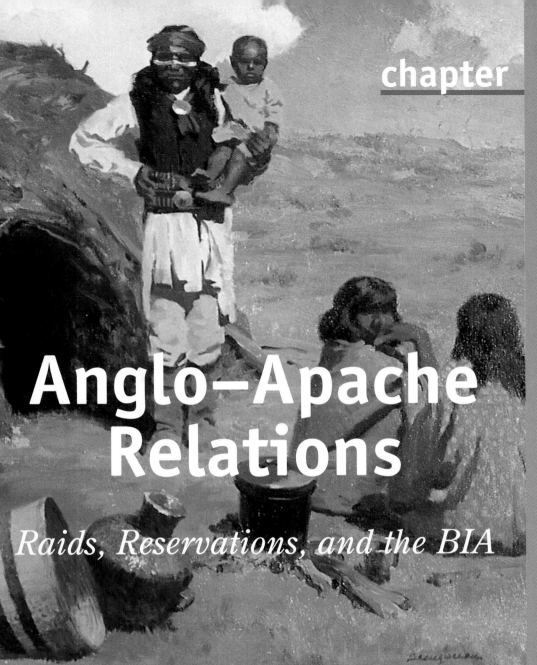

Anglo–Apache Relations

Raids, Reservations, and the BIA

TERMS TO UNDERSTAND
agile
resent
infantry
marauding
moral
indict
farce
justifiable
Indian agent
precipice
impregnable
ration
resurrection
contractor
exile
inaugural
vitality

Apaches often felt towards Anglo intruders. Notice the conical or dome-shaped wickiups.

1886
Geronimo surrenders twice.
Apaches are exiled to Florida.

1909 ➤
Geronimo dies at
Fort Sill, Oklahoma.

1885   **1890**   **1895**   **1900**

1894
Chiricauhuas are moved from
Florida to Oklahoma.

Apaches Fight for Their Way of Life

Geronimo (1823–1909) was a Chiricahua Apache war leader, not a chief.
(Stamp design 1994 U.S. Postal Service. Reproduced with permission. All rights reserved.)

Geronimo surrendered to General Nelson A. Miles.

GERONIMO, LEADER OF ARIZONA'S last Indian fighting force, surrenders! For eighteen months he has evaded thousands of soldiers bent upon capturing his tiny band of Apache warriors. The day: September 4, 1886. The place: Skeleton Canyon in southeastern Arizona.

"This is the fourth time I have surrendered," says Geronimo.

"And I think it is the last time," replies General Nelson A. Miles.

The next day they reach Fort Bowie and Miles wires a triumphant telegram across the country: "The Indians surrendered as prisoners of war . . . I intend to ship them to Florida without delay."

How did Geronimo and the Apaches come to this sad ending? Let's look back a few years and find out.

Apache Raiding

For centuries the Apache bands lived by hunting, gathering, subsistence farming, and raiding. Their homeland, in the rugged country of eastern Arizona, was ideal for hit-and-run raids. The warriors–*agile*, disciplined, and untiring–would sweep down from the mountains to run off horses and cattle at a ranch or to attack a wagon train. When chased by cavalry, the warriors lured pursuers into a canyon ambush or fled across the range. Very seldom did they fight in open battle.

To Anglo pioneers, the raiding lifestyle was wrong. They thought of the Apaches as an obstacle to progress. Apaches, on the other hand, *resented* the invasion of outsiders—first the Spanish and Mexicans, and then Americans. The warriors fought with merciless fury and cunning to keep their way of life.

The U.S. Army

The U.S. Army played an important role on the Arizona frontier. Cavalry and *infantry* units protected settlements, wagon trains, and Colorado River crossings. Army engineers built roads and telegraph lines. Life was dangerous for soldiers assigned to duty in Arizona. Their main job was to chase *marauding* Indians.

When the Military Department of Arizona was organized in 1870, Arizonans were protected by eighteen forts. General George Stoneman was in command. He had instructions to follow President Grant's Indian peace policy of "*moral* persuasion" and kindness. So Stoneman appeased the Apaches by giving them rations of food and clothing. The goal was to get Indians on reservations as soon as possible.

Meanwhile, Indians continued to raid up and down the Santa Cruz Valley south of Tucson. A rancher was killed near Tubac and a woman kidnapped. A raiding party drove off livestock from the San Xavier

Mission. The Tucson *Citizen* published a story blaming the Aravaipa Apaches near Camp Grant for the San Xavier raid. The Aravaipas had been given permission to live near Camp Grant on their old homelands in Aravaipa Canyon.

The Camp Grant Massacre

The Camp Grant Massacre was a low point in Anglo-Apache relations. The people in Tucson were angry because General Stoneman did not protect the settlers. Left to their own devices, William S. Oury and Jesus Maria Elías organized an expedition to attack the Aravaipa Apache camp. Oury was a former mayor of Tucson. The Elías family had a burning desire to get revenge against the Apaches. The family had been run out of the Tubac area by Apache raiders. At least three members of the Elías family had been killed.

In April, 1871, 148 men—94 Papagos, 48 Mexicans, and 6 Anglos—gathered outside Tucson. With guns, ammunition, and food, the expedition traveled by night on foot. About daybreak they reached Camp Grant and split into two groups. The Papagos attacked the sleeping Apaches in the Aravaipa camp with clubs. The Mexicans and Anglos waited on nearby bluffs and shot down any Apaches who managed to escape.

The assault was so swift and fierce that approximately one hundred were dead within a few minutes. The victims were mainly women and children, since most of the men were away hunting in the hills. Some of the Apache children were spared and turned over to the Papagos as slaves.

Back in Washington, President Grant was naturally shocked by the brutal massacre, calling it "purely murder." About a hundred men were *indicted*. Only one, Sidney R. DeLong, was tried in Tucson. All the parties involved agreed before the trial started that the fate of DeLong would be that of the others. The trial was a *farce*, just to satisfy the government in Washington. The jury found DeLong and the others not guilty.

It was almost impossible at that time to convict a person for killing an Apache. Even the judge was convinced the expedition was *justifiable*. The United States government, he said, did not give the Papago, Mexican, and American residents protection from Apache raids and murders. They had "a right to protect themselves and employ a force large enough for that purpose," he told the jury.

The Camp Grant Massacre has been called one of the bloodiest incidents in the white man's long and shameful relationship with the American Indians. By any standard of decent human conduct, it was one of the saddest days in Arizona history.

"I do not expect to see any of them [the attackers] punished . . . but I do ask you to get back fourteen of our children that they have taken captive."
—Eskiminzin, Aravaipa Apache chief

William S. Oury

The village of San Carlos is on the Apache reservation of the same name, 1880s.

Apaches Are Put on Reservations

The Camp Grant Massacre focused national attention on the Arizona Territory. General Stoneman was blamed by both those who sympathized with the Apaches and those who hated them for the army's ineffective way of dealing with the Apaches. He was replaced by General George Crook.

President Grant sent Vincent Colyer to Arizona as a peace commissioner. Colyer, a Quaker and Grant's principal adviser on Indian matters, had sympathy for the Indians. He hoped to make treaties with the Apaches and get them onto reservations. Newspaper editors in the territory were hostile to Colyer. They called for a strong military campaign against the Apaches. Colyer, however, proceeded with his peaceful work. By the time he departed in 1871, he had all the major Apache tribes except the Chiricahuas on reservations.

General O. O. Howard Meets with Cochise

Howard arrived the following year to continue Colyer's work. Howard was a one-armed Civil War hero known as "the Christian General." The Aravaipa Apaches were pleased when Howard arranged for the return of six captive children from Tucson residents. The Tucson families had adopted the children after the Camp Grant Massacre.

The most dramatic event of Howard's visit in Arizona was a meeting with Cochise. Cochise was led to the meeting by Tom Jeffords. Jeffords had sealed his friendship with Cochise by an Apache blood ceremony. Jeffords was probably the only white man who could have convinced Cochise to meet with Howard.

In the Dragoon Mountains, Cochise agreed to a treaty. He promised permanent peace in return for the Chiricahua Reservation in southeastern Arizona. Jeffords was appointed *Indian agent* there. "Hereafter," Cochise said in his native tongue, "the white man and the Indian are to drink the same water and eat the same bread."

Before Howard left Arizona he had all the Apaches concentrated on three reservations—White Mountain with its San Carlos subdivision, Camp Verde, and the Chiricahua.

General George Crook Defeats Apache Holdouts

After General Howard made peace with Cochise, General Crook was permitted to find and bring in all Apaches and Yavapais who were not living on reservations. While waiting for his chance, Crook trained an unusual but very efficient army of small, fast-moving units. Apache scouts were hired as trackers and were paid army wages. Crook himself wore a weather-beaten canvas suit with a Japanese style summer hat and rode a mule.

Meeting of Crook and Geronimo was painted by Francis H. Beaugureau.

Crook's first campaign was aimed at encircling Indians in the Tonto Basin area. The first major encounter was the Battle of Skull Cave. The Indians hid in a cave on a cliff near the Salt River. Twice they refused to surrender. The soldiers discovered that rifle bullets fired at the slanted ceiling of the cave would ricochet down on the Indians. When all the shooting was over, the troops found piles of dead bodies in the cave. Some seventy-five people had died. Only eighteen women and children lived long enough to leave the Salt River Canyon as captives.

Several months later, Crook's forces caught up with Apaches who had murdered three people near Wickenburg. One of the victims was an eighteen-year-old British immigrant. He was severely tortured—rolled in cactus, his ears and eyelids cut away, and his body stuck with burning splinters.

Crook, with the help of Indian scouts, tracked the renegades to Turret Peak, north of the Verde Valley. Crawling up the mountain on their stomachs at night, the soldiers charged the Apaches as the sun rose. Some of the Apaches were so panic-stricken they jumped off a steep *precipice* and were killed.

"During the heaviest part of the fighting a little boy ran out at the side of the cave and stood dumbfounded between the two sides. Nantje rushed forward, grasping the trembling infant by the arm, and escaped unhurt inside. . . . Our men suspended their firing to cheer Nantje. . . ."
—Captain John G. Bourke, who served with Crook

"I have come to surrender my people, because you have too many copper cartridges. . . . I want my women and children to be able to sleep at night and to make fires to cook their food. . . ."
—Cha-ut-lipun, chief of Tonto Basin Indians

"If your people will only behave yourselves and stop killing the whites, I will be the best friend you ever had. I will teach you to work, and will find you a market for everything you can sell."
—General George Crook

The Skull Cave and Turret Peak battles broke the resistance of the Tonto Apaches. They suffered great losses in strongholds considered to be *impregnable*. Defeated, the remaining Apaches began to assemble near Camp Verde. In return for food and protection, they agreed to remain on reservations.

Roads and a Telegraph

After the main Apache battles were over, General Crook gave attention to building first-class wagon roads to connect the military posts. He also brought in the first long telegraph line. It ran from San Diego to Fort Yuma and on to Maricopa Wells. One branch went to Fort Whipple and Prescott. Connecting lines were built later to other forts and towns.

Crook was popular with the people. Before leaving Arizona he was honored by Governor A. P. K. Safford and a large banquet crowd in Hatz's Hall in Prescott.

Martha Summerhayes wrote about her experiences as a young army bride.

Army Wife

Martha Summerhayes was a young army bride who lived with her husband Jack at military posts in Arizona during the 1870s. They arrived at Fort Yuma by the water route from San Francisco.

"And now began our real journey up the Colorado River on the steamer *Gila* with the barge full of soldiers towing after us, starting for Fort Mohave," Martha wrote in her book *Vanished Arizona*. It was "122 degrees in the shade," as the *Gila* puffed and clattered upstream.

After two months of rough travel, Martha and the lieutenant got to Fort Apache. Their home was a primitive log cabin. "I could never get accustomed to the wretched small space of one room . . . I had been born and brought up in a spacious house." While at Fort Apache Martha gave birth to a son. The wives of Apache chiefs gave her a "beautiful papoose-basket or cradle. . . . made of the lightest wood and covered with the finest skin of fawn."

Then came a hot time at Ehrenberg, a steamboat landing on the Colorado River. "Guests . . . were always astonished when the Cocopah Indian waited on them at table, for he wore nothing but his gee-string. . . . The Indian brought us water every morning in buckets from the river. It looked like melted chocolate."

At Fort McDowell "the men were kept busy, scouting and driving the renegades back to their reservation." Sleeping under the clear and starry Arizona sky was not always fun at the fort. Crawling ants had to be outwitted by placing each cot leg in a tin can of water. When the coyotes howled, chills ran up Martha's spine.

Jack's regiment was transferred to Texas until Geronimo went on the warpath for the last time in 1886. Then they returned. Martha wrote, "We traveled to Tucson in a Pullman car. . . . We went to take breakfast before driving out to the post of Fort Lowell. . . . Iced cantaloupe was served by a spic-span alert waiter. . . . then quail on toast . . . Ice in Arizona? It was a dream, and I remarked to Jack, 'This isn't the same Arizona we knew in '74'!'"

Bureau of Indian Affairs (BIA)

CONTRARY TO COMMON BELIEF, there were many whites who treated the Apaches kindly. General Crook was fair with Indians who lived peacefully. He offered to help them become self-supporting by buying all the corn and hay they could produce. Tom Jeffords did much for the Chiricahuas while he was agent. Another man who stands out is John P. Clum. He was only twenty-three when the Bureau of Indian Affairs (BIA) appointed him agent at San Carlos. A member of the Dutch Reformed Church, Clum was determined that Apaches would get a square deal.

Clum organized a small body of Indian policemen to replace supervision by soldiers. He gave the Apaches their own court. Clum had each band of Apaches elect a representative to meet with him as a council. More importantly, he persuaded the Apaches to turn in their guns. An Indian who wanted to go hunting could check out a rifle. Clum forbade the manufacture of "tiswin," an alcoholic drink. He found work for the Indians, principally in constructing agency buildings and living quarters. Many Apaches liked Clum and trusted him.

Indian agent John P. Clum posed with Apaches at San Carlos, 1875.

A Failed Policy

The Bureau of Indian Affairs tried to move most of the western Apaches to one reservation. Clum cooperated in this "removal policy." He thought he could control all the Indians at San Carlos without military help. The Camp Verde and most of the Fort Apache Indians were moved to San Carlos. During the next two years, Clum and his native Indian police force personally escorted the Chiricahuas to San Carlos.

Then Clum suggested that the army be ordered out of Arizona. He said the presence of troops made the Indians edgy. Clum claimed he could take care of all the Apaches with Indian police. When the BIA turned him down, he resigned as an Indian agent. He rode away from San Carlos to become editor of the Tombstone *Epitaph* and a friend of Wyatt Earp.

Before General Crook left Arizona, he protested against the herding of many different Apache tribes onto one reservation. The Apaches resented it too. At San Carlos they were overcrowded and often were shorted on *rations*. Some of the tribes and bands were suspicious and hostile toward each other. The Chiricahuas were especially unhappy at San Carlos.

Geronimo and his followers were troublemakers for a dozen years. They liked to make fun of men in other tribes who worked, calling them "squaws." Several times, Geronimo's band slipped away to Mexico.

What do you think?

• In Oklahoma, each tribal member was given his or her own land and the surplus land was sold. What would be the advantages and disadvantages of that system for American Indians in Arizona?
• Are there ways in which the reservations actually helped Indian people in Arizona? How were the people hurt by being forced to live on reservations?

Big Dry Wash

The Battle at Big Dry Wash

The White Mountain Apaches at the San Carlos Reservation were stirred up by Nock-ay-del-klinne, a medicine man. He had learned about Christianity at a school in Santa Fe and was impressed by the story of a *resurrection*. Nock-ay-del-klinne started his own religion and taught his followers a kind of ghost dance. He claimed power to bring two dead chiefs to life once all the whites were driven away.

Nock-ay-del-klinne was arrested by soldiers, then shot while trying to escape. The White Mountain Apaches then went on the warpath. They killed ranchers north of Globe and drove away stock. Cavalry troops caught up with the Apaches and defeated them at Big Dry Wash. This battle was the last major action between the U.S. military and the Apaches on Arizona soil.

Evolution of Apaches from warriors to Indian scouts to U.S. soldiers.
(Painting at the Fort Apache Museum)

U.S. Army Completes the Conquest of Apaches

"Dutchy" was a Chiricahua Apache Indian scout for the U.S. Army.

WITH THE CHIRICAHUAS IN MEXICO and other Apaches in a bad mood, General Crook was reassigned to Arizona. He listened to Indian grievances. Considering the way they were cheated on rations, Crook thought the Apaches had been very patient. Corrupt government *contractors* were bribing Indian agents to sign for more food than was delivered to the Indian people. Crook let the Indians scatter to the more fertile lands on the reservation so they could farm and become self-supporting.

Meanwhile, Geronimo, Juh, and Nachez led the Chiricahuas in raids north and south of the border. Not until January, 1884, did the combined pressure of American and Mexican soldiers force all the Apaches to surrender and return to San Carlos. Geronimo was angry because all the horses and cattle stolen in Mexico were taken away. He waited for a chance to escape again and looked for an incident to convince his followers to leave with him. That incident came the following year.

In violation of a reservation rule, the Chiricahuas made some tiswin and drank it. Fearing punishment, forty-two men, including Geronimo, fled to Sonora, taking ninety women and children with them. They left a trail of death and burning ranches.

Crook stationed himself at Fort Bowie and sent cavalry and Indian scouts into Mexico to chase Geronimo. Finally Geronimo agreed to meet with Crook just south of the border. He agreed to surrender his band on the condition that they could return to the reservation after two years of imprisonment.

While Crook was returning to Fort Bowie, however, Geronimo and a small group of his warriors bought some mescal from a traveling peddler and got drunk. Then they took off for their hideouts in Mexico.

General Crook sent cavalry and Indian scouts from Fort Bowie into Mexico to find Geronimo.

Anglo–Apache Relations

Geronimo Surrenders

General Crook resigned his Arizona command in disgust and was replaced by General Nelson Miles. For better communication, Miles set up an expensive message relay system. Messages were sent by mirrors from station to station until they got to the destination.

Miles selected a force of about a hundred soldiers and Indian scouts to track down Geronimo. Late in August, Lieutenant Charles B. Gatewood met with Geronimo under a flag of truce and secured his promise to meet with Miles. The final surrender took place in Skeleton Canyon north of the border. The Indians were taken to Bowie Station and put on a Southern Pacific train to Florida for *exile*. Then the peaceful Chiricahuas on the reservation were loaded on a train at Holbrook and sent to Florida.

Baldy Peak Heliograph Station shows how soldiers sent messages from camp to camp with mirror signals.
(Painting by Francis H. Beaugureau)

Movies, novels, and television have made Geronimo a famous American. His name was popularized during World War II by paratroopers who yelled "Geronimo!" after they jumped from an airplane.

Geronimo is featured in this poster advertising Pawnee Bill's Wild West Show.

Geronimo's Later Life

The Chiricahuas were never permitted to return to Arizona. In 1894 they were moved to Fort Sill in Oklahoma. Geronimo became a Christian for a while and confessed his many bloody deeds committed on the plunder trail. He urged his people to give up dancing and other worldly amusements and to repent for their sins.

Geronimo was in demand as a showman. The War Department permitted him to attend the St. Louis World's Fair. He sold the buttons off his shirt for a quarter apiece and carried a supply of replacements. In 1905 Geronimo rode with other Indians in President Theodore Roosevelt's *inaugural* parade. He died in Fort Sill, Oklahoma, in 1909.

Apache Art

Allan Houser was a world-famous painter and sculptor. A Chiricahua Apache, he was born at Fort Sill, Oklahoma, in 1915. He was a descendant of Geronimo. In this painting, Houser gives the viewer a feeling of motion and action. He captures on canvas the wildness of the fast-moving, high-stepping horses. You can feel the physical *vitality* and lively spirit of the Apaches in pursuit.

Wild horses were once free to roam the vast unfenced San Carlos Reservation. As cattle replaced horses on the grasslands, Apaches became known as the "Cowboy Indians of the West."

Like many Native American men, Apaches now wear Levi's, a brightly-colored shirt, boots, and a cowboy hat. They still love horses but are more likely to be seen driving a pickup truck. Peaceful and productive members of society, they work at a variety of occupations—cattle raising, mining, lumbering, tourism, and fighting forest fires. Apache cowboys, however, still ride wild horses at rodeos, a highlight of the annual tribal fair on the reservation.

The Wild Horses by Allan Houser (Courtesy The Heard Museum)

Points of Apache-Anglo Contact, 1870s and 1880s

Kingman

★ Fort Mohave

•*Williams*

Flagstaff

•*Winslow*

•*Holbrook*

Fort Whipple ★

•*Prescott*

Fort Verde ★

Big Dry Wash 1882 □

Turret Peak 1873 □

Fort Apache ★

Fort McDowell ★

□

Skull Cave
1872

★ Camp San Carlos

Fort Yuma ★

•*Yuma*

Gila Bend •

Camp Grant
Massacre 1871

□

Fort Thomas ★

★ Fort Grant

Fort Lowell ★

•*Tucson*

Fort Bowie ★

Cochise Stronghold
1872

Fort Huachuca ★

Mexico

Skeleton Canyon 1886 □

★	**U. S. Army Forts**
□	**Conflicts**
•	**Cities**

A Fort Apache summer shelter shows evidence of interraction
with white settlers.

Arizona Indian Reservations

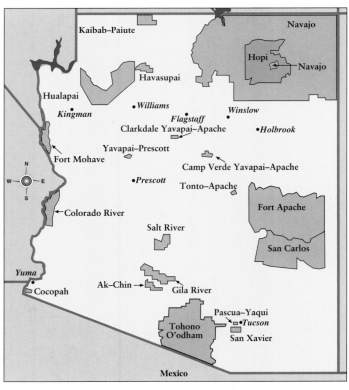

Kaibab–Paiute

Navajo

Hopi

Navajo

Havasupai

Hualapai

Kingman

•*Williams*

Winslow

Flagstaff

•*Holbrook*

Clarkdale Yavapai–Apache

Fort Mohave

Yavapai–Prescott

Camp Verde Yavapai–Apache

•*Prescott*

Tonto–Apache

Colorado River

Salt River

Fort Apache

San Carlos

Yuma

Ak–Chin →

Gila River

Cocopah

Pascua–Yaqui

•*Tucson*

Tohono
O'odham

San Xavier

Mexico

1. What was President Grant's Indian peace policy? Why did many Arizonans object to this policy?

2. Explain why the Camp Grant Massacre has been called one of the saddest days in Arizona history.

3. Why was Sidney DeLong the only member of the Camp Grant Massacre expedition who was tried?

4. Why was Vincent Colyer sent to Arizona?

5. What was the most dramatic event of General Howard's visit in Arizona?

6. What kind of army did General Crook train in Arizona? How was the army able to defeat the Apaches in the Battle of Skull Cave?

7. For what three reasons was General Crook popular in Arizona?

8. List four things John P. Clum did for the Apaches that earned their trust.

9. Why were many Apaches discontented on the San Carlos Reservation?

10. Where were the Chiricahua Apaches sent after Geronimo surrendered? Then what happened to them?

11. How was Geronimo made famous?

12. What are some things about the Apache man's life that Houser depicts in his painting? What feelings does the painting express?

Families who follow the old customs, and can afford the expense, take part in a "Coming of Age" ritual for their teenage daughters. The purpose of this ceremony, called the Sunrise Dance, is to ensure that the girl will enjoy good health, many friends, and a long life.

Chapter 8

THE TIME
1863–1912

PEOPLE TO KNOW
Jack Swilling
William Hellings
William Hancock
William J. Murphy
U.S. President Theodore
  Roosevelt
Jacob Hamblin
Ed Schieffelin
Lesinsky brothers
Henry C. Hooker
Dr. James Douglas
Juan Candelaria
Edward E. Ayers
Riordan brothers
Pearl Hart
Albert Steinfeld
P. R. Tully
Estevan Ochoa
John Wesley Powell

PLACES TO LOCATE
Salt River Valley
Wickenburg
Pipe Spring
Tombstone
Clifton
Morenci
Bisbee
Douglas
Globe
Jerome
Holbrook
Apache County
Flagstaff
Casa Grande
Maricopa
Benson
Willcox
Little Colorado River

	1870 William Hancock surveys the Phoenix townsite.		**1863—1912** Territory of Ariz **1877** Ed Schieffelin discovers the Tombstone Mine.
1860		**1870**	**1880**
1868 Jack Swilling completes an irrigation ditch in the Salt River Valley.	**1869** John Wesley Powell explores the Colorado River.	**1876** Mormons begin farming towns in Arizona. **1870s and 1880s** Ranchers overstock the open range with cattle	

Economic Growth

Water, Mining, Ranching, Lumbering, and Transportation

A wild ride on the stage from Tombstone to Tucson was painted by Olaf Wieghorst.

TERMS TO UNDERSTAND

transcontinental
opportunist
cultivate
unproductive
divert
gorge
glen
ethnology
integrity
polygamist
supplement
assayer
overproduction
profitable
agitator
homestead
consolidate
obsolete
notoriety
teamster
tandem

1882
E. E. Ayers builds a
sawmill in Flagstaff.

1887
Brand registration
is required by law.

1903
Copper miners at
Clifton and Morenci
go on strike.

1890

1900

1910

1920

1883
Santa Fe Railroad
is finished across
northern Arizona.

1885
Arizona Canal
is completed.

1892
Judge Kibbey decrees that
water belongs to the land.

1906
Construction
of Roosevelt
Dam begins.

1911
Roosevelt Dam
is completed.

The Phoenix
(Painting by Paul Coze in the
Phoenix Air Terminal)

The city of Phoenix rose from the old Hohokam ruins—just like the mythical Phoenix bird, rose from its own ashes.

Jack Swilling had visions of turning the
Salt River Valley into a prosperous
farming community by building canals
to bring water for irrigation.

Go West!

"GO WEST, YOUNG MAN, and grow up with the country!" said Horace Greeley, editor of the *New York Tribune*. Settlement of the West was a major trend in American history after the Civil War. The frontier disappeared forever as the West experienced a rapid increase in population and economic development. Within one generation, the West was carved into territories and states.

During the time Arizona was a territory, its non-Indian population grew from about 4,000 to 200,000. The new residents built towns, developed rich mines, irrigated farms, and filled in the open range land with livestock. Lumbering, Arizona's first major manufacturing industry, got a good start by sawing railroad ties.

Two *transcontinental* railroads were built across the territory. Branch rail lines and dirt wagon roads connected copper mines and farming communities to the main lines. At the beginning of the territorial period there was not even a stagecoach to ride. By 1912 Arizonans owned more than 1,800 automobiles. Airplanes were beginning to fly overhead.

Agriculture in the Salt River Valley

THOUGH UNOCCUPIED FOR CENTURIES after the Hohokam left, the Salt River Valley finally got some attention after the Civil War. In 1865 the U. S. Army established Fort McDowell and hired a man to cut hay for horses at the fort. He spotted some tall grass on the Salt River floodplain near present-day Sky Harbor Airport. After setting up a hay camp, he had a chance to visit with Jack Swilling, a red-headed giant of a man.

The Swilling Irrigation and Canal Company

Swilling talked excitedly about the remains of old Hohokam canals. Plans for a modern irrigation system were taking shape in his mind. An *opportunist*, he could foresee a great farming future for the Salt River Valley. He knew that the miners at Wickenburg were screaming for locally grown farm products. Grain and vegetables were expensive when hauled in by wagon from California.

Swilling went to Wickenburg to drum up enthusiasm for a canal company. He returned with some strong-backed workers and mule teams. The Swilling ditch was dug out of a Hohokam canal on the north side of the Salt River. Water flowed to freshly cleared land. In a few years, farmers *cultivated* and irrigated several thousand acres of wheat, barley, corn, beans, pumpkins, and other crops. More canals were dug as newcomers poured into the "garden of the territory."

Mill City was one of the names for a settlement that grew up near Swilling's ditch in present-day Phoenix. William Hellings built a flour mill there with expensive machinery purchased in San Francisco and hauled by wagon from the steamboat landing. Hellings produced six tons of flour every day. He fed the by-products—wheat germ, bran, and some flour—to hogs. Soon he had the first meat packing business in Arizona. Hellings sold smoked ham, sausage, bacon, and lard to stores all over the territory.

> **Linking the past and the present**
>
> Thomas Jefferson said, "Let our workshops [factories] remain in Europe." He wanted the United States to be an "agrarian" (farming) society. What did he mean? Would it be possible today?

The Phoenix Townsite

In 1870, prominent pioneers selected a townsite on higher ground where downtown Phoenix is located today. William Hancock, called the "father of Phoenix," surveyed the land. Mexican laborers hacked away desert growth to make wide streets. Sixty-three lots were sold at an average price of $40.

A year later, the Phoenix townsite was chosen as the county seat of newly-created Maricopa County. The first election for county officers turned to disaster when one candidate for sheriff killed his opponent following a violent argument.

The Arizona Canal

A large part of the Salt River Valley was still *unproductive* desert until William J. Murphy finished the Arizona Canal in 1885. Unlike other canals in the valley, this one did not follow Hohokam canal beds. Murphy had to construct a dam upriver to get water flowing at a higher elevation. His crew dug a thirty-five-mile canal to Scottsdale, Glendale, and other northern areas of the valley.

As the saying goes, "Where water flows, Arizona grows." Sure enough, many new settlers came to enjoy the advantages of what promoters called "a modern irrigation system in the agricultural capital of the Southwest."

> **Linking the past and the present**
>
> If William J. Murphy got his wish to see Arizona after "a hundred years" (right now), what do you think he would say?

ARIZONA PORTRAIT

William J. Murphy
(1839–1923)

William J. Murphy clerked in an Illinois hardware store and fought with the Union army during the Civil War. In 1881 he came to Arizona to level a section of roadbed for the Atlantic and Pacific (Santa Fe) Railroad.

Near Flagstaff, which was then a rowdy construction camp, he built a log cabin for his wife and children. They rode into town from New Mexico atop a wagon loaded with sacks of grain.

Two years later, Murphy was awarded the Arizona Canal contract and he and his family settled permanently in Phoenix. He bought sections of land north of downtown Phoenix to split into subdivisions and for vast citrus orchards. With an eye to beauty, he planted hundreds of ash trees to shade the streets.

Looking to the future, Murphy often said, "I would like to come back a hundred years from now and see this country."

Today the Salt River usually has a dry riverbed. Before Roosevelt Dam was built, however, water flowed through Phoenix. Early settlers saw "salmon" three or four feet long going upstream to spawn.

In the 1870s, fishermen in the Salt River sometimes used blasting powder to kill a lot of fish. People in Phoenix could hear the rumble of explosions from the river. The territorial legislature passed a law to forbid this method of fishing.

The dam for the Arizona Canal **diverted** some of the Salt River water for irrigation. Most of the river formed a beautiful foamy waterfall as it spilled over the dam and flowed downstream. But there was no fish ladder over the dam. Fish swimming upstream to spawn jumped into the air, trying in vain to climb up the waterfall. In 1888 the *Phoenix Herald* reported that "the river below the dam is filled with dead fish."

Big carp were plentiful in the irrigation canals. In 1892 a *Gazette* writer said, "The farmers who live next to the big canals say they never saw the like of fish coming down the canals. In irrigating, large numbers are left in the fields after the water soaks away. Small boys and Indians gather great lots of them and bring them to town. There are many fine large German carp."

Phoenix—A Flourishing Trade Center

By 1889 Phoenix was growing rapidly. Good dirt wagon roads ran in every direction. A railroad connected the town to the Southern Pacific Railroad. Clang, clang, clang went the trolleys on the streets. Phoenix was lighted by gas and electricity. Businesses included four banks, two ice plants, and good hotels. Residents had a choice of three daily newspapers—the *Republican*, *Gazette*, and *Herald*.

The town had three public elementary schools with 450 students.

It's time for a chat on a quiet day in Phoenix. The style for women in territorial days was a long skirt and tight-collared blouse. Men on business wore a jacket and tie. Both men and women always wore hats in public.

The people were thinking about a high school, but that was six years away. There were serious plans, however, for an Indian school north of town.

Real estate agents were advertising Phoenix as the "future metropolis of the territory." The legislature in Prescott must have been listening. The members voted to move the capital to Phoenix. The governor signed the bill as soon as it reached his desk.

Salt River Valley's Water Supply

Today the Salt River Valley has a big city population, swimming pools, and rich fields of alfalfa and cotton. Can you imagine that farmers were once troubled by an uncertain water supply—alternating disasters of flood and drought?

In 1891 water was plentiful—so plentiful that the Salt River overflowed its banks. At some places the river spread out eight miles wide. Raging waters washed out the Tempe railroad bridge, cutting Phoenix off from rail transportation. The flood gouged a new channel into a low section of Phoenix, forcing people to evacuate.

The great flood was followed by dry years in the 1890s. The Salt River could not fill all the canals that had been built. Armed, desperate men patrolled the canals to protect their water rights. At least a third of the farmland was forced out of cultivation. Livestock died. Orchards became firewood. Families packed and left, expecting Phoenix to die. Then the rains came. A flash flood destroyed the dirt dams. The water rushed on to the Gulf of California, wasted for all purposes except to dramatize the need to control water in the Salt River.

Roosevelt Dam

A huge storage dam was needed upstream to control flooding and to secure a dependable water supply for everyone. An organization of landowners, now known as the Salt River Project, pledged their land as security for a federal loan. Then the U.S. Reclamation Service began what would be the world's highest dam.

Much preliminary work had to be done. About 112 miles of access roads were built. The most important was Roosevelt Road, now called Apache Trail, from Mesa. Most of the construction machinery and supplies were hauled over this narrow, dangerous route in freight wagons pulled by twenty-mule teams. Work crews dug a 500-foot tunnel through solid rock to divert the river around the main dam site. Hot springs in the tunnel raised the temperature to as much as 130 degrees. The heat made work difficult.

A town called Roosevelt was built so construction workers would have a place to live. People who moved in knew that the town would be under water once the dam was completed.

A better location for Roosevelt Dam could not have been chosen. Today, the dam arches between steep canyon walls on a tough sandstone foundation. The 284-foot-high dam is 170 feet thick at the base and tapers to a 16-foot roadway at the top.

Former President Theodore Roosevelt dedicated the dam. People made the rough trip to the ceremony on horseback, in buggies, on bicycles, and in automobiles.

The Salt River flood of 1891 washed out the Tempe railroad bridge. Phoenix was without train service for several months.

Roosevelt Dam

The first stone of the Roosevelt Dam was laid in 1906. The dam was completed in 1911 at a cost of $10 million.

Former President Theodore Roosevelt (beside driver) was photographed on his way to dedicate Roosevelt Dam, 1911.

Brave Men in Wooden Boats

IN THE SUMMER OF 1869, Major John Wesley Powell led eight men in wooden boats down the Green and Colorado Rivers. This dangerous thousand-mile expedition took three months. Major Powell, a one-armed Civil War veteran and former Illinois science teacher, became a hero after he reached the west end of the Grand Canyon. His exciting journey erased the word "Unexplored" from early maps of this region.

Major Powell tried to learn as much about the geology as possible. A brave scientist, he climbed one steep cliff after another to observe the rock structure and to measure elevations. Once he got trapped on a wall, unable to move up or down. "I dare not let go with my hand," he shouted. "If I lose my hold I shall fall to the bottom!" At this critical moment, an ex-soldier in his group pulled him to safety by using a pair of long underwear as a rope.

Powell found only one major *gorge* which had no rapids. He named it Glen Canyon because of the cool green *glens* in the narrow side canyons. For a week, Powell and his men glided between the red and orange sandstone walls, some decorated with Indian pictographs. Here and there, they found the ruins of ancient Indian shelters.

The men marveled at the towering monuments, mossy alcoves, and water-carved spires, buttes, and rock overhangs. Powell wrote in his journal:

"We find ourselves in a vast chamber carved out of rock . . . more than two hundred feet high, five hundred feet long, . . . filled with sweet sounds. . . . We name it Music Temple."

A few days later, the Powell expedition began running the dangerous rapids of the Grand Canyon. "We rode the back of the Dragon," is the way one of the boatmen put it. Their wooden boats were overturned, caught in the whirlpools, and battered against the walls. The men ported the boats around the waterfalls or guided them down with ropes. By the time they got nearly a mile deep in the canyon, most of their food had been washed away.

Finally, all nine men reached a sandy shore where a clear creek emptied into the Colorado. Happy to be there, Powell named the creek Bright Angel. At this point, three of the river runners could endure no more. With Powell's blessing, they climbed out of the canyon, only to be killed later by Shivwits Indians.

Powell and five other men ran the remaining rapids to the mouth of the Virgin River, where Lake Mead is located today. The terrible ordeal was over. Powell had conquered the "Great Unknown"

wilderness along the Colorado. He had learned much concerning the geology of the earth's crust.

That afternoon the exhausted and hungry explorers feasted on fish, melons, and squash that Mormons brought by wagon from their settlement at St. Thomas.

Two years later, Powell began another scientific trip down the Green and Colorado Rivers. That time he rode in a chair strapped to his boat. While in the West, he also traveled overland to explore and map the Colorado Plateau region. With the help of Jacob Hamblin, he got acquainted with Indians in the region and learned to speak words in their languages.

Powell later continued his Indian studies as director of the Bureau of *Ethnology* in Washington, D.C. Under his leadership, the main job of the bureau was to classify all the American Indian tribes and their languages. He also headed the U. S. Geological Service for a while.

One of Powell's greatest achievements was to get the slow-to-act government interested in the conservation of land and the controlling of the limited water resources in the arid West. He said much of the land in the region should be left in its natural state. However, he wanted the federal government to build dams to store water, control flooding, and distribute irrigation water to farmers.

Powell posed for a photograph with a Paiute man after his 1869 expedition. The story goes that Powell wanted the Paiute to dress in his traditional clothing instead of the breechcloth he usually wore in the summer. Notice that Powell had lost part of his right arm in a Civil War battle.

Linking the past and the present

1. Would Major Powell be booed in the West today, as he was in 1893, for saying: "There is not enough water to irrigate all the lands in the West that can be farmed"? Explain.

2. Do you think Powell would have been in favor of building dams in Utah, Arizona, and Nevada? Why?

3. In the 1990s, Pima County tried "to rope off" the best desert lands (those that are the richest in natural vegetation) from housing developments. On which side of this issue do you think Powell would be? Why?

Jacob Hamblin
(1819–1886)

Jacob Hamblin came to Arizona to convert the American Indians to the Mormon faith. Hamblin explored the Colorado River area many times. He was the first white man to encircle the Grand Canyon. He blazed two well-traveled Mormon roads, one from Utah to California and another wagon road along the Little Colorado River in Arizona.

Hamblin became known for his influence with native peoples because of his *integrity* and his willingness to be a friend.

A *polygamist*, Hamblin married four wives and fathered twenty-four children. He moved his family from Utah into Arizona, New Mexico, and Mexico.

Hamblin spent his last years at Springerville, Arizona.

"This man, Hamblin, speaks their language well, and has great influence over all the Indians in the region. . . . He is a silent, reserved man, and when he speaks, it is in a slow, quiet way, that inspires awe. . . ."
—John Wesley Powell

Mormon Settlements

JACOB HAMBLIN WAS ONE of the most important pioneers in northern Arizona. Sometimes called the "Saint in Buckskin," Hamblin began exploring Arizona in the 1850s. He was the first American missionary to go among the Hopis and Navajos. Chief Tuba, a Hopi, became Hamblin's lifelong friend.

In 1870, the Navajos met with Hamblin and Grand Canyon explorer John Wesley Powell in a "big peace talk." The chief promised no more cattle stealing or raids against settlers.

Hamblin discovered Pipe Spring in the dry country north of the Grand Canyon. The Mormon settlers built a fort there and called it Windsor Castle. They raised cattle and made butter and cheese.

Hamblin blazed a wagon road from southern Utah to the Little Colorado River and followed the river southward. In 1876 about 200 Mormon families came to colonize along the river. They traveled along the Hamblin wagon road, crossing the Colorado River at Lee's Ferry. The colonists who settled at Allen's Camp lived in a fort of cottonwood logs. But after learning there was no Indian danger, they built stone houses away from the fort.

The Mormons planned to dam the Little Colorado River and irrigate crops. But they didn't know about the raging torrents that swept down the river in the flood season. One after another, seven dams were constructed and washed out. Four colonies were started but only Allen's Camp, now Joseph City, survived the floods.

Most towns in eastern Arizona were also founded by Mormons. The list is impressive: Woodruff, Pine, Heber, Shumway, Taylor, Snowflake, Springerville, Eager, St. Johns, Pima, and Thatcher.

Mormon families pose in front of the fort they called Windsor Castle, 1870s. The fort is now part of Pipe Spring National Monument.

Lehi and Mesa

In 1877 a wagon train of Mormon colonists founded the Lehi colony on the Salt River. They completed a four-mile irrigation canal and used the water for summer planting. Until their crops came in, the Lehi colonists depended on fish from the river to *supplement* their diet. With little leisure time, they set fish lines overnight. "When we got to camp, we placed all the morning catch side by side, ten or twelve big ones, but mine was the largest," wrote one man. The fish were sometimes as large as twenty-five pounds.

Upstream from Lehi, a group of Mormon men began digging the Mesa Canal. Enduring the hot summer sun, dust storms, rattlesnakes, and the many hardships of frontier life, they finished the canal and started work on the Mesa townsite. For the first year, according to one colonist, the Mesa settlers got by without any milk or dairy products. "We fell back on bread and beans and most of the bread was made from coarse flour."

> "As summer advanced, I often saturated my clothing with water before starting to hoe a row of corn forty rods long, and before reaching the end my clothes were entirely dry."
> —Joseph A. McRae, Mormon colonist at Mesa

> "Give me men with large families and small means, so that when we get there they will be too poor to come back, and will have to stay."
> —Daniel Webster Jones, leader of the Lehi colony, to Mormon leader Brigham Young

---

The Mormons

The Mormons were a religious group who started settling Utah in 1847. The word "Mormon" is a nickname for people who belong to The Church of Jesus Christ of Latter-day Saints. They started over 350 settlements in Utah, Idaho, Wyoming, Nevada, California, Arizona, and in Canada and Mexico.

Mormon men were often "called" by their leaders to do missionary work. They were also called to leave their new farms and homes and take their families to settle a new place. At certain times and places, the people were instructed by their religious leaders to live by the United Order. That meant they lived as one great family, working together and sharing the products of their labor. The United Order was not always used in Arizona towns, however.

Thatcher was one of many farming communities founded by Mormon families.

Ed Schieffelin's dream since boyhood was to discover a great mine. But he had nothing to show for years of prospecting. At age twenty-nine the dreamer left Oregon to seek his fortune, this time in southern Arizona. He made frequent trips from his base at Fort Huachuca into the rugged country bordering the San Pedro Valley.

"Have you found anything?" the soldiers would ask when Schieffelin came back now and then.

"Not yet," he replied, "but I will strike it one of these days."

"Yes, you'll find your tombstone," they retorted, reminding him of unfriendly Apaches in the area.

The word lingered in Schieffelin's mind, and after searching for six months he gave the name "Tombstone" to his first mining claim.

Tombstone in 1882. Silver mining put Tombstone on the map.

Mining in Territorial Days

HIGH SILVER PRICES AND RICH ORE discoveries attracted prospectors, miners, engineers, and investors to Arizona. Hardly a stone was left unturned as thousands of mine claims were filed.

The most famous silver strike was at present-day Tombstone. "I found some good float and several outcroppings," said Ed Schieffelin after months of prospecting in the rough country near the San Pedro River. He took the best samples to show his brother, Albert, who was working at the McCrackin mine. The *assayer* there was excited. He joined the Schieffelin brothers in a three-way partnership and accompanied them to Ed's Tombstone discovery.

Eureka! Ed found two richer mines with almost pure silver. He named them Lucky Cuss and Toughnut. Two years later, the Schieffelin brothers sold their interests to a group of eastern businessmen for $600,000. By that time, a mad silver rush was underway.

The town boomed, attracting thousands of hard-working miners, merchants, ranchers, and tradesmen. Almost overnight Tombstone became the biggest and rowdiest town in the territory. Two out of three buildings in the business section were saloons or gambling halls. The money rolled in as the mines produced $5 million worth of silver a year. Then a disaster struck. Tombstone's heyday was cut off in 1888 by underground water in the mines.

A tourist center today, the "town too tough to die" is better known for lawman Wyatt Earp and his brothers as well as a host of social parasites: gunslingers, gamblers, golddiggers, and cattle rustlers who drifted into town.

The McCrackin mine in Mohave County was one of Arizona's typical surface-rich silver mines. The ore was packed on burros to a stamping mill on the Big Sandy River eight miles away. Unlike many miners, Jackson McCrackin took his profits and retired to a ranch in northern California. A clever Scot was he!

The United States government quit buying silver in 1893. An *overproduction* of silver in the West had caused the market price to drop. The government could no longer afford to pay 1 ounce of gold for 16 ounces of silver, the set rate. Most silver miners began to prospect for gold.

Another famous Arizona mine was the Silver King, near Superior.
Silver worth millions of dollars was extracted there.

Copper Mining

Copper mining in Arizona was not *profitable* before railroads were built. Transportation costs were just too high. Copper ore mined in the rugged Clifton-Morenci area, for example, had to be shipped in wagons to Kansas City, about 1,200 miles away. That was a long haul.

Henry and Charles Lesinsky built a smelter at Clifton to process the ore. They also built a narrow-gauge railroad, the first in Arizona. It ran uphill about five miles from Clifton to the Longfellow mine. At first, mules pulled empty cars up to the mine and rode back on top of the ore. Later the mules were replaced with small locomotives.

Demand for copper picked up after the electric motor, telephone, and electric lights were invented. They all used copper wire and other copper parts. During the 1880s, Phelps Dodge and other eastern corporations began buying up copper mines for large-scale development.

Most of the early mines were the "bonanza" or high grade type. In this category were the famous Copper Queen in Bisbee, the Old Dominion at Globe, the United Verde at Jerome, and the Clifton-Morenci mines.

The railroad made copper mining profitable. Before trains, heavy ore had to be hauled long distances by wagons and mules.

Dr. James Douglas
(1837–1918)

Dr. James Douglas was a giant in Arizona's copper industry. Born in Canada, he graduated from medical school but turned to mining. From his brilliant mind came a new process for extracting copper from low-grade ores.

Douglas failed at first. He could not find a workable ore deposit in the Atlanta mine at Bisbee. After three years, the company gave him a choice—a cash payment for his services or a ten percent interest in the mine. "I chose to take the risk," Douglas said, "and my career depended on that hasty decision."

Miners soon struck a rich copper vein at the Atlanta mine. This discovery led to more success for Douglas at the Copper Queen in Bisbee and other mines. In 1908 he became president of Phelps Dodge Corporation. By that time, the city of Douglas had been named in his honor.

The Clifton-Morenci Strike

A law passed by the territorial legislature in 1903 resulted in a mine strike at Clifton-Morenci. The law set the legal working day for miners at eight hours instead of ten. The companies had been paying $2.50 for a ten-hour day. They offered a compromise of $2.25 a day, which was nine hours' pay for eight hours' work. But this offer gave miners a smaller total paycheck.

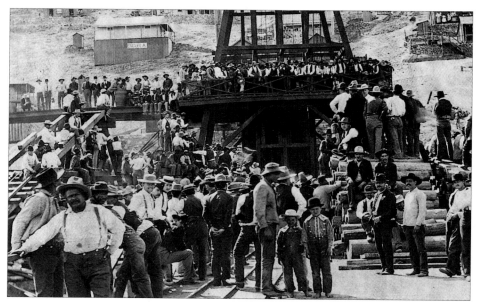

Miners joined forces during the Morenci strike of 1903.

Some of the 1,500 miners refused the offer and went on strike. Mobs formed on the streets and threatened to become violent. At that point, the acting governor sent in the Arizona Rangers and asked President Theodore Roosevelt for federal troops. Before the soldiers arrived, a large group of armed miners seized the Detroit Copper Company's mill at Morenci and disarmed the sheriff's deputies who were guarding it. The strike failed after the *agitators* were arrested.

Some newspapers in the state sided with the miners. *Our Mineral Wealth*, published in Mohave County, thought the company could pay higher wages. "Their company stores get back nearly all they pay out in wages," said the newspaper, "yet they buck and snort like they were in the last throes of poverty."

What do you think?

The Clifton-Morenci strike showed that miners and corporations were still not communicating. Neither side made an effort to sit down and discuss problems. Does this happen today? How can people solve problems in a way that is good for both sides?

Poor George

The colorful, bearded prospectors with their faithful burros have a special niche in the history of Arizona and the West. With only rule-of-thumb geology, they located rich mines without knowing their real value. Take the case of George Warren. He and some friends found copper in the present-day Bisbee area. They staked out claims and named the place Warren Mining District.

On the Fourth of July, George went on one of his frequent gambling binges. In a footrace between himself and a man on horseback, George bet a claim that later became the Copper Queen Mine. He lost the race and lost the mine.

The claim's eventual worth was millions of dollars. Dr. James Douglas and Phelps Dodge Mining Company began large-scale operations at the underground Copper Queen. Poor George soon drank himself insane, eking out a meager living on a little pension from the mines.

George Warren's photograph was used by the artist who drew the miner on the state seal.

Henry C. Hooker operated the huge Sierra Bonita Ranch.

The Cattle Industry

DURING THE 1850S, MOST OF THE CATTLE in Arizona were just passing through. Cowboys drove large herds of Texas cattle across Arizona to California. So many cattle reached the market, in fact, that prices dropped from $500 to $6 a head. Other herds were driven to Arizona to supply beef to stage stations and the army.

In the 1870s and 1880s, hundreds of ranchers were attracted to Arizona by the abundance of grasses, mild climate, and open spaces. One of the most successful pioneer ranchers was Colonel Henry Hooker. He got his start by driving Texas longhorns to supply beef to army posts and Indian reservations. Hooker *homesteaded* in southeastern Arizona. In a few years he controlled all the surrounding grazing lands—about 800 square miles.

By 1880, stock raising had become one of Arizona's leading industries. But many grasslands were soon overstocked. Range land on which nature

"Down to Winter Pasture" was painted by Joe Beeler. It shows cowboys driving cattle from the high country to winter grass in the valley.

had put a few hundred game animals was overrun with thousands of cattle and sheep. The animals soon destroyed much of the natural vegetation. Valleys once covered with high rich grasses were taken over by mesquite, sage, and greasewood.

A severe drought in 1885 and another in the early 1890s caused a grass shortage. Thousands of cattle died. Cattlemen were forced to sell their steers at greatly reduced prices to avoid further losses.

The destruction of grasslands resulted in changes in the Arizona cattle industry. Most cattlemen cut the size of their herds and changed from raising and selling beef to raising calves. Yearlings were then sold for fattening on feeding lots. Stockmen introduced purebred cattle, particularly Herefords. Small cattle companies *consolidated*, giving them more capital to make ranch improvements. Steam pumps and windmills were installed and dirt reservoirs constructed.

Cattle Feeding in the Salt River Valley

In 1888, Colonel Hooker drove 12,000 steers from Graham County to the Salt River Valley to fatten on alfalfa. The same year, Walter Vail shipped seventeen carloads of cattle from his huge Empire Ranch to pasture on farms near Tempe. In the 1890s, grain and cottonseed products became cheaply available. The cattle-feeding business then began operating on a large scale in the Phoenix area.

The Aztec Land and Cattle Company

This company operated a huge ranch in northern Arizona. Better known as the Hashknife outfit, the company ran 60,000 head of cattle with the famous Hashknife brand. The ranch stretched along the railroad from Holbrook almost to Flagstaff.

When rustling became a problem, the Aztec company hired some Texas gunmen to protect the livestock. The thievery was not stopped, however, until Burt Mossman took charge. He personally escorted to jail three neighboring ranchers caught butchering Hashknife cattle. With the help of sheriffs and civic leaders, Mossman was able to send a large number of rustlers to the territorial prison in Yuma.

The Cowboy: Fact and Fiction

Branding was a hot, dirty job. In fact, very little of the cow boy's work was romantic. His life was one of loneliness and drudgery. He worked long hours, and often seven days a week. He dug holes for fence posts, repaired fences, cleaned corrals, cared for injured or sick stock, shoed horses, fixed windmills, hauled salt, and even milked cows.

Most of the early cowboys were drifters with very little education. Their pay was low. Through Western novels and movies the cowboy has been pictured as a noble outdoors man who protects the weak and fights against wrongs. He was big-hearted, free, and happy-go-lucky.

What do you think?

The cowboy, not his rancher boss, has become the folk hero of the cattle industry. Was the cowboy's job more "romantic," or is there some other reason to explain why this is true?

Branding!

Branding was especially important in Arizona because of the open range system of grazing. The vast public domain was roamed by cattle of many different owners. When disputes arose, the brand was the only proof of ownership. Cattlemen worked together in spring and fall roundups. Each calf was branded like the mother cow.

Beginning in 1887, all ranchers were required by territorial law to register their brands and earmarks. At one time there were 17,000 brands listed. With so many on the book, it became difficult to devise a new brand.

The brand language involved circles, boxes, diamonds, bars, triangles, or crosses. Hearts are still popular. The old Empire Ranch heart brand is the most famous. There are numerous character brands: rocking chair, umbrella, tepee, half moon, coffee pot, anvil, violin, and many interesting Mexican designs. Initials are commonly used. One rancher used the "ICU" brand. Some cowpoke with a sense of humor caught one of the calves and added a number to make the brand read "ICU2."

There is a trick to branding properly. The first essential is a proper iron. If the iron is too narrow and sharp it cuts and goes in too deep. A fairly wide brand holds the heat better. Some cattlemen use a "running iron" and simply draw the brand on a calf. When the branding iron is cherry red, it doesn't have to be held against the calf very long. With a little salve or grease spread over the brand, the burn is healed in a week.

Branding cattle was a tiring job for ranch hands.

Cowboys on a large ranch pose for a photograph in 1897.

The Sheep Industry

THE SHEEP INDUSTRY THRIVED IN northern Arizona. The Hopis and Navajos had learned sheep raising from the Spaniards. But the commercial sheep industry got started when Juan Candelaria and his brothers started a ranch in present-day Apache County. A few years later, in the early 1870s, many sheep were driven to northern Arizona after a severe drought hit California. The incoming flocks carried alfilaria seed in their wool. The "filaree," as it is called, started growing here and is now a valuable plant on the sheep ranges.

Flagstaff became the center of the sheep industry. The biggest producers were the three Daggs brothers, who ran as many as 50,000 animals on the Colorado Plateau. They used purebred Merino rams to improve their flocks. The five Babbitt brothers also ran a lot of sheep which could be identified, according to a popular joke, by the sound of "Baa-ab-itt, Baa-ab-itt."

The sheep population exploded in the 1880s and northern Arizona sheep ranchers began a new practice. When frost hit the mountains, they drove their sheep to winter alfalfa pastures in the warmer southern regions. The sheep spread out and slowly ate their way through the public grazing lands. After cattlemen protested, the U. S. Forest Service marked off driveways for the sheep and required herders to move the animals at least five miles a day. Now, of course, most sheep are moved by truck or train to save time.

Many early sheep ranchers hired Basque herders from Spain. The Basques were used to the lonely job of tending sheep. Many of the Basques became sheep ranchers themselves.

By the late 1870s, wool became an important Arizona export. "A barge with 26 bales of wool arrived in Yuma from upriver. . . . The Lord & Williams wagon train arrived with 39 bales."

—*Arizona Sentinel* (Yuma), 1887

Navajo families were the first sheep ranchers in Arizona.

The Ostrich Industry

"ONE EGG OR TWO, SIR?" That was a favorite joke on ostrich ranches when an unsuspecting guest showed up for breakfast. An ostrich egg weighs three pounds and could easily provide a delicious omelet for a dozen people.

By the early 1900s, ostriches were thriving on alfalfa fields near Phoenix and Yuma. They were raised for their feathers and sold as breeders. Every fashionable lady in the country wanted a plume in her hat and maybe a feather scarf, known as a boa. During World War I, feathers in women's clothing fell out of style. The ostrich industry went bust, leaving Arizona growers with thousands of almost worthless birds to feed. Many ostriches were slaughtered and used for fertilizer.

In the 1980s, ostrich raising returned to the Southwest. As in the early days, ostriches for breeding bring a high price. Other birds are grown for their plumes, low-fat meat, and hides. The hides are popular with footwear makers because the high quality leather has an unusual pattern created by the quill holes.

Nona Marshall proudly wears an ostrich feather on her hat.

An ostrich farm near Phoenix was profitable until ostrich feathers went out of style.

Linking the past and the present

The ostrich industry was doomed to be short-lived because it depended on the fashion business. Give examples of other style changes that have made some items of clothing, and the materials that were used to provide them, *obsolete*.

The Red House

In 1904, Michael and Timothy Riordan built a spacious log mansion in Flagstaff and named it Kinlicki, a Navajo word for "red house." The home had separate living quarters for the two families and a common area in the center. Today the mansion is the Riordan State Historic Park. Visitors can see the home's original furnishings and illustrations of the lifestyle enjoyed by a well-to-do territorial family.

Lumber: Arizona's First Major Manufactured Product

WITH THE SANTA FE RAILROAD as a customer and the world's largest stand of ponderosa pines nearby, what more could a lumberman in northern Arizona ask for?

Edward E. Ayers built a large sawmill in Flagstaff. The Ayers mill made railroad ties for the Santa Fe Railroad. Ayers also sawed ties and telegraph poles for the Mexican Central Railroad. He shipped lumber from the "big yellow bellies," as the great orange-barked ponderosa pines were called, to mines and towns in the Arizona Territory and to his yards in Los Angeles and New Mexico.

The Riordan brothers bought the Ayers' business. Denis, Michael, and Timothy Riordan incorporated under the name Arizona Lumber and Timber Company. This company got its timber from private lands. With no need for the timber on public lands, Denis Riordan supported the forest conservation policy of Teddy Roosevelt and other presidents. The federal government, over the protest of most loggers and cattlemen, set aside 73 percent of Arizona's timberlands in forest reserves. Loggers were forbidden to cut timber on these reserves.

Railroads were important to the lumber industry. In the 1880s, the sawmills made wood ties for the railroads. Later, logs and lumber were hauled on trains like this one.

Transportation In Territorial Days

Stagecoach Travel

The traveler could not be choosy. He had to be thankful for anything that moved on wheels. After a while, most of Arizona's towns and mining districts were served by small stage lines. The stage business actually picked up after railroads arrived in the 1880s. The stages brought hundreds of people who needed transportation to places not on the railroad.

Stagecoach travel was slow and uncomfortable. Five miles an hour was a typical speed, though it seemed much faster to a weary passenger bouncing around like a rubber ball. Buckboards, buggies, wagons, and homemade vehicles were more common than the classic Concord coach seen in western movies. In most coaches the passengers sat on hard seats and were crowded like sardines. The roads were rough and dusty. There was always the odor of foul-smelling cigars and unbathed traveling companions. Stage holdups were frequent, especially on lines that carried mail and Wells Fargo payroll boxes.

Stage stops were famous for bad food. The usual fare was beef jerky, salt pork, stale bread, bad coffee, and beans. A Chicago reporter wrote about a traveling salesman who refused to eat beans at one Arizona stage stop. When the traveler demanded something better, a local man thrust a revolver in his face and said, "Stranger, eat them beans!" And he did!

Wise travelers carried some food with them. A man coming from California to Tucson wrote: "There was a German with us who brought loaves of rye bread and a bundle of limburger cheese and he saved our lives even if we did make him tie the cheese on the axle back of the stage."

Stage stops were short. After a fresh team was hitched, passengers would hear the driver yell, "Time to go again! All aboard! Got my orders!" Then, as soon as the stage was loaded, crack! crack! went the whip. "Git up! Hi Yi! Yip Yip!"

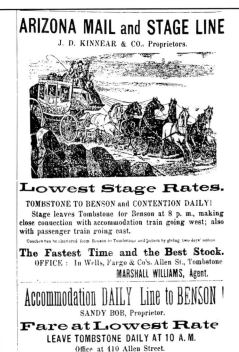

ARIZONA MAIL and STAGE LINE
J. D. KINNEAR & CO., Proprietors.

Lowest Stage Rates.

TOMBSTONE TO BENSON and CONTENTION DAILY!
Stage leaves Tombstone for Benson at 8 p. m., making close connection with accommodation train going west; also with passenger train going east.

Coaches can be chartered from Benson to Tombstone and return by giving two days' notice.

The Fastest Time and the Best Stock.
OFFICE : In Wells, Fargo & Co's. Allen St., Tombstone
MARSHALL WILLIAMS, Agent.

Accommodation DAILY Line to BENSON !
SANDY BOB, Proprietor.
Fare at Lowest Rate
LEAVE TOMBSTONE DAILY AT 10 A. M.
Office at 410 Allen Street.

This advertisement appeared in the *Tombstone Epitaph* January 11, 1892. What would the stages carry? What cities did the stage line connect?

She Was a Bad Guy

Not all stagecoach robbers were men, but Pearl Hart disguised herself as one. In 1899, Hart and a male friend held up the Globe stage, making off with about $400, watches, and jewelry. The sheriff followed their tracks and arrested them.

Pearl, who could barely write her own name, got national *notoriety* for this one botched holdup. Reporters dramatized her into a colorful character. Hart played along, hoping for a "big break" into theater. She posed for photos heavily armed in masculine attire or sitting modestly in a long dress.

Joe Boot, her robbery partner, was tried and sentenced to thirty years at the Yuma penitentiary. A jury freed Pearl on the stage holdup charge, but found her guilty of stealing the stage driver's pistol. She served about three years at the Yuma penitentiary.

After release, Pearl and her sister acted in a stage holdup skit around the country. She then disappeared from the public eye.

Wagon Freighting

In the 1870s it took sixty to ninety days to get merchandise from San Francisco. Before railroads, all overland freight was hauled by wagon. Some goods came by ship to the mouth of the Colorado River. There the cargo was loaded on barges and pulled up river by steamboat to depots at Yuma, Ehrenberg, or Hardyville. Wagons then hauled the goods over a cobweb of trails to places in Arizona.

Other shipments came overland all the way. P. R. Tully and Estevan Ochoa of Tucson were the merchant princes in the Southwest. They employed hundreds of men to haul goods from Kansas City over the Santa Fe Trail and from Mexico. The Tully & Ochoa Company also had freighting contracts with the U. S. government to supply forts.

A typical freight outfit might consist of two wagons pulled by oxen, mules, or horses. But a *tandem* of three or four huge high-sided wagons hitched to twenty or thirty mules was not uncommon. Mules were more expensive than oxen but were faster and needed less water. The smartest pair was put in front and the strongest pair next to the wagon. A wagoner needed great skill to drive a team over a mountain road with sharp curves. Usually he had one or more helpers to handle the brakes and other chores.

Some drivers owned their own rigs, but most of them worked for freighting companies. These companies did a thriving business serving the towns and mines of the territory. Every major town had freight depots, wagon and harness shops, blacksmiths, and big corrals for the mules.

After railroads came to Arizona, wagons were used mainly for short hauls. Freight ran the gamut from barbed wire and machines to clothing, flour, canned goods, and "U-Needa-Biscuit" frosted cookies.

A wagoner and his mules pose for a picture in the Salt River Valley.

The Southern Pacific and Santa Fe Railroads

"The Chariot of Fire (locomotive) has arrived in Tucson on its way across the continent. We welcome the railroad . . . we welcome the builders," said Charles Poston to a celebrating crowd on March 20, 1880.

The Southern Pacific Railroad was laying track from the California coast to El Paso. A crew of 200 Anglos and 1,100 Chinese laid down a mile of track a day out of Yuma. Then construction stopped at Casa Grande for eight months because of extreme summer heat. During that time, most of the Chinese workers scattered to find work in mining camps and to open restaurants, laundries, or other businesses. When the railroad was finally completed, Casa Grande, as well as Maricopa, Tucson, Benson, and Willcox, became important shipping points along the Southern Pacific Railroad.

In 1883 the Santa Fe Railroad completed the second trans–continental line across the Arizona territory. Tracklayers, moving westward across northern Arizona from New Mexico, faced a major obstacle at Canyon Diablo. For six months they struggled to bridge this 550-feet-wide gorge. More bridges and tunnels lay ahead before workers spanned the Colorado River and joined a Southern Pacific line. New railroad towns sprang up from Holbrook to Kingman. The economy of Flagstaff was given a boost by the railroad.

An accident in 1880 symbolized the beginning of a new transportation era in Arizona. A Southern Pacific locomotive smashed into two Tully & Ochoa Company freight wagons, killing the mules. Animal power could not compete with steam.

What do you think?

The Santa Fe Railroad received free land from the government. The company got twenty alternate sections of land (like a checkerboard) for each mile of track. A section is one square mile. Why do you think the federal government was willing to give the railroad so much land?

A Santa Fe train crosses Canyon Diablo in this postcard from 1905.

Holbrook grew up along the Santa Fe Railroad, 1887.

The First Automobiles in Arizona

In 1899, Barnum and Bailey Circus brought a steam car to Phoenix and Tucson. The same year, Dr. Hiram W. Fenner had the parts for a steam-powered Locomobile shipped from Boston and assembled in Tucson. Unfortunately, Fenner ran the car into a saguaro cactus on his first ride.

The first "gas buggies" were sold as a sideline by bicycle stores and wagon makers. Drugstores put in a stock of gasoline and motor oil. Livery stables were converted into garages. Blacksmiths learned how to repair broken parts. The earliest automobiles—whether steam, electric, or gasoline-powered—were little more than amusing playthings. Gradually, however, eastern automakers produced cars that were more powerful, dependable, and affordable. Soon, people were driving cars on dusty wagon roads in nearly every part of the territory. At the time of statehood in 1912, there were 1,852 automobiles in Arizona.

Once cars were accepted, drivers demanded highways. Phoenix businessmen promoted good roads by organizing an annual auto race from Los Angeles to the Phoenix fairground. Each town along the way put up prize money for the first driver to arrive. Local people used mule teams and shovels to smooth out the road in their area. As roads improved, the winning time was cut from $41^1/2$ hours in 1908 to $20^1/2$ hours in 1911. You will read more about early automobiles in a later chapter.

Three families take a ride near Prescott in the early 1900s. There were few roads then.

1. Explain why Jack Swilling is a very important person in the history of the Salt River Valley.

2. Why was the name Phoenix chosen for the city?

3. Explain why Roosevelt Dam was needed.

4. List some of the achievements of Jacob Hamblin.

5. List five towns in Arizona that were settled by Mormons.

6. Where was Arizona's best-known silver strike? Who discovered it?

7. What caused silver mining to decline in the 1890s?

8. For what reasons did copper mining develop slowly at first?

9. Where were some of the big bonanza mines located?

10. What did Henry Hooker do, and where?

11. For what reason did grasslands deteriorate in the 1880s?

12. Which large cattle ranch in northern Arizona stretched from Holbrook almost to Flagstaff?

13. Why did the open range system of grazing make branding especially important in Arizona?

14. From what country did the Basque sheep ranchers come?

15. For what achievement does Edward E. Ayers deserve a prominent place in Arizona history?

16. List five discomforts of stagecoach travel.

17. How did the first railroad lines in Arizona help the wagon freighting business?

18. What brought the first car to Phoenix and Tucson?

Dr. Hiram Fenner shows off his steam Locomobile.

PEOPLE TO KNOW

Lucy Flake
Nellie Cashman
Hutchlon Ohnick
Sue H. Summers
Rev. Joseph P. Machebeuf
Bishop Jean Salpointe
Rev. David Tuthill
Rev. William Meyer
Endicott Peabody
R.A. Windes
Charles D. Poston
Uriah Gregory
Winfield Scott
Samuel Drachman
Morris Goldwater
Ben McClendon
William and Ann Neal
John Swain
Sgt. Benjamin Brown
Cpl. Isaiah Mays
Booker T. Washington
Burt Mossman
Thomas Rynning
 Harry Wheeler

TERMS TO UNDERSTAND

lye
alkali
desert refrigerator
evict
sociable
parish
chaplain
tabernacle
denomination
immigrant
civic
porter
regiment
buffalo soldier
abolish

1868
Jean Baptiste Salpointe is the first
Catholic bishop in Arizona.

1881
The Earps shoot it out
with their enemies in
Tombstone.

1860   1870   1880

1881
Tucson gets the first commercial
telephone switchboard in Arizona.

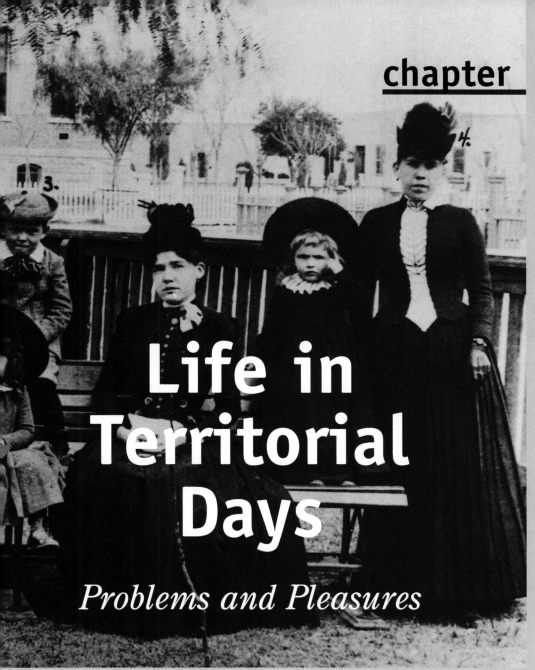

Life in Territorial Days

Problems and Pleasures

Members of the Orndorff family are dressed in their Sunday best in Tucson, 1889.

PLACES TO LOCATE

Snowflake
Tombstone
Flagstaff
Williams
Florence
Jerome
Oatman
Pearce
Congress
Stanton
Yuma
Phoenix
Tucson
Prescott
Bisbee
Warren
Douglas
Globe
Clifton
Scottsdale
Mammoth
Oracle
Holbrook
Nogales

1863—1912
Territory of Arizona

1890s
Football comes to Arizona schools.

1892
Arizona Medical Association is formed.

1907
The territorial legislature makes gambling illegal.

1890   **1900**   **1910**   **1920**

1885
The all-black 10th Cavalry is assigned to Arizona.

1895
The Neals open the Mountain View Hotel in Oracle.

1901—1909
Arizona Rangers arrest cattle thieves and outlaws.

Women on the Frontier

FRONTIER ARIZONA was a land of mining camps, army posts, lonely ranches, farms, and scattered villages or towns. Everyone faced discomforts and hardships, but women especially endured a harsh life. Pioneer women coped with homemaking, farm chores, gardening, canning, and raising children under primitive conditions. Just getting safe clean drinking water was a challenge. Outbreaks of typhoid fever and other diseases took a toll, mainly among children.

Lucy Flake's life on a farm near Snowflake was typical for women on the frontier. Let's take a peek at her diary entry for an ordinary day, May 16, 1896:

> **"I will just write my morning chores. Get up and turn out the chickens, draw a pail of watter . . . make a fire, put potatoes to cook, then brush and sweep half inch of dust off the floor and everything, feed three litters of chickens, then mix biscuits, get breakfast, milk besides work in the house, and this morning had to go half mile after calves. This is the way of life on the farm."**

Women dreaded wash day wherever they were. Here is how Marguerite Noble, recalling her own family memories, described laundry day in her famous novel *Filaree*:

> **"Melissa carried sloshing pails of water (from the creek) and filled a black washpot to boil the clothes. The wood resisted burning. . . . With her sunbonnet she fanned the flames. Smoke choked her and perspiration covered her face. She put a can of *lye* in the boiling water, and when the scum formed, removed it. With a butcher knife she shaved a bar of homemade soap into slivers, dropping the fragments into the water. Then she settled her washboard into a tub of warm water and scrubbed the clothes against the ripples of brass. The harshness of the soap irritated her hands."**

Making chicken soup for supper was not like a quick trip to the supermarket:

> **"Grabbing the fowl by the legs, she carried it squawking and flapping to the yard. With an experienced twist of her hand and wrist, she wrung the hen's neck. The body flopped in the dirt. Melissa scalded, plucked, singed, and cleaned the bird and took it inside to boil. . . . "**

Washing clothes was a dreaded chore for women.

Women in the Hall of Fame

Every year, deserving women are inducted into the Arizona Hall of Fame. A broad spectrum of women have been honored. The museum is located in the old Carnegie Library near the State Capitol.

Indian women have kept house, provided food and clothing, and raised children in Arizona for 500 generations. The first Hispanic women arrived at Tubac in 1752. They lived with their Spanish soldier husbands and children in adobe huts around the presidio.

Anglo women began coming in great numbers after the railroads were built in the 1880s. Women of all races and religious faiths endured hardships on the Arizona frontier.

This cartoon appeared in *The Phoenix Gazette*.
The lady's dress was considered bold in territorial days.

Territorial Towns

MOST OF ARIZONA'S TOWNS were founded during territorial days. Towns sprang up near mines, along railroads, or in valleys where farming was the main industry. A combination of railroad, lumbering, and livestock put Flagstaff and Williams on the map.

As the territorial towns grew, annual festivals and celebrations became traditional. People developed a sense of community pride. The general store was still the pioneer's main shopping center, but specialty stores were beginning to open.

By 1892 there were enough doctors in the towns to form the Arizona Medical Association. This group got the legislature to set higher qualifications for doctors and to pass health laws.

Flagstaff is a good example of an early Arizona town. This is what it looked like in 1882.

Born in Ireland, Nellie Cashman was the first woman to stake a gold claim in the Yukon Territory (northwestern Canada). She was also the first to start her own business in Tucson. She opened Delmonico Restaurant, advertising the "best meals in town." Nellie moved to Tombstone during the silver rush of 1880.

Called the "Angel of Tombstone," Nellie raised her sister's five orphaned children. She became a one-woman director of charities wherever she was. When a man fell into a mine shaft, breaking both legs, she quickly raised $500 for his care and comfort.

In 1898 Nellie returned to the Yukon, started a hotel in Alaska, and raised money for a hospital.

> "Florence is a dreamy, quiet, restful farming town. There is no rush, not much noise. . . . Crowing roosters and squeaking pump handles awaken the people."
> —*Weekly Enterprise, 1883*

Most towns had a general store, where people could buy the things they needed. What are some of the items for sale here?

Ghost Towns

Besides the territorial towns that have grown and prospered, Arizona has at least 130 ghost towns. Some, like Jerome, still have life left.

Most of the ghost towns have only a few buildings or mounds of adobe bricks to show where miners or stage station operators once lived and worked. Congress, for example, was the site of a celebrated gold mine. In 1900 the town had a mill, hospital, homes, boarding houses, Chinese and Mexican restaurants, Catholic and Presbyterian churches, a three-teacher school, saloons, telegraph and telephone connections, and its own electric light plant. Today, only a few broken-down buildings remain.

Stanton is now a ghost town.

The Railroad Brings Change

Railroads made Arizona more like the rest of the country. Throngs of people from the States began migrating to Arizona to make their homes. More women and families moved into the territory. Churches began to compete with saloons for the attention of sinners. Eastern styles of clothing, food, and architecture appeared. The close business and social ties with Mexico were weakened. The *peso*, called the "dobe dollar," lost its value in trade. Anglo-Mexican marriages became less common.

ARIZONA: A Journey of Discovery

Water, Sanitation, and Cooling Problems

Very few towns had a pure water supply. Water from shallow wells was often contaminated by nearby privies. This lack of sanitation caused typhoid fever epidemics. Typhoid was especially bad in Yuma because the prison dumped waste into the Gila River, upstream from where Yuma residents got their water supply.

Some Phoenix residents used the water in the town's irrigation ditch even though good well water was available. Water in the ditch was polluted by livestock, by people who bathed in it at night, and by saloon keepers who washed their spittoons in it.

In Tucson, *alkali* got into the underground wells. For a while, enterprising Mexicans hauled water from springs and sold it for five cents a pail. Add soap at 50 cents a bar and bathing was considered a luxury. Water was finally piped in, but it contained "vegetative matter" and had a bad odor.

Tombstone had Arizona's best waterworks, costing half a million dollars. Water was piped twenty-one miles from a reservoir in the Huachuca Mountains. The system not only provided water for drinking and bathing, but had enough pressure to put out fires. Twice the Tombstone business district had burned down.

Keeping cool in the desert was another challenge. Houses with thick adobe walls were the coolest. A wide porch for shade helped, too. In the summertime nearly everyone slept outdoors or on a screened porch. The fancy Hotel Adams in Phoenix cooled the lobby by placing around the room huge pans, each with a block of ice and a fan blowing over it.

Ice companies operated in the larger towns, but most families used an outdoor "desert refrigerator" to preserve food that could spoil. A wooden frame was covered with burlap on all sides. The burlap was always kept damp by water dripping from a container on top. Natural breezes were the "fan."

Mexicans adapted to the hot climate better than most Anglos. They wore lightweight clothing, sandals, and wide-brimmed sombreros. Well-to-do businessmen sometimes put their wives and children on a stagecoach or train and sent them to the mountains or seashore for the summer.

> "The water was a little too thick for navigation and rather thin for real estate. It was totally unfit for use."
> —*Tucson Citizen*, 1885

The desert refrigerator helped to keep milk, butter, and meat from spoiling in hot weather.

Linking the past and the present
Clean safe drinking water is still not easy for some Arizona cities and towns to get. Find out what some of the problems are in your community or the places surrounding it.

A Phoenix telephone installer in the early 1900s carried phones over his shoulders and tools around his waist.

"The streetcars had their shortcomings for they were noisy, hot in summer, cold in winter, sometimes had flat wheels and the ride could be rough. They did, however, go anywhere worth going in their day, and for only five cents."

—Lawrence J. Fleming
Ride a Mile and Smile the While

Bisbee residents celebrate the opening of the new Warren-Bisbee Street Railway in 1908.

Telephones

In the East, the telephone was invented by Alexander Graham Bell in 1876. Five years later, the first commercial telephone switchboard in Arizona was installed at the stage station in Tucson. The first two phones in Phoenix connected an ice factory to the owner's home. Like other towns in the territory, Phoenix later had several phone companies. Each company had its own phone book. Residents had to buy phone service from every company if they wanted to talk to all possible phone customers.

Prescott was also equipped with "hello" lines, some of the home-grown variety. Frank Wright's little company was a good example. Wright did some unusual things, at least by today's standards. On one occasion he hired a two-man orchestra to play music to his fifty telephone customers. (The radio had not been invented yet.) Wright also installed a free phone on a tree in the town plaza. He and another company helped to save the town on July 4, 1900. Together they alerted the fire-fighting teams when a great fire raced up Whiskey Row on Montezuma Street.

All the phone companies in Arizona were finally combined by Mountain States Telephone and Telegraph Company. This company started in Bisbee-Douglas and expanded to give Arizona one telephone system. Bell phones and switchboards were installed in nearly every town. The work was completed in 1912, the year Arizona became a state.

Streetcars

At least five towns had electric trolleys—Bisbee-Warren, Douglas, Phoenix, Prescott, and Tucson. Some of the lines started out as mule or horse-drawn streetcars. The animal-pulled cars in Phoenix had open sides. Two back-to-back seats ran the full length of the car. Tucson began operating horse and mule cars between the Southern Pacific Railroad depot and the University of Arizona campus. Student pranksters sometimes removed the lightweight car from the track at night and pushed it onto the campus. The trolley company didn't think that was funny.

In 1893 an electric railway was launched. The cars were connected by a pole to an electric wire overhead. Riders on Tucson's electric trolley called it "Izzer" because of the sound it made. Prescott had electric streetcars along Gurley Street to Fort Whipple. The Prescott line was used mainly by school children and by soldiers at the fort.

Fun Times in Frontier Towns

LIFE IN TERRITORIAL DAYS was not all work. The pioneers knew how to have fun in their leisure time. They enjoyed picnics, square dances with old-time fiddling, horse races, rodeos, and contests for the young such as sack races, burro races, and tugs of war. Holidays and festivals were always fun times.

Fourth of July Celebrations

Most towns had parades on the Fourth of July. A typical parade in Tucson might be half a mile long. A snappy brass band led horse-drawn carriages and floats trimmed in red, white, and blue. An afternoon baseball game at Military Plaza always drew a crowd. In the evening, the military band from Fort Lowell usually played a concert of patriotic music.

In mining towns, hard rock drilling contests were popular. Mine companies sponsored their best drillers and put up big prize money for the winners. In the double jack contests, one man would hold and turn a steel drill while his partner swung a sledge hammer to pound it into a block of stone. There was danger that the hammer man would miss the center of the drill and smash the holder's hand or head. The winners of a contest in Bisbee one year drilled a record hole of forty-six and three-fourths inches.

A special event in most northern Arizona towns was the fire hose race. Each team pulled a two-wheeled cart with a reel of hose to a fire hydrant, hooked up the hose, and turned on the water. The team with the fastest time won. The rivalry between teams from Jerome and Prescott was especially keen. Big areas in both towns had burned down and the people realized the importance of speed in putting out a fire.

Bisbee Boys Band

ARIZONA PORTRAIT

Hutchlon Ohnick

Hachiro Onuki came to the U.S. from Japan in 1876 to visit the Centennial Exhibition at Philadelphia. He stayed, took part in the Tombstone silver boom, and changed his name to Hutchlon Ohnick, which sounded more American.

Ohnick gave up mining to manufacture gas from crude petroleum in Phoenix. Six explosions of coal oil lamps in one week made his gas plant a welcome sight. "This town can't afford to burn coal oil any longer," said a local newspaper. Ohnick installed pipes and fixtures in time to illuminate stores during the 1886 Christmas season. His best customer was the Capital Saloon, which had fancy gas lamps.

Later, Ohnick worked as a superintendent of the Phoenix Electric Light Company. This company generated electricity with steam engines. Ohnick has been described as "the foreigner who launched this desert city into an era of prosperity."

San Juan's Day

Two of the favorite Mexican holidays were *Cinco de Mayo* and the *Fiesta de San Juan*. In 1883 about 1,500 people enjoyed the San Juan's festival in Phoenix. They bought huge glasses of lemonade at booths, danced to the music of a six-piece band, and gambled. Most of the crowd at the bullfight jeered. Some of the bulls were ferocious but their horns had been sawed off.

Another event was the *corriendo de gallo*. A rooster was buried in the ground, except for the head. The object of the contest was for a horseback rider to pull the rooster from the ground as he sped by on a running horse. Many grabs were made before a rider pulled the bird out. This cruelty to animals would not be allowed today.

Sports

Baseball was not as well organized in territorial days as it is today. Most games were of the pickup variety. In Jerome the young miners and merchants would pile on wagons and ride downhill to a flat spot near the Verde River. There they marked off a diamond. Mine companies soon realized the importance of entertainment for their employees and began promoting baseball leagues. After statehood, Jerome and Clarkdale each won the state baseball championship.

Football became a sport in high schools and colleges in the 1890s. The Phoenix Union High School team played four games in 1898, two with Phoenix Indian School and two with Tempe Normal School (now ASU). The Phoenix Union team won three and tied one. The last game with the Indian School ended in a five-to-five tie. (A touchdown counted five points then.) The Phoenix Indians used a play called the "revolving wedge." All the players stood up around the center. As they moved down field they whirled together like a cyclone.

Some schools had girls' teams. This is the 1912 Phoenix High School girls' basketball team. What do you think of their uniforms?

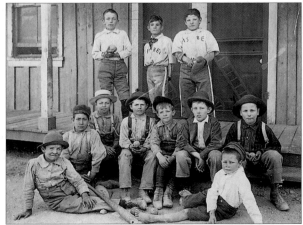

This Bisbee baseball team got together for a picture in 1898. How do their hats and uniforms differ from those we see today?

The Theater

Hispanics in Tucson enjoyed night plays performed outdoors in a park. A favorite was *Elena y Jorge*. The beautiful Elena had a wicked uncle who wanted to sell her for gold. But the plot ended happily when her true lover, the handsome Jorge, won her hand.

Traveling entertainers came to the fancy saloons and theaters to perform. Tombstone had several theaters. Schieffelin Hall, named after the man who discovered silver at Tombstone, could seat 700 people. Plays, operas, musicals, and lectures were booked there.

Many miners and cowboys preferred the famous Bird Cage Theatre in Tombstone. The entertainment was not highbrow. Comedians, girl dancers, and variety shows were well received. When the popular play *Uncle Tom's Cabin* was performed at the Bird Cage, a drunken cowboy got too involved. He shot the bloodhound that was pursuing Eliza, a runaway slave, as she crossed the icy Ohio River.

A similar incident took place at the rival Crystal Palace. On the stage a poor orphan girl was about to be *evicted* by a hard-hearted landlady. A miner, unable to hold back his feelings any longer, stood up, threw a large coin to the girl, and exclaimed, "Here, Sis, take that and pay the old she-devil!" The sympathetic audience applauded loudly.

Most of the towns also had local entertainers. Glee clubs, brass bands, and amateur actors performed. John P. Clum, the former Indian agent and editor of the *Tombstone Epitaph*, had a role in several plays.

The famous Nola Forest sang at the Bird Cage Theatre.

The Bird Cage Theatre still stands today. Now a museum, it is one of Tombstone's most popular tourist attractions.

Linking the past and the present

Today, Arizona has many museums in towns and cities around the state. What are some things you would expect to find in one of these places to remind you of life in territorial days?

Saloons and Gambling Halls

Nearly every town had at least one saloon, if not a whole row of them. Prescott's Montezuma Street was called "Whiskey Row" because saloons outnumbered other businesses. The saloon was the social center for many cowboys, miners, teamsters, businessmen, politicians, and professional men.

Tombstone had more than a hundred saloons. The town's first big fire was caused by its favorite beverage. An open barrel of whiskey exploded when a bartender got too close with a lighted cigar in his mouth. By supper time, four square blocks of buildings were in smoking ruins.

Some of the earliest saloons were no more than a tent with a rough board for a bar. There were also fancy places, such as the Crystal Palace in Tombstone, Congress Hall in Tucson, the Fashion in Jerome, the Gold Coin in Globe, and the Blue Goose in Clifton. These saloons often had velvet drapes, expensive glassware, and a polished wood bar with heavy brass rails. Some had a mirror large enough for a man to see his image from hat and moustache to boots.

Gambling provided entertainment in many saloons. Most of the owners made the games as crooked as they could and still attract customers. Roulette wheels were rigged so the operator could stop the marble where he wanted it. Loaded dice were used. Card sharks marked or trimmed the corners of important cards. The losers were the cowboys, soldiers, and wagon freighters who came in with their hard-earned wages. In 1907 the territorial legislature made gambling illegal in Arizona. Seven years later the people voted to close saloons.

Gamblers play a game called faro in Morenci.

The Street Fight (Painting by Don Perceval)

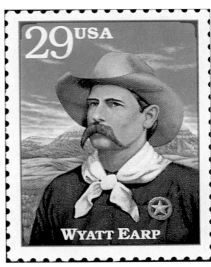

Wyatt Earp and the Tombstone Street Fight

THE WILD WEST'S BEST-REMEMBERED GUNFIGHT took place on October 26, 1881. The shoot-out was never called anything except "the street fight" in thousands of words of court testimony. But fiction writers and movie makers invented the catchy phrase, "Gunfight at the OK Corral."

Historians still argue about the causes of the fight. They often ask, "Will the real Wyatt Earp please stand up?" Was Earp the fine, fearless, frontier peace officer portrayed today in television programs? Or were he and his brothers the gamblers, thieves, and bullies who hid behind their badges? The truth may be somewhere in between.

First came the argument, then the shooting, and then the burying. We know that the Earp and Clanton families carried long-simmering grudges. Both sides hurled challenges to "make a fight." The bad blood reached a climax as nine men played roles in a real-life drama. On one side were Wyatt, Virgil, and Morgan Earp plus their friend Doc Holliday. On the other side were Ike and Billy Clanton, Tom and Frank McLaury (McLowry), and Billy Claiborne.

The half-minute gunfight erupted on a vacant lot and spread out onto Fremont Street. Three men died and two of the Earp brothers were wounded. The Earps testified at their trial that they meant only to disarm the gang. The judge ruled the killings "a necessary act done in the discharge of official business."

Within months, Virgil Earp was shot in the back after dark and was crippled for life. Morgan was killed in a pool room by an unknown assassin. Wyatt Earp left Tombstone and became a legend.

Religious Groups

Catholics

"I am happy the Papago Indians can sing in a tolerable manner and remember some of the Spanish prayers they had been taught," said Reverend Joseph P. Machebeuf in 1859. He was the first American Catholic priest assigned to Arizona. His church was a converted two-room house in Tucson.

Almost ten years later, Jean Baptiste Salpointe arrived as Arizona's first Catholic missionary bishop. San Augustine in Tucson was his home church. Salpointe recruited six young priests from France and sent them to start *parishes* in the territory's largest settlements. He also brought in nuns to start St. Joseph's Academy for Girls and St. Mary's Hospital in Tucson. Years later, the Sisters of Mercy started St. Joseph's Hospital in Phoenix.

Under Salpointe and his successors, the Catholic Church continued to expand, keeping pace with the growth of the territory. The church worked to improve the education and health of the people as well as their souls.

Bishop Salpointe helped build the Catholic Church in the territory.

Methodists and Presbyterians

When Arizona became a territory, it was one of the least known and most thinly populated areas in the United States. Protestant missionary groups in the East had difficulty finding ministers to serve in this isolated territory. Thus, a handful of churches had to compete with hundreds of saloons for the attention of sinners.

> **"The first time the Gospel has ever been preached [in what is now Arizona] by a Protestant clergyman was in Tubac this week. The Rev. David Tuthill will preach at regular intervals in Tucson, Tubac, Calabasas, and Fort Buchanan."**

This earliest account of a Methodist circuit preacher at work in Arizona was printed in the Tubac *Arizonan*, 1859. Before churches were built, people gathered under a shady cottonwood tree or in a home, store, or courthouse to hear a traveling preacher or an army *chaplain* deliver a sermon. Tuthill preached his sermon at a hotel in Tubac.

The Methodist church grew rapidly after Reverend George H. Adams built churches in a dozen towns, from Kingman and Winslow in the north to Yuma and Willcox in the south. A real go-getter, he once walked into a Tucson saloon and "passed the hat" among gamblers to raise money for the First Methodist Church.

One of the early churches was the First Presbyterian in Phoenix, organized by Reverend William Meyer. Then a twenty-nine-year-old bachelor, Meyer delivered his first sermon standing on a barrel in a warehouse. In a few months "Preacher Bill" had a congregation of eight members and built an oval-shaped *tabernacle* in downtown Phoenix. Cottonwood poles supported a roof of leafy brush. The walls were made of ocotillo cactus stems placed upright and laced together.

All the *denominations* struggled to exist in the early years. After the railroads were built, women and families came to Arizona in greater numbers. Then more ministers were willing to serve in this frontier region. The organization of each church brought both spiritual fellowship and opportunity for wholesome social gatherings.

The first Presbyterian Church of Phoenix was organized in this building. Reverend William Meyer (left) directed the construction. Shortly after marrying his New York sweetheart, Meyer left Phoenix, discouraged by his work. "In a year and a half," he said, "only one new member has come in." Future growth of his church, however, proved that Meyer had done a better job than he knew.

Episcopalians and Baptists

The Episcopalians sent out missionary priests. Young Endicott Peabody was the most famous. A muscular, educated man from Boston, Peabody rode into Tombstone on a stagecoach. Soon to be respected by the town's toughest as a heavyweight boxer and a baseball umpire, he held religious services in the courthouse. Later, St. Paul's Episcopal Church was built. It is Arizona's oldest Protestant church still in use. An iron picket fence around the church was donated by poker players at the Crystal Palace Saloon.

R. A. Windes brought his family to Arizona from Chicago in a two-mule wagon. He organized seven Baptist churches, beginning with the Lone Star Baptist in Prescott. This church had only one hymnal book. Windes, with a twinkle in his eye, said that the congregation "sang with enthusiasm and volume, but not much tune." He founded the First Baptist Church in Phoenix. Charles D. Poston, the "father of Arizona" was a member.

The next year, a nice frame church was built and Uriah Gregory was chosen to be pastor. Gregory, a bearded and distinguished-looking former teacher and lawyer, came from Tucson. There he had worked with Mexican bricklayers to build an adobe Baptist church. Like other ministers, Gregory was concerned about the influence of saloons and the twenty-four-hour gambling halls in Arizona's towns.

Life in Territorial Days

ARIZONA PORTRAIT

Winfield Scott
1837–1910

Reverend Winfield Scott, a Baptist preacher in the Phoenix area, was a man with many interests. A wounded Civil War veteran and a retired army chaplain, Scott filled pulpits in Phoenix, Tempe, and Prescott. He also grew citrus and other crops on his Scottsdale farm. Active in civic affairs, he was president of the first Scottsdale board of education, a member of the territorial legislature, and a member of the college board.

The city of Scottsdale is named for this busy man.

Scottsdale

Many Mormon families like this one came south from Utah to settle in the territory.

Jacob Isaacson, a Jewish pioneer, founded the town of Isaacson. It was later renamed Nogales.

Latter-Day Saints (Mormons)

By the 1880s, the second largest religious group in the territory was The Church of Jesus Christ of Latter-day Saints. The people were usually called "Mormons." Religion played an important part in the lives of Mormon settlers. The Mormons were the closest-knit religious group in Arizona. The Mormon bishop supervised the travel to Arizona and the settlement of *immigrant* families. He was also in charge of farming and other economic work, as well as running the local church. In a Mormon community, the bishop and other religious leaders were also the *civic* leaders. They ran for office and played a very important part in local politics.

Polygamy, or the religious practice of a man marrying more than one wife at a time, was practiced by a few of the Mormon people. New polygamous marriages were forbidden by the church in the 1890s.

Jewish Pioneers

Jewish settlers, though small in number, made a strong impact on the economic growth of Arizona. Most of the Jewish pioneers, like the Goldwaters in Prescott and the Drachmans in Tucson, were merchants. At least four gave their names to towns—Herman Ehrenberg, Isador Solomon, Joe Mayer, and Jacob Isaacson. David Abraham built wagon roads. Henry and Charles Lesinsky owned a copper smelter at Clifton. Selim Franklin led the legislative fight to create the University of Arizona.

There were no rabbis or synagogues in those days, so casual services were held in homes. In Tucson, Samuel Drachman led prayers and songs for the High Holy Days. He also presided over Jewish weddings. Morris Goldwater performed the same duties in Prescott.

African Americans

AFRICAN AMERICAN PIONEERS, cowboys, and soldiers took part in developing the West. The first big westward movement of blacks came from the southern states after the Civil War freed them from slavery. Some black cowboys tended huge herds of longhorns on ranches in Texas. Others settled in Indian Territory (now eastern Oklahoma) where some married into Indian tribes. Eventually, the more adventurous drifted westward into Arizona.

Black pioneers often started working at jobs they had learned in the South. They were cooks, barbers, laborers, teamsters, maids, table waiters, and *porters*. Charley Embers was typical of some early blacks in the territory. He cooked for a mining camp at Ajo for a while. His next job was unloading freight at the Maricopa Wells stage station. Like many pioneers, Embers married a girl of Mexican descent.

Before long, however, blacks were on the scene as cowpunchers, soldiers, merchants, gold prospectors, stagecoach drivers, and musicians. Ben McClendon was one of the first black prospectors. A runaway slave, he came to Yuma in 1862. There he joined a party of prospectors and shared in rich gold discoveries in the Prescott area. Later, Ben found a gold mine but never revealed its location. He would hang around Wickenburg until his money was spent and then disappear into the hills. Before long the town residents would see him return with a burro loaded with ore. The rocks were smashed and the gold washed out. But on one trip, Ben never returned. His body was found near his dead burro a few miles from town. To this day no one has located his mine.

William "Curley Bill" Neal was one of the most well-to-do blacks in territorial days. Born of a black father and a Cherokee mother, Neal had an Indian name, "Bear Sitting Down." Starting as a cook in a Tucson hotel, Neal next went into the freight business. He supplied fuel wood to copper smelters and hauled ore from the mines at Mammoth. For a time, he carried the mail between Tucson and Oracle.

In 1895 Curley Bill and Ann, his young wife, opened the Mountain View Hotel in Oracle as a year-round resort. Arizonans went there in the summertime to enjoy the cool crisp air of the Santa Catalina Mountains. Winter visitors from the East rode to the resort from Tucson in one of Neal's stagecoaches. Mrs. Neal was a gracious hostess and kept the guests occupied with picnics, horseback riding, and other activities. "Buffalo Bill" Cody was a frequent visitor.

Black Cowboys

William Neal was a rancher, running thousands of cattle on his ranch at Oracle. Most black cattlemen in territorial Arizona, however, worked as cowboys. John Swain punched cattle for John Slaughter in southeastern Arizona. Known as "Sweeney" and "Little John," he was born a slave on Slaughter's ranch in Texas. Given his freedom after the Civil War, he chose to remain with Slaughter. Swain helped drive huge herds of longhorns from Texas. He tracked and shot rustlers. One of his jobs was to protect his boss on trips into Mexico to recover stolen cattle.

Some black cowboys went by only a first name. Jim was another cowpuncher who came from Texas with John Slaughter. A giant of a man, he once fought John L. Sullivan, the famous heavyweight boxing champion. In Tombstone, Jim staggered Sullivan with a roundhouse swing, but then the great Sullivan quickly knocked him out. Old-timers around Tombstone talked about the fight for years.

Sweeney and Jim were real live cowboys. Dozens like them played an important part in the history of the Arizona cattle industry.

John "Sweeney" Swain wanted to live long enough to ride a bronco on his 100th birthday. If it pitched him into the next world, he said, that would be all right. Swain missed his 100th by only a few months.

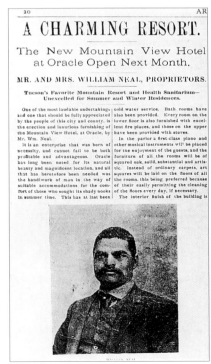

William and Ann Neal opened the Mountain View Hotel in Oracle.

"Arizona Joe" was the hero of a story in an 1887 western magazine. Many black cowboys worked on the frontier.

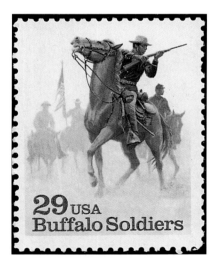
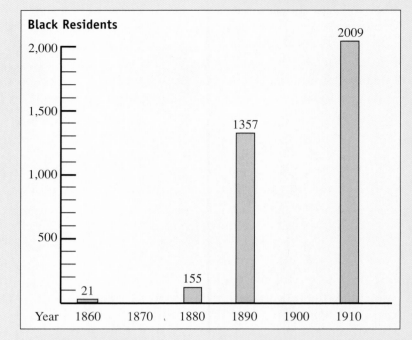

activity

African Americans in the Territory

Black Residents

(Bar graph showing number of black residents by year)

Year	Residents
1860	21
1880	155
1890	1357
1910	2009

1. According to the information on the graph, is the following statement true or false? "The black population in Arizona grew from 21 people in 1860 to 2,009 people in 1910."

2. How much did the black population increase between 1880 and 1890?

Buffalo Soldiers

After the Civil War, the U. S. Army was reorganized to include black *regiments*. The 9th and 10th Cavalry and the 24th and 25th Infantry were all black with white officers. The black troops were assigned to the western frontier. The Indians called them "buffalo soldiers" because of their short curly hair.

In 1885, the 10th Cavalry was transferred from Texas to Arizona. Nearly 700 enlisted men and 38 white officers followed the Southern Pacific Railroad tracks to Bowie Station. There the regiment was split and went to other forts (see the map on page 136). The buffalo soldiers soon joined other cavalry units in search of Geronimo, whose band was off the reservation raiding. The black soldiers also guarded waterholes along the border and fought skirmishes with Apaches. After Geronimo's surrender, the buffalo soldiers got the unwelcome job of rounding up 400 peaceful Chiricahuas at Fort Apache and putting them on a Florida-bound train at Holbrook.

Frederic Remington, the great artist of the frontier West, accompanied a unit of the 10th Cavalry on patrol in Arizona. Remington said that the buffalo soldiers were not only good fighters but also "charming men with whom to serve." He painted *The Holdup* showing the payroll robbery between Fort Grant and Fort Thomas in 1889.

Two black soldiers, Sergeant Benjamin Brown and Corporal Isaiah Mays, were awarded the Congressional Medal of Honor. They were guarding the army payroll—$26,000 in gold and silver. Robbers fired down from a rocky ledge, forcing the soldiers to retreat to a dry creek bed and leave the money wagon unattended. In the fight that followed, eight soldiers were hit. Brown and Mays continued to return fire after being severely wounded. Suspects—a gang of Gila Valley farmers and stockmen—were later arrested and tried for the robbery. Defended by a capable lawyer, they were freed.

Booker T. Washington

"**Phoenix is a melting pot. I am impressed by the way people get along. . . . During the three-day celebration I witnessed a foot race in which an Indian, a white, and a Mexican took part. The timekeeper was black.**"

Booker T. Washington, the famous African American educator and ex-slave, visited Phoenix in 1911. He was happy to see that blacks there were moving into a variety of jobs. One man owned the Home Kitchen Restaurant. Another was one of three fruit merchants in the city. Black people owned most of the barbershops.

Of the Chinese people Washington said, "They run all but two of the restaurants and control most of the truck gardens in the suburbs. The Chinese farmers deliver vegetables in horse-drawn wagons. . . . There are many Chinese merchants too."

Washington could not help but note the sad plight of the Indians. "I saw hundreds of them standing about on street corners in their picturesque Indian costumes. They idly watch the strange spectacle of a new civilization pouring into this new country, sweeping away their primitive life," he said.

Chinese people began coming to Arizona in the 1880s to work on railroads and in mining towns. Often they worked as cooks or in laundries. Many of them had been merchants in China. Once settled in the territory, they began to open restaurants, grocery stores, and laundries. Over time the Chinese entered other occupations and professions.

Life in Territorial Days

The Arizona Rangers

FOURTEEN STOUT-HEARTED MEN called the Arizona Rangers helped establish law and order in the Arizona Territory. Could a police force with so few officers rid the vast territory of cattle thieves and outlaws?

By 1900 rustling near the Mexican border was forcing some cattlemen out of business. Train robberies were another problem. A Southern Pacific train was held up at Cochise Station and a train between Nogales and Benson was robbed. These crimes frightened the railroad companies. They joined cattlemen and miners in asking the legislature to create a ranger force. In 1901 the territorial legislature established the Arizona Rangers.

The Arizona Rangers worked to establish law and order in the territory. There was no uniform, though the rangers tended to dress alike. After the first year they wore a five-pointed star that was sometimes hidden under a vest or jacket.

Burton C. Mossman

Burt Mossman had experience in dealing with cattle rustlers when he was in charge of the Hashknife ranch near Holbrook. "I selected Rangers who were good ropers, riders, shooters, and trackers," said Mossman.

Their first headquarters was at Bisbee, near the Mexican border. The rangers cooperated with the *Rurales*, a Mexican soldier-police force, to rid the country of bandits and smugglers. Mossman, a fearless leader, personally handled the toughest case. The target was Augustino Chacón, a ruthless killer who once confessed to having murdered fifteen Americans and thirty-seven Mexicans. Chacón dug his way out of an adobe jail ten days before his scheduled hanging. Mossman, posing as an escapee from a Tucson jail, tracked down the killer in Mexico, got acquainted, and then arrested him. He forced Chacón to ride handcuffed, with a rope around his neck, into Arizona. This time Chacón was hanged in Solomonville. Just before the trap door was dropped, he looked the sheriff in the eye and said, *"Adios, amigo."*

Burton C. Mossman was the first captain of the Arizona Rangers.

Thomas Rynning

"The captain shall select as his base the most unprotected and exposed settlement of the frontier." So read the law. When Thomas Rynning, a former Rough Rider, took over the rangers in 1902, he moved the headquarters to Douglas. This town, then one of the toughest places in the West, attracted cattle thieves and known killers to its saloons, dance halls, and gambling joints. The Cowboy Saloon and others were run by men who boasted of notches on their six-shooters. But the rangers slowly cleaned out Douglas and turned their attention elsewhere.

The rangers learned that cattle thieves who posed as honest ranchers were not easily caught. The neighbors of a man named Taylor in Cochise County, for example, had been unable to convict him of branding their calves. So the rangers thought of a clever way of detecting him. They roped thirteen unbranded calves belonging to the neighbors, made a slit in the gullet (the skin around the throat) of each, and pushed in a Mexican coin. After driving the animals toward Taylor's land, the rangers left.

They returned several months later to check things out. Finding the calves with Taylor's brand, the rangers hauled them to Tombstone and arrested Taylor. They gave a dramatic demonstration of cutting the coin out of the gullet of one of the calves. When the evidence was shown, Taylor promised to leave the country if he could sell his ranch and cattle. He did sell them, but at a fraction of their real value. The neighbors happily accepted this bargain. "Taylor's ranch will no longer have miracle cows that produce a dozen calves a year," said one rancher.

The rangers worked hard, making more than 1,000 arrests in one year. In 1905 Rynning reported to the governor that "cattle stealing was practically wiped out in Arizona."

Thomas H. Rynning was the second captain of the Arizona Rangers.

Harry Wheeler

Harry Wheeler was another fearless ranger leader. During his exciting career he was forced several times to shoot it out with desperate men. On one occasion, Wheeler shot a robber in the Palace Saloon in Tucson. The robber had the saloon customers lined up against the wall at gunpoint when Wheeler pushed open the swinging doors. The two men exchanged fire, but the sure-shooting Wheeler hit his target as the robber's bullet whistled harmlessly by.

Bold and daring, Wheeler liked his job. No one was more disappointed when the territorial legislature *abolished* the rangers in 1909. The colorful rangers had performed a great service in helping to bring law and order to the territory.

Harry Wheeler was the last captain of the Arizona Rangers and later the sheriff of Cochise County.

activity

Another Century

1. What would you add to this list of territorial items that are no longer used today?

2. List five things you currently use that you think will no longer be used a hundred years from now.

activity

Chart Arizona Towns

On a separate piece of paper, make an "Origin of Arizona Towns" chart. Use the column headings shown in the example below. (Hint: some helpful aids would be an Arizona highway map and the book *Arizona Place Names*.)

Town	Farming	Mining	Railroad	Cattle	Ghost Towns
Duncan	✔				

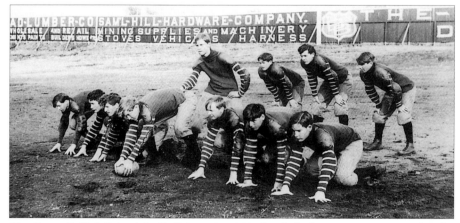

The Prescott High School football team in 1908. Football players wore canvas suits. At first they had no headgear and no protective pads. Special hand grips were attached to the trousers of linemen. Backfield men could grab these grips and be pulled for extra yardage. There was lots of slugging, kicking, and biting in the pileups. A play was not dead until the runner could no longer move, or until he said "down."

1. How was life on the frontier difficult for women?

2. List three types of places where towns got started during territorial days.

3. How did Tombstone solve its water problem?

4. What did Arizona families use to preserve food that might spoil?

5. Why is Hutchlon Ohnick important in Arizona history?

6. When and where was the first telephone switchboard installed in Arizona? What was a major problem for early phone users?

7. Name five Arizona towns that had electric trolleys.

8. List five popular fun activities in territorial towns.

9. What were the two favorite Mexican holidays? Is that true today?

10. List two popular places of entertainment in Tombstone.

11. For what accomplishments are the following leaders remembered? Bishop Salpointe, Endicott Peabody, George H. Adams, R. A. Windes, Winfield Scott, and Samuel Drachman.

12. Who was William Neal? List some of his business activities.

13. Why were black soldiers called "buffalo soldiers?"

14. Why were the Arizona Rangers organized?

Phoenix residents in the 1900s were proud of their modern trolley cars.

President Taft signed the statehood proclamation on February 14, 1912.

1901
President McKinley
visits Arizona.

1906
Arizonans vote against
joint statehood with
New Mexico.

1910
Charles K. Hamilton
makes the first flight
in Arizona.

1911
Constitution
convention
meets in
Phoenix.

1900

1905

1910

1910
Congress passes the Enabling
Act, making it possible for
Arizona to become a state.

1910
Civil war in
Mexico

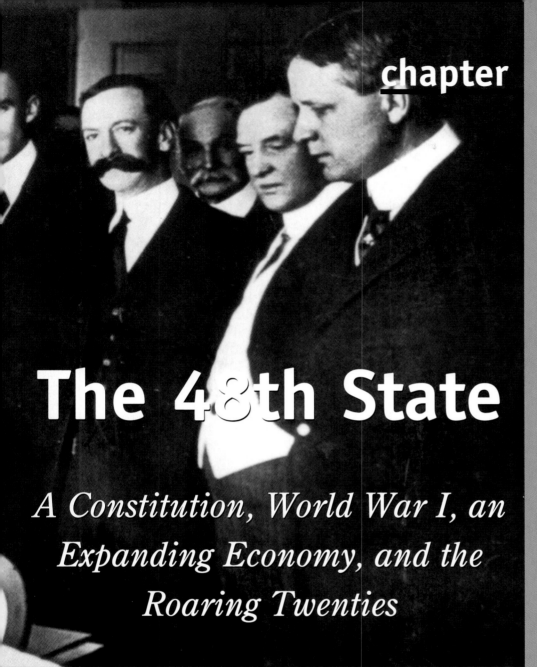

10

TERMS TO UNDERSTAND
amendment
joint statehood
progressive
recall
impartial
thrift
women's suffrage
organized labor
humanitarian
armistice
liberty bond
aviation
quarantine
boll
radical
IWW
treason
Tin Lizzie

The 48th State

A Constitution, World War I, an Expanding Economy, and the Roaring Twenties

Delegate Ralph Cameron of Flagstaff stands on Taft's right .

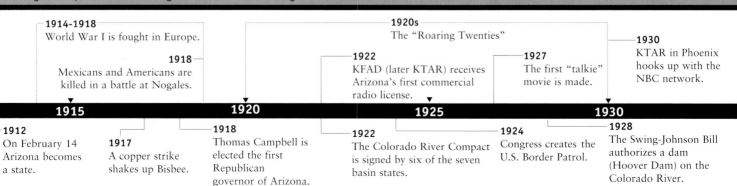

1914-1918 World War I is fought in Europe.		1920s The "Roaring Twenties"		1930 KTAR in Phoenix hooks up with the NBC network.

1918
Mexicans and Americans are killed in a battle at Nogales.

1922
KFAD (later KTAR) receives Arizona's first commercial radio license.

1927
The first "talkie" movie is made.

1915 — **1920** — **1925** — **1930**

1912
On February 14 Arizona becomes a state.

1917
A copper strike shakes up Bisbee.

1918
Thomas Campbell is elected the first Republican governor of Arizona.

1922
The Colorado River Compact is signed by six of the seven basin states.

1924
Congress creates the U.S. Border Patrol.

1928
The Swing-Johnson Bill authorizes a dam (Hoover Dam) on the Colorado River.

Preparing for Statehood

President William McKinley visited Arizona in 1901. Four months later, he was assassinated in New York.

PRESIDENT WILLIAM MCKINLEY rolled into Phoenix on a Southern Pacific train to take a look at the territory. He toured the brand new capitol building and visited the Indian School. On a side trip to the Congress Mine, the president's party was shown how gold is mined. The First Lady was presented with a small gold bar as a souvenir. McKinley was accompanied by reporters from every major news service. For a brief moment in 1901, the eyes of the nation were focused on Arizona.

As the twentieth century began, the territory was making rapid progress. Arizona led the nation in copper production. The Roosevelt Dam would soon give the Salt River Valley a dependable water supply. The people could boast of sixty newspapers published here. There was a good school system with three schools of higher learning.

By 1912 the population grew to 204,000. The three largest cities were Tucson, Bisbee and its suburbs, and Phoenix. By any standard, Arizona was ready for statehood. But the U.S. Senate and Easterners were slow to accept the idea of Arizona as an equal in the family of states.

Joint Statehood Is Defeated

Opponents of separate statehood for Arizona and New Mexico tried to combine the territories into one huge Texas-size state. This strategy would cut the number of new senators from four to two. The name of the super state would be "Arizona" but the capital would be in Santa Fe.

Arizonans, both Democrats and Republicans, did not want joint statehood. They signed petitions against it. Almost every club, church, and organization in the territory worked to defeat it. Arizona got support from Senator Joseph B. Foraker of Ohio. He introduced an *amendment* to the joint statehood bill that permitted voters in both territories to vote yes or no on joint statehood. Either territory could stop Arizona and New Mexico from being combined. As the election turned out, Arizonans voted against joint statehood 16,265 to 3,141. New Mexico, on the other hand, favored it by a big margin.

The Arizona Constitutional Convention

Congress finally passed the Enabling Act, a law that made it possible for Arizona to become a state. Soon Arizonans were busy electing delegates to represent them at a convention. There the state constitution would be written and approved. Most of the delegates were *progressives* who wanted to give ordinary people a bigger voice in government.

The delegates began their work at the capitol in Phoenix. They elected George W. P. Hunt, a progressive Democrat from Globe, to preside over the convention. They also hired clerks at five dollars per

This cartoon was titled "A Flag Day Dream." Just what are the men dreaming of? Do they want joint statehood or separate statehood? How can you tell?

day, a dollar more than the delegates received. Morris Goldwater jokingly offered to resign as a delegate in order to take a job as a clerk. Miss Ethel Ming, a real clerk, smiled but reminded Goldwater that "the delegates get big chunks of honor," which was worth something.

George W. P. Hunt presided over the constitutional convention.

Morris Goldwater from Prescott was a delegate to the constitutional convention.

This was the headline in *The Arizona Republican* on December 5, 1910.

In this cartoon, the "big question" is whether or not the delegates will give up statehood (the bone) for a constitution with all the various reforms that were popular (the image in the water). The cartoonist suggests that Arizona can't have both. How was this "big question" answered?
—from *The Arizona Republican*, October 9, 1910

Progressives

The nation was in the mood for change when Arizona became a state. People who favored reforms such as women's suffrage, conservation of forests, pure food laws, better working conditions in factories and mines, and regulation of the railroads were called progressives.

Popular Progressive Reforms

Committees worked on different parts of the constitution. When the delegates got around to voting, they approved the initiative, referendum, *recall*, and direct primary. Labor unions, which had a strong influence with progressive delegates, insisted on the people's right to recall (remove from office) judges who gave court orders to stop strikes.

The delegates, however, defeated two popular reforms of the day: prohibition of liquor and women's suffrage (the right to vote). A majority of them ignored a prohibition petition signed by thousands of women asking that the sale of intoxicating beverages be forbidden.

A special postcard pleading for women's suffrage also failed to influence enough delegates. The card had a picture of a drunk opposite a young mother. The caption said, "This man can vote. This woman can not." Later, at the first state election, Arizona's male voters approved an amendment giving women the right to vote and to hold office. Eight years later, the U.S. Constitution was amended to give women these rights nationwide.

What do you think?

President Taft believed a judge should be "independent, *impartial* . . . and have the courage to make an unpopular decision without being 'recalled,' or taken out of office." How might the threat of recall affect a judge's decision?

Here is a cartoon version of President Taft opposing the recall provision in the Arizona constitution. How is the Arizonan portrayed?
—the *Washington Evening Star*, April 11, 1911

President Taft Delays Statehood

The convention put together a constitution, which the voters approved. After a long delay in Washington, D.C., President Taft signed a document making Arizona a state on one condition. The recall-of-judges provision had to be stricken from the state constitution by a vote of the people.

Tired of waiting for statehood, Arizonans reluctantly voted to remove the section at a special election. The voters also chose their official state officers. George W. P. Hunt would be the first governor. The two U.S. Senate seats went to Marcus Smith and Henry Ashurst. Sheriff Carl Hayden easily won Arizona's only seat in the U.S. House of Representatives. Hayden would serve in Congress longer than any person in American history—seven terms each in the House and Senate between 1912 and 1969.

After Arizona became a state, the people voted to put the recall back into the constitution. The whole controversy turned out to be a big deal over nothing. Only one judge has been recalled.

Statehood at Last!

O N VALENTINE'S DAY, February 14, 1912, at 10:02 A.M., President Taft picked up a gold pen and scratched his signature on an imposing-looking paper. He signed the proclamation admitting Arizona into the Union as the forty-eighth state.

The good news reached Phoenix by telegraph. Steam whistles blasted away. People took to the streets to celebrate and share their joy with others. Soon the whole state knew. In Globe, a cannon sounded the people's approval forty-eight times. Bisbee residents exploded a stack of dynamite on Copper Queen Mountain. Prescott's pistol-firing celebrants slowed down just long enough to watch schoolchildren plant a native white oak on the courthouse plaza.

People in Phoenix were still shouting when Governor Hunt appeared in the lobby of the Ford Hotel. He walked to the capitol. His purpose was to set an example of *thrift* for everyone. Dressed in a brown suit with a carnation in the lapel, Hunt smiled and doffed his woolly hat as drivers in touring cars stopped to offer him a ride. As soon as the governor reached the capitol, his walking days were over. Thereafter he was chauffeured in a $3,000 automobile that cost the taxpayers $300 a month.

Following Hunt's inauguration and speech, there was a parade in downtown Phoenix. William Jennings Bryan, the well known "silver-tongued orator" from Nebraska, spoke for two hours to a crowd at the city plaza. The crowning event of the day was the inaugural ball held on

"If you want to be certain that I will veto your constitution, just go ahead and put judicial recall into it."
—President Taft, in Arizona for a visit

The scorn of many Arizonans for Taft's opposition to the recall and his delay of statehood was expressed in a poem published in the Florence *Blade-Tribune*:

Ode to Billy Taft

We will tolerate your gall
   and surrender our recall
Till safe within the statehood
   stall,
Billy Taft, Billy Taft.

Then we'll fairly drive you daft
With the ring of our
   horse-laugh
Billy Taft, Billy Taft.

As we joyously re-install
By the vote of one and all,
That ever-glorious recall,
Billy Taft, Billy Taft.

Frances Willard Munds
1866–1948

Frances, daughter of well-known cattleman John Willard, began teaching in Yavapai County at the age of nineteen. By the time she married John L. Munds, a future county sheriff, she was deeply involved in the women's suffrage movement. In 1914, two years after Arizona women got the right to vote, Frances easily won a seat in the state senate. By then a grandmother, she was the first woman senator in Arizona and only the second in the United States.

Like Governor Hunt, Senator Munds was a progressive Democrat. In her two-year term, she led the education committee and worked to get a bill passed that cut the property tax for widows.

the pavement in front of the Hotel Adams. A brass band from the Indian School played for a jubilant crowd. The next morning, Governor Hunt was at his desk in the capitol at 6:30 a.m. Most Arizonans thought the "baby state" was off to a good start.

Arizona's First Congressional Delegation

| Senator Henry Fountain Ashurst, Prescott | Senator Marcus Smith, Tombstone | Representative Carl Hayden, Maricopa County |

Governor George W. P. Hunt

George Hunt was wearing overalls and leading a burro when he arrived in Globe as a young man. He became a wealthy merchant and banker. In politics, however, he chose to speak for *organized labor* and the common man. The voters were not bothered by his bad grammar and elected him governor seven times.

Hunt was against capital punishment (the death penalty). He compared it to the "hanging of witches." He fought with his fellow Democrats in the legislature when they passed a death penalty law. Hunt had other *humanitarian* ideas too. He put prisoners to work on state roads and did away with striped uniforms. He made the national news by staying overnight in a cell at the state prison in Florence.

Hunt helped to write the state constitution, but he came to realize that it doesn't give the governor's office enough power. The legislature has been the strongest branch in state government. Hunt said the legislators did what the copper companies, railroads, and ranchers told them to do. The people didn't complain much. In those days, their jobs and businesses depended on the mines, railroads, farms, and ranches.

> **What do you think?**
> Governor Hunt was against capital punishment, or the death penalty. How do you feel about this form of justice?

Governor Hunt On His Famous Economy Walk to the Capitol. He Uses An Auto Now and It Costs the Taxpayers $300.00 a Month

This cartoon is from the *Arizona Gazette*.

The First Republican Governors

Two Republicans interrupted Governor Hunt's long service as governor in the 1920s. Thomas E. Campbell defeated Hunt in 1918 and won again two years later. A native son from Prescott, Campbell was the first Republican and the first Catholic to be governor. The state senate also went Republican in 1920, the only time between 1912 and 1966.

Campbell wanted to end chaos in state government by reorganizing some fifty independent agencies into a few departments. He would appoint an administrator for each department. "Whoa!" said the House of Representatives. "This plan will transform Arizona from a democracy into a kingdom." Campbell was nearly fifty years ahead of his time.

In 1928, John C. Phillips beat out Governor Hunt. His victory was remarkable considering that Democrats outnumbered Republicans two to one at that time. In office for only two years, Phillips was mainly concerned with the lingering Colorado River controversy.

Thomas E. Campbell

John C. Phillips

Linking the past and the present

Governor "Honest John" Phillips often joked that he was once voted the "homeliest man in Maricopa County" at the territorial fair. Are a candidate's looks more important today than they were in the 1920s? Should it be that way?

The 48th State

The Colorado River Controversy

ARIZONA IS ONE OF SEVEN STATES drained by the Colorado River. In 1922, these states agreed that a dam should be built on the river in northern Arizona to prevent flooding of California's Imperial Valley downstream.

Another agreement, the Colorado River Compact, would give half the river's water to the upper basin states and half to the lower basin states (Arizona, California, and Nevada). That is where the controversy began. All the states' legislatures ratified the agreement except one. Governor Hunt and the Arizona legislature feared that Arizona would not get its fair share of water. California was ready to use all the water the state could get. Hunt argued that "Arizona's future economy would depend on Colorado River water for irrigation and hydroelectric power." No one, of course, could predict Arizona's immense population growth.

Congress went ahead without Arizona's approval and passed the Swing-Johnson Bill. This law authorized the building of a high dam (now known as Hoover Dam) on the Colorado River. Congress suggested a specific amount of the river's water for each state. California would get the most and Nevada the least. California and Arizona would split any surplus water. Only states that signed the Colorado River Compact could take water from the river.

The Arizona legislature did not ratify the compact until 1944. Meanwhile, Hoover Dam was completed and giant turbines began generating electricity there in 1937. The sale of power eventually paid for the entire cost of building the dam.

Hoover Dam

Colorado River Basin States

Problems on the Border

CIVIL WAR BROKE OUT IN MEXICO after the people overthrew their leader in 1910. Pancho Villa's bandit army fought Mexico's federal troops in Sonora. One day, bullets were whizzing across the border into Naco, Arizona. Sheriff Harry Wheeler rode bravely between the lines with a white handkerchief on a stick. Both sides stopped fighting until Wheeler explained the situation. The Mexicans apologized and changed the line of fire. The Naco battle attracted curious sightseers from Bisbee. They came to visit with American soldiers and observe the Mexican Revolution firsthand.

Battle at Nogales
For a brief time, Nogales became an international battleground. The trouble started when a Mexican ammunition smuggler was shot while crawling under a border fence. Citizens began taking shots at each other across the border. When Mexican and American soldiers arrived on the scene, they also exchanged fire. Nearly eighty Mexicans and more than thirty Americans were killed. After four bloody days, an *armistice* was arranged by Governor Hunt and the governor of Sonora.

The Pershing Expedition
Pancho Villa blamed the United States for helping President Carranza gain power in Mexico. In revenge, he led bandits in raids along the border. They shot up the town of Columbus, New Mexico, leaving behind seventeen dead Americans and many injured people.

President Woodrow Wilson sent General John "Black Jack" Pershing into Mexico with an army to capture Villa dead or alive. This American force included the all-black 10th Cavalry from Fort Huachuca. The army kept Villa on the run but could not catch him.

The U.S. Border Patrol
A few years later, Congress created the Border Patrol, mainly to stop foreign citizens from illegally entering the United States. This was no easy task. More than a million Mexican citizens, legal and illegal, entered this country between 1910 and 1930.

Another problem arose when Mexican border states decided that Chinese people owned too many restaurants and other stores. They began harassing them with arrests and fines. One grocer was fined for keeping a cat, while others were fined for not having cats to keep down the mice. Many Chinese entered the United States with the help of smugglers. They came to places like Tucson, Phoenix, Globe, Florence, Prescott, and Flagstaff, where local Chinese people could find jobs for them. Many Chinese Americans had secret hideouts under their stores. Trap doors opened to underground tunnels running to other buildings.

General Francisco "Pancho" Villa led raids along the Arizona-Mexico border.

Once when Pancho Villa was watching the Americans from atop a hill in Mexico, he said (in Spanish), "I wish I had an army like that!"

The 48th State

World War I

WORLD WAR I STARTED in Europe in 1914, but the United States did not enter the war until 1917. Most people in this country were very patriotic and eager to "save the world for democracy." Americans fought on the side of Britain, France, and their allies. The other side was led by Germany.

Arizona contributed a larger percent of soldiers per capita than any state in the Union. More than 12,000 men were drafted or enlisted. Mathew B. Juan, a Pima Indian, was the first of 321 Arizona men killed in World War I. He had shown his patriotism by volunteering for the army. The 158th Infantry, an Arizona National Guard unit, was selected as President Wilson's special honor guard at the Paris Peace Conference.

America's Singingest War

During World War I the entire nation caught the spirit of patriotism and burst into song. Popular songs on the serious side were "Keep the Home Fires Burning," "It's a Long Way to Tipperary," "There's a Long, Long Trail," and George M. Cohan's spine-tingling "Over There."

Over There

Over there, over there
Send the word, send the
    word over there
That the Yanks are coming,
    the Yanks are coming.
The drums rum-tumming
    everywhere.

So prepare, send a prayer.
Send the word, send the
    word to beware.
We'll be over, we're coming
    over
And we won't come back, till
    it's over, over there.

This poster was displayed in Arizona during the war. What does the word "stamina" mean? How is "victory . . . a question of stamina?"

During World War I, patriotic Arizonans took part in national bond drives to raise money for the war. They bought bonds with their savings and proudly wore liberty buttons.

Arizonans Show Their Patriotism

Arizonans were eager to help in the war effort. They went along with the nation in staging a big Liberty Day parade. Every economic, ethnic, and age group participated. In Phoenix an Indian band, Civil War veterans, a Girls' Loyalty League from the high school, and many others marched or rode in the parade.

Mexicans from *Liga Protectora Latina* carried flags and *señoritas* dropped flowers along the parade route. The *Liga*, an organization to protect the rights of Mexican Americans, urged its members to buy U. S. Liberty bonds, save food, and keep peace between labor and management because "it will win the war."

Arizonans were expected to buy bonds according to their wealth. Many bought $100 bonds and joined the 100% American Club. School children in Chandler bought $1,155 in thrift stamps with money they earned themselves. Albert Steinfeld of Tucson led the big buyers with a $25,000 bond purchase.

Volunteer speakers, known as "Four Minute Men," gave patriotic pep talks and kept people informed about the war. They handed out red, white, and blue pamphlets. Patriotic movies were shown in movie houses. The Hip Theater in Phoenix ran *The Kaiser, the Beast of Berlin*. Commenting on this film, a reporter for *The Arizona Republican* said, "No American, unless his blood be made of ice water, can remain in his chair as this smashing story unfolds."

"Food Will Win the War—Don't Waste It." This sign was seen everywhere. Arizonans helped save the extra food needed for our allies in Europe. Housewives signed pledge cards. They promised to cooperate with the government's "wheatless" and "meatless" days. Cornmeal was in demand in Arizona grocery stores as a substitute for wheat bread. Even children, when eating an apple, were encouraged to be "patriotic to the core."

Peace at Last

Germany surrendered on November 11, 1918, ending the war. "The armistice has been signed!" shouted a Phoenix reporter. He was phoning the engineer at the waterworks. "Let her go!" he yelled. The engineer let go with a loud blast from the fire whistle to inform the whole town, "the great war is over and the boys are coming home."

Members of the 158th Infantry make their way home after the armistice. People all across the country welcomed the soldiers home with parades and celebrations.

Lieutenant Frank Luke Jr.

Frank Luke Jr. was one of America's greatest **aviation** heroes. Known as the "Balloon Buster from Arizona," he was the first American airman to receive the Congressional Medal of Honor. In his short but gallant career he destroyed fourteen observation balloons and four air planes in the skies above France.

Luke had been an athlete at Phoenix Union High School. After pilot training he was assigned to combat duty and decided to specialize in shooting down balloons. This was one of the most dangerous jobs for a pilot. He had to swoop down near the earth and expose his airplane to accurate ground fire.

On September 29, 1918, Luke shot down three balloons. Pursued by German planes and wounded by ground fire, he made a forced landing in his Spad XIII behind German lines. Refusing to surrender, Luke died defending himself with a pistol.

Two other Arizona pilots were American air aces. Lieutenant Ralph O'Neill shot down five planes. Major Reed Chambers had seven planes to his credit.

Frank Luke Jr. stands with his airplane. Today, a statue honors him at the Arizona State Capitol. How are war planes today different from his plane?

The Spanish Flu

A SPANISH FLU EPIDEMIC took its toll as the war ended. Throughout the world, an estimated 22 million died. The flu virus swept across America like wildfire. When it reached Flagstaff, students at the college were put under *quarantine*. Winslow had several hundred people down with the flu almost overnight.

Public gatherings were forbidden. Schools, churches, and movie theaters were closed. The state fair was canceled. In Winslow, Jerome, and other towns, school buildings were turned into hospitals. Phoenix and Tucson looked like mass holdup scenes when adults were required to wear gauze masks while on the street. To keep the flu from spreading, even handshaking was discouraged.

By the end of January the epidemic was over. Somehow the virus had changed form. It began attacking pigs and chickens.

WWI Gives Industry a Boost

WARTIME PRICES FOR COTTON, copper, cattle, and lumber soared to new high points. Horses and mules were also in great demand. Arizonans were busy trying to meet the demands.

Cotton Farming—Boom and Bust

In the years after Arizona became a state, cotton farming in this area was changing from a curiosity to the major source of income. World War I gave the industry a big boost. Pima cotton was used for cotton cord in automobile tires and as a substitute fabric for scarce linen to cover airplane wings. The price of the cotton went up to about a dollar a pound. More and more acres of cotton were planted.

Oddly enough, Arizona's first real cotton king was not a farmer at all. He was Paul W. Litchfield, an official of the Goodyear Tire and Rubber Company. Litchfield bought 24,000 acres in the Salt River Valley. He put his cousin, a New York fruit farmer named Kenneth McMickin, in charge of planting and irrigating Goodyear's desert land. McMickin soon became a cotton expert and the recognized "father of the cotton industry" in Arizona.

Other companies, such as Firestone, Fisk, and Dunlop, entered the race to buy Arizona's cotton crop. The price went sky high. The next year nearly every farmer in Arizona planted cotton. They plowed under alfalfa crops and sold their dairy herds. Banks eagerly loaned money to cotton growers, who developed new lands along the Santa Cruz south of Tucson. Land prices doubled.

Then came the crash. Why? For one thing, the military no longer

---

"We'd heard about the flu hitting all over. But nothing happened here until Winslow High School came to play the university football team. One of the Winslow players had just recovered from the flu. . . . In the evening they had a dance. The next day they called me to the university. There were some sick boys. Soon the number grew. The school was quarantined. We brought nurses from Los Angeles. They all got sick. Then the epidemic started in the city. . . . It got so bad the Health Department put in cots at Emerson School for sick people. . . . I don't know how many died, perhaps a hundred. It was an awful thing."

—Dr. Martin Fronske, the only healthy doctor in Flagstaff after the flu hit

ARIZONA: A Journey of Discovery

needed cotton when the war ended. Also, cheaper cotton from Egypt became available. With less demand, cotton prices fell and much of the latest crop could not be sold. Loans went unpaid.

The state legislature tried to help by forming the Arizona Pima Cotton Growers' Association. This organization decided not to dump the surplus cotton on the market. Instead, it shipped a trainload to Massachusetts for storage near the mills. The surplus was eventually sold. But low prices wiped out most of the small farmers.

Goodyear led the way in *mechanizing* cotton farming. During World War I, the Goodyear farms had about 1,200 mules at work. But tractors replaced mules in the 1920s. After 1932, most tractors and other farm vehicles had rubber tires. For several years Litchfield Park was the center for Goodyear's tractor, truck, and automobile tire testing.

Cotton was king and **bolls** of it burst out all over Arizona's desert valleys. In this picture, wagon loads arrive at a Phoenix cotton gin. Soon after the boom, prices dropped and farmers went bust.

A Big Demand for Copper

When American factories got into full production during WWI, there was a big demand for copper to make shells and other war materials. Arizona's mining industry responded by producing record amounts of copper. In 1917, steam shovels were first introduced for stripping ore at the Ajo open pit copper mine. Other mines increased production by making greater use of the flotation process to separate copper from crushed ore.

Arizona was plagued by trouble in the mines during the war. A copper strike at Jerome appeared to be settled when a *radical* miner's union tried to take over. The Industrial Workers of the World (IWW), better known as Wobblies, were also anti-war. They staged another strike at Jerome, but loyal miners would not tolerate it. They loaded the

The Morenci open pit copper mine is the largest in Arizona and the second largest in the country. What can you learn about the method of open pit mining from this picture?

ARIZONA: A Journey of Discovery

Wobblies on boxcars and shipped them out of town.

The IWW led copper miners at Bisbee on strike for higher wages and other demands. To the public, this wartime halt in copper production seemed nothing short of *treason*. Sheriff Harry Wheeler and the armed Bisbee Citizens Protective League rounded up about 2,000 workers and took them to the Warren ballpark during the night. Most of the surprised men were IWW strikers, but some were unorganized miners or innocent bystanders.

After they were in the ballpark stockade, the men were given a chance to go back to work. Some of the workers promised to do so and were released. The others, however, answered with jeers, curses, and singing. By noon, the group was pared down to 1,185 men. Dirty, hungry, half-clothed, but high-spirited, they were loaded on boxcars, some with manure still on the floor, and shipped to a small New Mexico town. Their civil rights were overlooked in the atmosphere of war excitement.

What do you think?
Do you think the Bisbee copper strike was handled properly?
Explain your answer.

Bisbee citizens watch as a trainload of IWWs departs for New Mexico.

The Roaring Twenties

THE 1920S WERE A TIME of prosperity and exciting changes in lifestyle and attitudes. The automobile replaced the horse as assembly line production reduced the cost of cars. Factories turned out hundreds of new consumer products ranging from cellophane wrapping to linoleum. Radios, washing machines, refrigerators, vacuum cleaners, and other appliances made home life more pleasant. Merchants made it easier for consumers to buy on the installment plan—"buy now, pay later."

If there was a symbol of the twenties, it was the flapper—the restless young woman always eager to try something new. She cut her hair short, wore short dresses, and used kiss-proof lipstick. She danced the arm-flinging, leg-pitching Charleston, the most popular dance craze. Her music was jazz, a lively, ever-changing music born in the South and made famous worldwide by Louis Armstrong with his trumpet. A popular song described the flapper girl as having "turned-up nose" and "turned-down hose." She was, the singer said, a "flapper, yes sir, one of those." And then he asked, "Has anybody seen my gal?"

The latest appliances were displayed in this Bisbee store in 1929. How do they compare to appliances today?

The "Frolic" was a popular ballroom in Phoenix in the 1920s.

Automobiles Change Arizona

The last horse-drawn cab in Phoenix went out of business in 1917. For years, foot-weary pedestrians could find Slim Cooper's horse and buggy in front of Doyle's cigar stand. But Cooper finally gave in to the gasoline age and bought a Buick 6. In the 1920s a large number of Model T Fords were sold around the state. Henry Ford's assembly line turned out these hand-cranked "Tin Lizzies" quickly and sold them for less than $300. Ford said a buyer could have any color he wanted, as long as it was black.

The automobile had a tremendous impact on Arizona. Thousands of people got new jobs selling or servicing cars and trucks. The auto manufacturers bought huge amounts of raw materials, including Arizona's copper and cotton. New businesses opened. Filling stations, garages, tourist cabins, billboards, and hamburger drive-ins dotted the roadside. The auto let people live farther from their work. Auto and bus travel ended the isolation of many Arizonans. The economic center of rural life began to shift from the crossroads store to larger towns where people went to shop. More Arizonans took vacations to the mountains or the Grand Canyon.

Soon car owners demanded better roads. The only improved roads in the 1920s were near larger cities. Maricopa County set an example for the rest of the state, raising money through the sale of bonds to build 300 miles of concrete roads. By the end of the 20s, the state highway system was surfaced with gravel and suitable for only a few cars at a time.

Even if the road ran smoothly, the car often did not. The low-powered engines overheated. High-pressure tires were easily punctured. A motorist going very far was advised to carry spare tires, a pile of inner tubes, a tire repair kit, a tool box, a tow rope, chains, mud hooks to get the car out of ruts, emergency gaskets, extra spark plugs, a box of wheel cup grease, an oil can, and extra oil and water. Weather was a problem since most of the cars were open with only a canvas top.

The Model T Ford

"The car chuckled, jiggled, and clattered happily as though it was working for a man who loved and understood it," wrote John Steinbeck, a famous author, about a Model T Ford whose owner kept it in good repair. To Steinbeck, the car was almost human.

To start the Model T, a driver had to adjust the petrol and spark levers just right, walk to the front of the car, and crank it by hand. The reverse gear gave the car some flexibility. When the brake was gone, the driver could stop the car by shifting to reverse. Also, when the low gear was too worn to pull uphill, the driver could turn the Model T around and back up.

Thanks to Henry Ford, Arizona and the rest of the country had automobiles before good roads were built. The "Tin Lizzie" or "Flivver" became part of the nation's folklore.

Two young women wash their Model T in Scottsdale.

> **"The only thing I fear is sneezing,"** said the young risk-taking Stinson. **"Seconds lost in an aerial maneuver would throw my craft out of control."**
>
> —from an interview

Katherine Stinson delivered the first airmail to Tucson.

On November 2, 1911, the people of Phoenix forgot politics for a while. They waited on rooftops, not wanting to miss the unusual sight of an airplane. Famous flyer Cal Rodgers, slowly making a coast-to-coast journey, landed on an alfalfa field south of the fairground.

Early Aviation in Arizona

In the early 1900s the airplane was used primarily for stunts and amusements. Charles K. Hamilton made the first flight in Arizona at the state fairgrounds in Phoenix. He flew a bamboo and silk contraption, beating a Studebaker car in a five-mile race, only to lose the next day.

Hamilton was a barnstormer, going from town to town to entertain people. From Phoenix he shipped his plane by rail to Tucson where he thrilled another crowd. He reached an altitude of 900 feet and a speed of forty miles an hour. Tickets were sold for the spectacle. To prevent gate crashing, the pilot was required to take off and land his flimsy, awkward plane in a very small field surrounded by a board fence.

Katherine Stinson, advertised as the "Flying Schoolgirl," thrilled Tucson fair crowds. The nineteen-year-old did loop-the-loops and a death dip, which was a steep power dive toward the crowd. After the show, Stinson flew a sack of air mail from the fairgrounds in south Tucson and dropped it at the downtown post office. The U. S. Postal Service went along with the stunt and approved it as the first "official" airmail flight in Arizona.

In 1919 the City of Tucson built the nation's first local airport on the Nogales highway south of town. Years later, a new airport named Davis-Monthan was built. Charles Lindbergh came to town for the dedication, just four months after his historic solo flight across the Atlantic Ocean. Thousands of people were waiting at the airport when Lindbergh landed his famous silver-tinted plane, *The Spirit of St. Louis*.

Commercial air service in Arizona began in 1927 when Aero Corporation scheduled a seven-passenger plane from Los Angeles to Phoenix and on to Tucson. The flight took seven hours and ten minutes. Scenic Airways, another early airline, carried passengers to view the Grand Canyon in Ford tri-motored planes, called "the gooses." Scenic also built an airport, the present Sky Harbor in Phoenix.

Charles Hamilton made the first flight in Arizona.

A good seat in the balcony at the Grand Theater in Douglas cost ten cents. The theater is now preserved as a national historic site.

Picture Shows

The first movies had no sound. Viewers read subtitles to keep up with the plot. Some theaters had a piano or organ for background music. Many of these "silents" were filmed in Arizona. A popular Tucson-made movie, *The Sleeper,* told the story of a luckless old prospector who finally struck it rich. Several hundred local residents, working as "extras," took part in a gold rush. Dressed in old clothes, they jumped off a chugging Southern Pacific train and headed for the "gold fields."

Arizona provided more than extras, trains, and scenery for the "flickers." Writers such as Zane Grey and Harold Bell Wright wrote western stories that were used in movie scripts. Wright's *Son of His Father* was filmed at a ranch on the Mexican border. Arizonans were angered by the film company's publicity release. "The actors," said the report, "had to ride eighteen miles on pack mules to reach the location, existed on food supplies dropped from an airplane, and were constantly in danger of attack by Mexican bandits." The company apologized for this false report and threw a party for the state's residents at the Blue Moon Ballroom in Tucson.

The first "talkie," or movie with sound, was *The Jazz Singer* starring Al Jolson. It was shown in Arizona in the late 20s. By that time, every major town had at least one "picture show" theater. The fancy ones, like the Orpheum in Phoenix, were called "movie palaces." Audiences at the Orpheum marveled at the fountains, art work, and ceiling with its sky effect of rolling clouds and blinking stars.

Movies made it possible for Arizonans to see on the screen how the rest of the country lived, dressed, and traveled.

Leo: Lion or Pussycat?

Leo was his name. He was the African lion that roars at the beginning of many movies made by Metro Goldwyn Mayer (MGM). As a publicity stunt, MGM decided to fly the 400-pound Leo nonstop from California to New York. Thus began a funny event in Arizona's aviation and movie history.

The lion was placed in a comfortable cage on a Ryan airplane. This plane was similar to the one Charles Lindbergh used on his historic flight across the Atlantic Ocean.

Martin Jensen, a dashing barnstormer, was the pilot. Five hours after leaving San Diego, Jensen was approaching the Mogollon Rim. When he realized the plane couldn't get high enough to clear the mountains, he stalled the engine and landed on top of a large tree east of Payson. The fall was broken. Jensen was unhurt except for a minor cut. Leo was fine, though a bit grumpy.

Jensen fed and watered Leo and began walking for help. After three days he reached the H-Bar Ranch. The rancher took phone messages for Jensen's wife and MGM to Globe. When news of the accident spread, everyone wanted into the act. Some local cowboys talked about holding Leo for ransom. They backed off when told that the animal was a fierce African lion.

One of the rescuers, however, said Leo "was a nice tame old boy. He just rolled over like a pussy-cat."

MGM got more publicity from this accident than if the stunt had been successful as planned. In gratitude, Leo was incorporated into the company's logo.

Tom Mix
1880–1940

Tom Mix, the most famous silent film star, lived in Prescott when he was making westerns there. A 1913 film was called *The Sheriff of Yavapai County*. In all his films, Mix set the standard for movie cowboys. A dashing daredevil, he did all his own stunts with his famous wonder horse Tony. Mix didn't smoke, drink, or swear on screen. "I aim to set a good example for young people," he said. "I keep my   pictures clean."

Mix grew up in a Pennsylvania coal mining town. At an early age he joined the army and was wounded in the Spanish-American War. Later, he punched cows in Oklahoma, became a national rodeo champion, and performed in Miller's Wild West Show.

After his movie career was over, Mix was killed when his speeding convertible turned over on the highway south of Florence.

Radio Links Arizona to the Rest of the Nation

The radio was the most exciting invention of the 1920s. Its popularity spread across the United States with amazing speed. A new style of life developed as families clustered around the radio to listen to their favorite music, comedy series, or spine-tingling mystery.

The first amateur station in Arizona was 6BBH. A young Barry Goldwater was one of several radio operators involved with 6BBH. The listeners were "ham operators" with crystal sets and earphones. KFAD of Phoenix was Arizona's first licensed commercial station. Later, the call letters were changed to KTAR, standing for "Keep Taking the Arizona Republic." The newspaper was part owner of the station.

Not many people owned a radio set in the 1920s. The census of 1930 revealed that only 18.1 percent of Arizona's families had a radio. That is why public listening areas were set up with loudspeakers in some towns. They were favorite listening spots for younger people who could not have "radio parties" at home. About 10,000 excited boxing fans crowded Phoenix's Central Avenue to hear a broadcast of the Dempsey-Tunney fight. *The Arizona Republic* used a public address system to share the fight with the cheering, rain-dampened crowd. In 1930, KTAR was welcomed as the newest member of the NBC network. Arizona was in tune with the rest of the nation.

People in Arizona used to listen to radio programs much like families today gather to watch TV.

1. For what reasons was Arizona ready for statehood in 1912?

2. Give three examples of progressive ideas that were put in the Arizona constitution. Which one of these reforms did the labor unions want? Why?

3. Name two popular reforms of the day that were not included in the original constitution.

4. Why did President Taft delay Arizona statehood?

5. When did Arizona become a state?

6. What was the Colorado River Compact? Why didn't the Arizona governor and the legislature want to sign it?

7. Why was the U.S. Border Patrol created?

8. Why did many Chinese people leave Mexico?

9. List three ways in which Arizonans demonstrated patriotism during World War I.

10. List two uses of Pima cotton during World War I. How did cotton farming change after the war?

11. How did World War I affect the copper industry in Arizona?

12. List five ways the automobile changed Arizona.

13. What company built an airport where Phoenix Sky Harbor is located today?

14. What was Arizona's first licensed commercial radio station? When did it join the NBC network?

Cecil B. de Mille, the great film director, took a train from the East to make his movie *Squaw Man* in Flagstaff. But a bad storm was raging when the train arrived. To avoid the storm, De Mille stayed on board and continued to Los Angeles. Except for that unfortunate storm, Flagstaff might have been the movie capital of the world instead of Hollywood.
—*Phoenix Gazette*

This stamp honors the veterans of World War I.
(Stamp design ©1985 U.S. Postal Service.
Reproduced with permission. All rights reserved.)

The 48th State

THE TIME
1930s

PEOPLE TO KNOW
Walter Bimson
Carl Bimson
Governor B. B. Moeur
U.S. President Herbert
   Hoover
U.S. President Franklin
   Roosevelt
I. E. Solomon
Harold Bell Wright
Ross Santee
Lewis Douglas
Isabella Greenway
John Greenway
Oscar C. Palmer
Dr. Willis Carrier
Frank Lloyd Wright
Clarence B. Kelland

PLACES TO LOCATE
Yavapai County
Prescott
Mesa
Tucson
Parker Dam
Phoenix
Flagstaff
Douglas
Hoover Dam
Tempe
Yuma
Grand Canyon
Paradise Valley
Scottsdale

1929
Stock market crashes.
First refrigerated air conditioning
in the state is installed in
Phoenix.

1932
President Hoover provides
emergency relief money to the
states.
Harold Bell Wright heads a
charity drive in Tucson.

| 1929 | 1930 | 1931 | 1932 | 19 |

1931
Arizona Highway
Patrol is created.

1933
Franklin D. Roosevelt
becomes U.S. president.

Governor Moeur and
President Roosevelt declare
bank holidays.

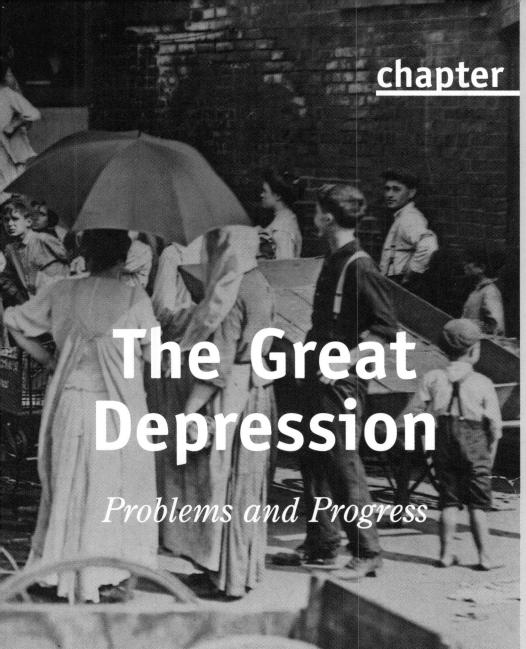

TERMS TO UNDERSTAND
recession
depression
transient
installment
undaunted
"fireside chat"
FDIC
trestle
PWA
WPA
armory
CCC
dependent
eradicate
scarcity
AAA
induct
bureaucrat
IRA

The Great Depression

Problems and Progress

During the Great Depression, people lined up to get free food from charities.

3
bella Greenway is
first woman
ted to Congress
n Arizona.

1939
Columbia Pictures
builds Old Tucson.

| 1934 | 1935 | 1936 | 1937 | 1938 | 1939 |

1934
The U.S. Congress creates
the Federal Housing
Administration.
Indian New Deal laws are
passed.

1936
Frank Lloyd Wright
begins building Taliesen
West in Paradise Valley.

The Great Depression

AN OLD RIDDLE goes like this: "When is an economic downturn a *recession* and when is it a **depression**?" The answer is: "It's a recession when you are out of work; it's a depression when I am out of work."

The prosperity of the 1920s turned suddenly to depression in the 1930s. The Great Depression was more severe, lasted longer, and affected more people than any in history. About 15 million Americans were out of work. Hundreds of banks failed, and people lost their savings. Prices of farm products dropped. Many mines and factories closed. Foreign trade came to a standstill. Many jobless people roamed the country looking for work. The people in Arizona shared the misery of the rest of the nation.

Arizona not only had to help its own unemployed workers, but also *transients* looking for a warm climate. The need for relief was great. Private groups, public charities, and the state and national governments waged a war on the depression. Somehow life went on.

"No one thinks of those depression days as happy times, but in retrospect they were not all bad. We all learned things about work and self-sufficiency and pulling together and appreciation and making the most of what we had."
—Helen E. Bunnell

Gasoline was fifteen cents a gallon at this downtown Phoenix service station, 1933.

Causes of the Great Depression

The causes of the Great Depression were complex. Economists still argue about the causes, but they agree that the following factors were involved:

1. **Overproduction** by both farms and factories was a major cause. More was produced than consumers could afford to buy. Not enough profit went into wages to increase the buying power of workers.

2. **Too much credit** was another cause. The "easy money" policy of the banks led consumers to buy goods on the *installment* plan. By 1929, many consumers were in debt. They had to stop spending. When they did, there was a sudden drop in the sales of automobiles, radios, and other goods. Then factories had to close down and there were more unemployed people.

3. **Too much speculation** was a third major cause of the depression. Thousands of people gambled on the stock market in the 1920s. Hoping to get rich quickly, they borrowed money to buy stocks. The big demand for stocks raised the price higher than the stocks were worth.

The bottom finally fell out of the stock market in 1929. In panic, everyone tried to sell. As stock prices fell, some people lost everything they had. The Wall Street stock market crash signalled the beginning of the depression.

The first-place winner of the high school Rotary speech contest in Phoenix said there must be "a wise limitation of credit" to keep the economy steady. Too much buying on credit leads to overproduction, which is followed by layoffs, unemployment, and depression.
—*The Arizona Republic,*
March 26, 1931

Depression Cycle

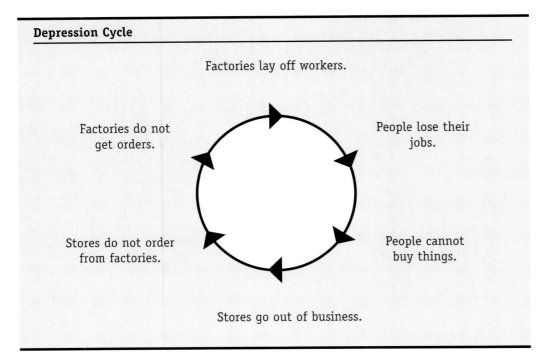

Factories lay off workers.

Factories do not get orders.

People lose their jobs.

Stores do not order from factories.

People cannot buy things.

Stores go out of business.

A Jolt to Arizona's Economy

The mining industry was hit hard. When eastern factories shut down, they stopped buying Arizona copper. With little demand for copper, the price fell from eighteen cents a pound in 1929 to five cents in 1932. At this price the mines could not make a reasonable profit. Many companies laid off miners and closed their mines.

Farmers and ranchers struggled with low selling prices for their products, interest payments on loans, and taxes on their land. The cotton growers were hurt the most. The price for cotton dropped from nineteen to six cents a pound.

Cattle and sheep ranchers suffered as beef and wool prices tumbled. Beef prices got so low that some cattlemen gave their animals away. The Yavapai County Cattle Growers in Prescott supplied the Salvation Army in Prescott with beef for the poor.

School and population trends were like weather vanes for the depression. School enrollment dropped as workers and their families moved away. Migrant children were in and out of schools.

The Man Who Killed Santa Claus

In 1932, merchants in Mesa were suffering for lack of business. John McPhee, colorful editor of the *Mesa Tribune*, offered a novel idea to attract a crowd to the annual Christmas parade that went down the street in front of the stores. He hoped that if more people came to the parade, they would spend money at the stores.

"Why not have Santa Claus jump from an airplane and lead the parade?" McPhee asked. Parachuting was considered a dangerous stunt in the 1930s. Merchants liked the idea, and they hired a stunt man to make the jump. But there was one problem—on parade day the parachutist was drunk. McPhee was disappointed, but **undaunted**. He borrowed a department store dummy Santa and told the pilot to push it, with parachute attached, from the plane. "I will then appear in a Santa costume and lead the parade," McPhee explained.

People had brought their children from miles around Mesa to watch Santa's unusual arrival. The crowd gazed skyward as the plane flew over and Santa jumped. But there was another problem. The parachute didn't open. Down, down, down, the dummy fell. It splattered on the field in front of hundreds of bawling children and horrified adults.

Trying to recover from the incident, McPhee appeared dressed as Santa to ride in the parade. The stunned public, however, was in no mood to accept a substitute. McPhee skipped town for a few days, but people would not forget the incident, then or ever. The editor is still remembered as "the man who killed Santa Claus."

Bank Holidays

During hard times, people often withdraw their savings from the bank. They also make fewer deposits. Between 1929 and 1932, bank deposits in Arizona dropped in half. This large withdrawal of money added to the large number of uncollectible loans and put some banks out of business. In three years, thirteen banks in Arizona closed their doors. Many small banks merged with others rather than close.

Walter Bimson, the new president of Valley National Bank, had reason to worry one morning in March, 1933. Over the phone came word that the governor of California had temporarily closed all banks in that state. The California and Arizona banks were closely linked. Bimson feared that the California banks would start withdrawing money from Arizona's banks. He persuaded Governor Moeur to close the banks for three days. The bank holiday prevented a possible epidemic of bank withdrawals and failures.

On March 6, 1933, U.S. President Franklin D. Roosevelt declared a national bank holiday. In a "fireside chat," over the radio he explained that all banks would be examined. Only the sound ones would reopen. Most banks were soon back in business.

Confident Arizonans greeted the end of the bank holiday by depositing much more than they withdrew. On the first day of business at a Tucson bank, an orchestra played "Happy Days Are Here Again." This spirited tune matched the mood of several thousand smiling bank patrons.

A short time later, Congress set up the FDIC (Federal Deposit Insurance Corporation) to protect bank deposits. People were guaranteed that if they deposited money, they could get it back even if there were bank problems. This restored the public's confidence in banks.

Walter Bimson was president of the Valley National Bank during the Great Depression. He collected many fine paintings.

"'Put me down for $10,000,' cattleman John Udall of Springerville said. Udall was pledging every cent he had to save the town's only bank."
—Ernest J. Hopkins, bank historian

"Customers in line at a Phoenix bank held envelopes and sacks of money for deposit. They gawked at a shabbily dressed elderly man holding a glass jar with both hands. This man opened a new account, pulling $500 gold certificates from the jar. Like most of the customers, he probably had heard President Roosevelt say on the radio, 'Your money will be safer in a re-opened bank than under a mattress.'"
—Reporters from the *Tucson Citizen* and *The Arizona Republic*, March 1933

Governor Benjamin B. Moeur.
A country doctor at Tempe, he was elected governor in 1932 and 1934.

Valley National Bank

The Valley National Bank was Arizona's most successful financial institution during the 1930s. Bimson made it the "people's bank" by stressing small installment loans. To do this he had the help of two federal agencies, the Reconstruction Finance Corporation (RFC) and the Federal Housing Administration (FHA).

One way banks make money is by charging interest on loans. Bimson borrowed money from the RFC. With new money to lend to customers, he conducted a vigorous advertising campaign. The key slogan was: "Yes, Mr. Jones, We Will Gladly Make That Loan!" Needless to say, the bank got a lot of new customers.

The United States Congress helped banks and the construction industry by creating the FHA in 1934. The FHA guaranteed bank loans for new houses and home improvements. Valley National Bank employees walked around the city and rang doorbells. They talked to people about new porches, plumbing repairs, and cooling systems. The bank made one of the first FHA loans in the nation. The money was borrowed by a young couple with a new baby. They got a loan to add a room to their house.

Parker is the world's deepest dam. Crews dug down 233 feet before reaching bedrock.

Battle at Parker Dam

Dr. B. B. Moeur was Arizona's governor during the depression. The most exciting event of his administration was the "Colorado River Affair." The national spotlight was focused on Moeur when he tried to stop a Los Angeles company from building a dam on the Colorado River.

"California will get no more water until Arizona is guaranteed 2,800,000 acre feet a year," Governor Moeur said. He sent a National Guard squad to patrol the site. He was embarrassed when the soldiers tried to inspect the site in two antique steamboats. The boats got entangled in a cable and the "desert sailors" had to be rescued by the "enemy" Californians. Newspapers naturally poked fun at the "Arizona navy" and its "battleships."

Later in the year, workers began building a *trestle* bridge from the California side of the river. Moeur sent sixty soldiers to the river "front." To avoid trouble, all construction at the dam site was stopped. The battle then moved to the U. S. Supreme Court. The court ordered Arizona not to interfere with the building of Parker Dam. Work went ahead. The dam was completed in 1938.

Private and Local Charities

FEW PEOPLE LOOKED TO THE GOVERNMENT for help in the early years of the depression. Poverty-stricken families just stopped buying. Old clothes were remade and mended. Entertainment was centered in the home. The pioneer practice of "use it up, wear it out, make it do, or do without" became a saying in many households. Each family took care of its own problems.

Groups of people organized to help the needy in their town. In Phoenix, homeless men chopped wood each morning at a local woodyard in return for housing and food. Phil Tovrea, who was connected to the meat packing industry, pledged 1,000 pounds of meat daily for the unemployed. Phoenix high school and college students took part in a three-day "Create-a-Job" campaign. The students contacted everybody in Phoenix and listed all the odd jobs available.

In 1930 the Tucson Chamber of Commerce registered 1,100 out-of-work men. "This is a good time to have the fence painted and a new roof put on the garage—if you have the money," said Isabella Greenway in a speech at the Rotary Club. She worked with civic leaders to raise money and find jobs for needy people.

Tucson writer Harold Bell Wright headed a committee that raised money to assist several thousand unemployed people. In one month, nearly forty tons of food were distributed. The unemployed earned the food by working on public projects.

At Flagstaff, college students were permitted to pay tuition fees with hay, oats, or turnips instead of cash. The college dairy made good use of these fees.

For the first time in history, President Herbert Hoover's administration provided some federal emergency relief money to the states. Each county set up a welfare board to distribute any state or federal relief funds available. But the counties shouldered the primary relief burden during the early years of the depression.

The New Deal

THE NEW DEAL was a national effort to overcome the depression. Franklin D. Roosevelt, often called FDR, became president in March, 1933. He took a trial-and-error approach to the nation's problems. "Try something," he said. "If it fails, try another."

The first task was to care for jobless people. The New Deal tried giving money to the states. The money was handed out but the people wanted jobs, not charity.

ARIZONA PORTRAIT

Harold Bell Wright
1872-1944

(Drawing by F. Graham Cootes)

Harold Bell Wright, a New York native and self-educated author, said he learned to "scribble" during his years as a preacher in the Ozark Mountains.

One of his first books, *Shepherd of the Hills*, got him started on a long list of best-selling novels. The characters in his books are simple, honest, hard-working people. Some of the novels were based on Arizona stories and Indian legends.

While still a young man, Wright moved to the dry Arizona desert to recover from tuberculosis.

A skilled artisan, he carved the ornamental woodwork and forged the iron for his home in Tucson. During the depression, Wright was admired as Tucson's "first citizen" for his charity work in helping children with tuberculosis, the unemployed, and other needy people.

President Roosevelt wanted to give the American people a "new deal of the cards." His plan was called the New Deal.

Listening to the radio was the most popular form of family entertainment during the depression. President Roosevelt used radio to inform people about what he was doing to help them.

The next New Deal relief programs were "make work" projects such as raking leaves and picking up litter in parks. Finally, programs were designed to provide socially useful work. Many aspects of the New Deal were of lasting value for Arizona. Many of the construction projects are still in use. Reforms in banking and housing head the list. Conservation got a big boost.

Fireside Chats

During the Great Depression, President Roosevelt spoke to the American people on the radio. He always started the programs by saying, "Good evening, friends." He told the people he was trying to help them, and explained what he was doing to help the nation get out of the depression.

In 1932, Arizona Democratic leaders met with presidential candidate Franklin D. Roosevelt at the Greenway Ranch. Clockwise from the left are F. A. McKinney, Senator Carl Hayden, Major Oscar F. Temple, Governor Hunt, Roosevelt, Governor-to-be B. B. Moeur, and Congressman Lewis W. Douglas.

The PWA

The Public Works Administration (PWA) created jobs through contracts to private industry. A large part of Arizona's PWA funds was spent on the completion of Boulder (Hoover) Dam. Other projects improved the sites of ancient Indian dwellings and the Tumacácori Mission. The university and colleges got some new buildings.

The WPA

The Works Progress Administration (WPA) was based on the belief that everyone has the right to useful work. It soon became the nation's chief relief agency. WPA workers improved the state highway system. They constructed school buildings, post offices, libraries, the National Guard *armory* in Phoenix, water systems, sidewalks, bridges, and government buildings. One of the bigger WPA jobs was the state fairgrounds project. Workmen built a racetrack, grandstand, and exhibit halls.

The WPA gave people with talents a chance to practice their skills. One of the more interesting WPA programs was the Federal Writers Project. Under the direction of Ross Santee, researchers and writers gathered data all over the state and prepared a *State Guide*. The Federal Music Project presented over a thousand concerts in Arizona. Jobs were given to actors, artists, and teachers.

A popular jingle went like this:

We work all day
For the WPA
Let the market crash
We collect our cash.

WPA workers build a sidewalk.

A WPA music concert in Phoenix. Howard Pyle, a popular KTAR radio announcer and future governor, is at the microphone.

A plaque at the South Rim of the Grand Canyon honors CCC men who worked on canyon trails in the 1930s.

The CCC

The Civilian Conservation Corps (CCC) was one of the most popular of the federal relief programs. It gave work and job training to young men between the ages of eighteen and twenty-five. At the same time, the CCC promoted a nationwide program of conservation. Some 1,500 camps were built, mainly in forested areas. The men lived under army discipline. They were supervised by the federal agency to which they were assigned. The pay was $30 a month. Out of this amount, $22 to $25 a month was sent home to parents or *dependents.* The men also received food, clothing, shelter, medical attention, and education.

One of the first jobs of the CCC men assigned to the Forest Service was to *eradicate* twig-blight disease. This fungus threatened to destroy the state's huge ponderosa pine forests. The only known way to combat the disease was to remove infected twigs and trees. The CCC also planted 7.5 million trees and constructed nearly 6,000 miles of forest roads in Arizona.

The CCC restored range lands. Check dams were built in eroded gullies. Overgrazed land was reseeded in grass and fenced off. Stock ponds were constructed. CCC men near Tempe and Yuma cleaned out irrigation systems and lined canals with concrete. The CCC built a trail in the Grand Canyon and a scenic road in the Petrified Forest. Tucson Mountain Park was reseeded with native grasses and fenced. New trails and guard rails were built in Colossal Cave near Tucson.

1933-1983

Civilian Conservation Corps USA 20c

The CCC provided jobs for young men during the Great Depression.

"Life was rough. I couldn't find a job. My parents lost their farm. For me and three million other young men, the CCC was the high point of our lives. Through hard work and camp life, the C's, as we called ourselves, learned discipline and leadership."

—Lewis Erdos, interview

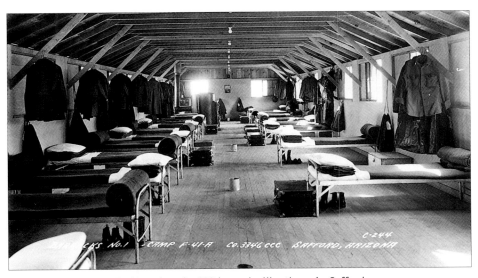

Workers slept in CCC barracks like these in Safford.

"'Daddy, do something! The man is shooting our cattle!' It is hard to explain to an eight-year-old why the government was buying cattle and killing them to raise beef prices, especially if we didn't understand it ourselves."

—Nel S. Cooper, ranch woman, interview

The AAA

The "Triple A" (Agricultural Adjustment Administration) paid farmers to plow under part of their crops. The first year, cotton farmers in Maricopa County, for example, got $125,000 to take 9,000 acres out of cultivation. Why? The idea was to raise crop prices by creating *scarcity*. The AAA also bought and killed livestock, including thousands of Navajo sheep and goats. Critics often asked, "Why destroy food when many Americans are hungry?" Yet, the plan seemed to work—at least for farmers.

The Great Depression

Isabella Greenway

What do you think?
Until the 1930s, most Americans believed that the federal government should keep its hands off the economy and business of a state. How did the government programs of the Great Depression change this attitude?

John and Isabella Greenway

"Isabella, . . . Eleanor and I think you should run for an upcoming seat in Congress," pleaded President Franklin D. Roosevelt in 1933. Isabella Selmes Greenway, a bridesmaid at the Roosevelt wedding and a longtime friend, ran and won. She was the first woman to represent Arizona in Congress.

After the death of her first husband from tuberculosis, Isabella married Colonel John C. Greenway, a dashing and wealthy bachelor. Their honeymoon to the Grand Canyon was her introduction to Arizona. John took his bride to Ajo, where he was part owner of the copper mine.

"Fighting Jack" Greenway had earned the rank of colonel on the battlefields of France during WWI. A wound and poison gas had weakened his robust health. Four years after his death, a statue of John Greenway was placed in our nation's capitol building.

Isabella moved to Tucson, where she built a furniture factory to employ disabled veterans. She and Bill Gilpin, John's private pilot, started the G and G Airlines Company. In 1931 Isabella built the Arizona Inn. This quiet, elegant inn attracted well-to-do visitors and celebrities. During the depression, Isabella sometimes called meetings of civic leaders at the inn to plan fundraisers for charity.

Isabella Greenway was *inducted* into the Arizona Women's Hall of Fame.

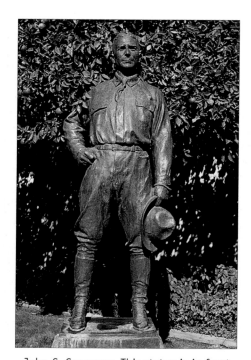

John C. Greenway. This statue is in front of the Arizona Historical Society in Tucson. A replica of the statue is in our nation's capitol building in Washington, D.C.

A War Ends the Great Depression

The scope of the New Deal was immense. Its programs brought relief to millions. Some critics, however, said the New Deal didn't go far enough. But others argued Roosevelt's "one-man super-government" was running up a huge debt and destroying the free enterprise system. "The American people, once self-reliant citizens, are getting a bad case of the 'gimmes,'" said one critic. The problems of farm surpluses and unemployment were not solved until the United States entered World War II.

American Indians Get a New Deal

IN 1924 CONGRESS gave all native-born Indians American citizenship. But having citizenship changed their lives very little. Many Indians lived in poverty. On the reservations they were controlled by federal *bureaucrats*. The U. S. Senate investigated the so-called "Indian Problem" and recommended an "Indian New Deal."

The Indian Reorganization Act

The Indian Reorganization Act (IRA) of 1934 was the most important New Deal act for Arizona Indian tribes. It encouraged them to continue their tribal organization. The tribes began to adopt their own tribal constitutions, hire lawyers, and form business corporations. They were given the right to practice their own native religions and tribal customs on the reservations.

The IRA also made the federal government responsible for preventing erosion and overgrazing on the reservations. Nearly 2,000 American Indians were soon employed in the Indian division of the CCC. They built check dams to stop erosion and to conserve water supplies, constructed reservoirs and truck trails, and reseeded thousands of acres on the reservations.

The Johnson-O'Malley Act

The Johnson-O'Malley Act of 1934 provided funds for school districts willing to enroll Indians. Before this law, Indian children could not attend public schools because Indians did not have to pay state and local property taxes on reservation land.

Today the State of Arizona applies for Johnson-O'Malley federal money each year. As a result, Native American boys and girls are in public schools all over the state.

Mabel Anton was a Tohono O'odham judge.

On the reservation, many Native Americans, such as this Pima girl, were able to hold on to much of their native culture.

Tribal Government

Each Arizona tribe set up an elective government. Nearly all of the tribes adopted a constitution, using the U. S. Constitution as a model. A tribal chairman was elected to head the executive branch. A council was the legislative body. In later years, nearly every reservation organized a police force and tribal courts with Indian judges. Today these courts handle only misdemeanors and offenses against tribal law. More serious crimes are tried in state or federal courts.

At first, self-government was not easy for the American Indians. For generations they were forced to be dependent on the federal government for food, clothing, and money. Strong tribal leaders did not emerge until the 1950s and 1960s.

Since the 1930s, the federal government has allowed American Indians to be Indians. Community day schools have replaced many boarding schools. An Indian Arts and Crafts Board works for the preservation of American Indian culture.

This is a Navajo tribal council in session. Can you see the influence of hogan architecture in this council chamber at Window Rock?

ARIZONA: A Journey of Discovery

Life Goes on in the 1930s

NOT ALL LIFE IN THE THIRTIES was gloom and doom. "Picture shows" provided entertainment, though it was more of a luxury to see one. Drug stores continued to sell fountain drinks, chocolate bars, and magazines. Free baseball games gained more spectators and competition improved. People still drove automobiles, but they kept them longer. Newspapers stayed in business, though they often lost subscribers or had to cut down on the size of the paper.

Without much money, people turned to things that were either free or inexpensive. Reading, jigsaw puzzles, card games, stamp collecting, and radio programs were popular. Families enjoyed radio shows like the *Major Bowes Amateur Hour, George Burns and Gracie Allen, Fibber McGee and Molly, Kate Smith, The Lone Ranger,* and many others. Sports fans followed their heroes—Babe Ruth, Dizzy Dean, Jesse Owens, Bill Tilden, and Joe Louis to name a few. Both children and adults looked forward to the weekly color comics: "Little Orphan Annie," "Dick Tracy," "Mutt and Jeff," and "Gasoline Alley."

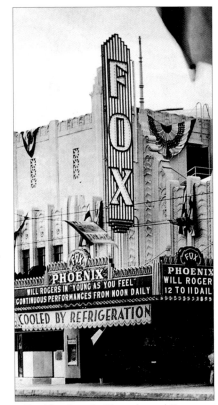

Fox Theaters in Phoenix and Tucson were air conditioned in the 1930s.

The 1934 state champion Funk Jewelers softball team of Phoenix reached the national semifinals in Chicago. Paul Fannin (top row, third from right) was a pitcher. Later, he was elected governor and then U.S. Senator.

"Hundreds of children, each bringing some article of food for the price of admission, attended the Fox Grand Theater special performance for the benefit of needy families in Douglas."
—*Tucson Daily Citizen,*
December 23, 1930

The first coolers were homemade. Excelsior (wood fibers) soon replaced charcoal in coolers.

Keeping Cool

Old-timers remember hot summers in Arizona's desert towns when they were kids. Rosemary Henderson of Tucson recalls how some children kept cool. "The theaters had refrigeration. It was cooler there during the summer, so the theaters were our babysitters. My little brother and I would go to the theater. We would sit there and watch the movies during the hot part of the day."

Fred Kalil's family got out of town. "My father would send my mother and brother and me to California," he said. "We'd rent an apartment right on the sand [beach]. We stayed there from the time school let out until school started again.

My dad had the store and he stayed in Tucson in order to sell a nickel's worth of something. But nobody was here. Everybody went out of town. You could shoot a cannonball down Congress Street and you wouldn't hit a fly."

Evaporative (Swamp) Coolers and Air Conditioning

Room coolers were first used in Arizona in the 1930s. The first ones were homemade wooden boxes installed in windows. A garden hose, hung at the top of the box, dripped water into a layer of charcoal packed between pieces of chicken wire on one side. An electric fan drew air through the charcoal. Phoenix soon had 5,000 of these window coolers, now commonly called swamp coolers. Other desert towns followed suit.

Oscar C. Palmer began the assembly line production of coolers in Phoenix in the 1930s. The Goettl brothers also started manufacturing coolers about the same time. Soon Phoenix was the "Cooler Capital of the World."

The first refrigerated air conditioning in the state was installed in Phoenix in 1929. Hotel Westward Ho, the Mountain States Telephone Company office, and the Orpheum Theater led the way. Before long, other hotels, theaters, and businesses had to install some kind of cooling to attract customers.

Dr. Willis Carrier designed air conditioning equipment for the Magma Copper Mine near Superior. The rock temperature at the 4,000 foot level was lowered from 140 to 93 degrees. Carrier was the first person in North America to use air conditioning to cool a mine shaft.

Young Oscar Palmer (far right) stands beside his father in this 1913 photo of the Phoenix Sheet Metals Company shop. As a teenager, Oscar made his experimental coolers in this shop.

Frank Lloyd Wright

FRANK LLOYD WRIGHT, one of the world's greatest architects, was attracted to the desert. He brought his students here and together they built Taliesen West. From this workshop, and Wright's other home in Wisconsin, came designs for some of the world's most famous buildings.

Wright believed that a building should be built of native materials and blend with the environment. He preferred the use of native trees and plants for landscaping around desert homes. Today, people in water-short areas of Arizona are learning to appreciate both the beauty and necessity of what Wright was saying in the 1930s.

The beautiful Grady Gammage Auditorium on the campus of Arizona State University at Tempe was designed by Frank Lloyd Wright.

These architects are working at Taliesen West in Paradise Valley just north of Scottsdale.

"What a scientific marvel of construction the long-lived saguaro! Or the latticed stalk of the cholla! A building in the desert should also be nobly simple, sturdy, and harmonize with the surrounding environment."
—Frank Lloyd Wright

Old Tucson

The Last Round-Up was filmed at Old Tucson and the San Xavier Mission in 1947.

OLD TUCSON WAS BUILT IN 1939 by Columbia Pictures. The adobe and wood village, a popular tourist attraction, is a replica of an Arizona town as it might have appeared in the 1860s. It was constructed for the filming of *Arizona*. The movie was based on a thrilling novel by Clarence Buddington Kelland, who moved to Arizona in a trailer in the 1930s. The heroine is Phoebe Titus, who is stranded in Old Tucson when her father dies. Phoebe bakes pies for a living. She also runs a freighting business and survives Indian attacks. The story is made doubly attractive by a tender romance between Phoebe and Peter Muncie.

Since 1940, hundreds of western movies and TV films have been produced at Old Tucson. John Wayne probably made more movies here than any other star. The first was *Tall in the Saddle*.

Other Important Events of the 1930s

Arizona Highway Patrol

The Arizona Highway Patrol was created by the legislature in 1931. Its primary function in the beginning was to increase the registration of vehicles. Hundreds of out-of-state car owners were forced to buy Arizona plates. Within a month after the Highway Patrol was started, more than 17,000 drivers in Maricopa County alone applied for a driver's license. At least that number had been driving illegally without a license.

Gradually the patrol was able to give more attention to enforcement of traffic laws. Safety programs and auto inspections became important duties of the Highway Patrol.

The Modern Miracle Drug

Penicillin is a powerful drug used to treat infections. It was the first antibiotic used successfully in the treatment of serious disease in human beings. The drug was introduced in the West in the 1930s, shortly after it was discovered by a British scientist.

The End of Prohibition

The U.S. Constitution's Eighteenth Amendment (1919) banned the sale or manufacture of intoxicating beverages. But the amendment was not enforceable and only encouraged drinkers, moonshiners, and bootleggers to disobey the law. As president, Franklin Roosevelt got prohibition repealed by the Twenty-First Amendment (1933). Roosevelt said the legal sale of alcohol would give the government badly needed tax revenues, create new jobs, and provide farmers another market for grains.

Arizona's Western Stars

The first Arizonan to star in westerns was a cowgirl from Prescott, Dorothy Fay Southwick, who dropped her last name. A doctor's daughter, Dorothy Fay learned to ride and rope on her uncle's ranch. She became Tex Ritter's leading lady in movies and his wife in the real world.

Rex Allen, known as the "Arizona Cowboy," sang his way to stardom atop his wonderful horse Koko. The annual Rex Allen Days festival now attracts many visitors to his hometown of Willcox.

Another singing cowboy, Marty Robbins of Glendale, started his career on a Phoenix television station in the 1950s. Andy Devine of Kingman made his mark as a sidekick who talked in a gravelly, high-pitched voice.

Jack Elam, a native of Miami who attended Phoenix Union High School, was a crazy-eyed villain in many westerns.

Chain Reaction—Cause and Effect

The Great Depression was a series of events that happened like a maze of falling dominoes. As one system fell, it caused others to fall. It took the efforts of many people working hard and donating to charity, strong government programs, and eventually a war, to gradually end the depression.

On a separate piece of paper, arrange the causes and effects below in a possible order of the chain reaction of the Great Depression (some causes had several effects).

Workers produce too many goods and farm products.
People borrow too much money.
The New Deal is established.
Many businesses are bankrupt.
Millions of people are jobless.
People borrow money to buy stocks.
Great Depression deepens.
Banking system nears collapse.
FDR becomes president.
The stock market crashes.
Factories close.
World War II begins.

Chapter 11 Review

1. List three causes for the Great Depression.

2. In what ways was Arizona's copper industry affected by the depression?

3. Why did some banks fail during the depression?

4. Who was Dr. B.B. Moeur?

5. Why were Phil Tovrea and Harold Bell Wright "very important people"?

6. List five examples of WPA projects in Arizona.

7. What does CCC stand for? Explain the purpose of the CCC.

8. What world event brought the end of the Great Depression?

9. How did the Johnson-O'Malley Act and the Indian Reorganization Act help American Indians?

10. Why is Phoenix called the "Cooler Capital of the World"?

11. What was Frank Lloyd Wright's profession?

12. Why was Old Tucson built?

THE TIME
1939—1945

PEOPLE TO KNOW
General Hideki Tojo
Benito Mussolini
Adolf Hitler
U.S. President Franklin
     Roosevelt
Arthur Benko
Bill Mauldin
Barry Goldwater
General George F. Patton
Ira H. Hayes
Lew Davis
Epimenio Rubi
Sergeant Manuel Mendoza
Silvestre Herrera
The Nakagawa family
Jurgen Wattenberg
Molly Crouch
General Dwight D.
     Eisenhower
U.S. President Harry S.
     Truman
Mikhail Gorbachev

PLACES TO LOCATE
Europe
Germany
Poland
Great Britain
Africa
Ethiopia
Asia
Soviet Union (Russia)
Pacific Ocean
Iwo Jima
Japan
Hawaii
Panama

1941 DECEMBER 7
Japanese planes bomb Pearl Harbor.
The U.S. enters World War II.

1939   1940   1941

1939 - 1945
World War II is fought in Europe and Asia.

The Arizona Daily Star

JAP BOMBS SMASH AT HAWAII
BEFORE TOKYO DECLARES WAR

HUNDREDS ARE KILLED
AND DAMAGE IS HEAVY
IN SURPRISE ASSAULT

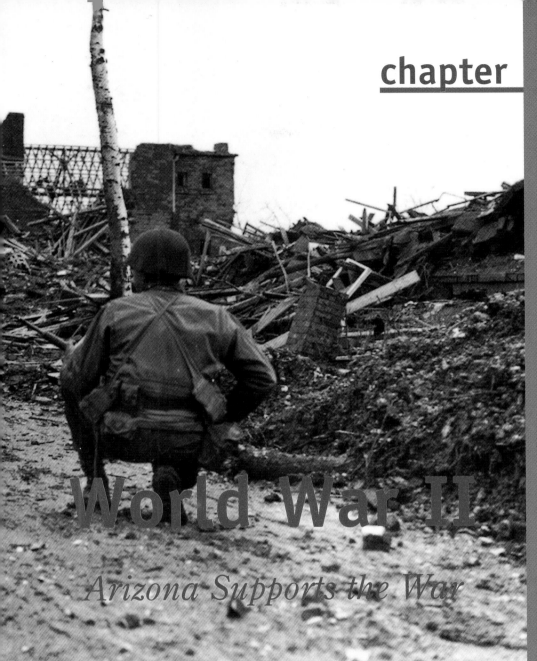

TERMS TO UNDERSTAND
dictator
infamy
installation
turret
pontoon
ration stamps
gunnery
syndicated
deploy
propaganda
relocation
compensate
POW
concentration camp
Axis
communist
arms race

World War II

Arizona Supports the War

World War II bombs destroyed cities and villages in European countries.

1942
Japanese Americans
are moved to
relocation camps.
Ration books
are issued.

1944 June 6
American and British soldiers land on
the beaches of Normandy, France, on
what is now called "D-Day."

1945
President Roosevelt dies;
Harry Truman is president.

1945 August 6
U.S. drops atomic bomb
on Hiroshima, Japan.

1942   **1943**   **1944**   **1945**

1943
Italian and German prisoners are
brought to Arizona POW camps.

1945 May 8
Germany surrenders.

1945 August 14
Japan surrenders.
The war is over.

Setting the Stage for War

WHILE AMERICANS WERE FIGHTING the Great Depression in the 1930s, three *dictators* were boldly pushing the world into the worst war in human history. Tojo's Japanese troops invaded Chinese territory. Mussolini conquered Ethiopia's barefooted army in Africa. Germany's aggressive Adolf Hitler gobbled up helpless Austria and Czechoslovakia. He began his ruthless persecution and programmed murder of European Jews.

In 1939, Hitler smashed into Poland with planes, tanks, and infantry. World War II "officially" began two days later when Great Britain and France declared war on Germany. Most Americans sympathized with Britain, France, and their allies. President Franklin Roosevelt provided these countries with aid, but America did not enter the war.

Remember Pearl Harbor!

Two years later, the day dawned bright and sunny over U.S. battleships neatly anchored in Pearl Harbor, Hawaii. The radar screen showed a few blips, but no one suspected what was about to happen. Japanese bombers, sneaking in from distant aircraft carriers, attacked without warning on Sunday morning, December 7, 1941. This was a date, as President Roosevelt told Congress, "which will live in *infamy.*"

The bombers wiped out our Pacific battleship fleet and killed or wounded more than 3,000 sailors, soldiers, and civilians. Over 150 American planes were destroyed at the air base before they could get off the ground. The United States had suffered severe damage. The next day Congress declared war on Japan and, several days later, on Germany and Italy. The United States then began fighting two wars at the same time—one in Europe and one in the Pacific region.

"Tora! Tora! Tora!" With this code word, Mitsuo Fuchida notified his commander that the surprise attack on Pearl Harbor had begun.

"When school ended in 1943, I joined the 442nd. . . . Two of my wife's brothers also went overseas with the unit. I was the only one in our family to come home."
—Bill Kajikawa, former coach at Arizona State University

The Arizona Daily Star
TUCSON, ARIZONA, MONDAY MORNING, DECEMBER 8, 1941

JAP BOMBS SMASH AT HAWAII BEFORE TOKYO DECLARES WAR

HUNDREDS ARE KILLED AND DAMAGE IS HEAVY IN SURPRISE ASSAULT

This was the newspaper headline the day after Japan's sneak attack on Pearl Harbor.

ARIZONA: A Journey of Discovery

USS Arizona

The battleship *USS Arizona* was the hardest hit of all the ships at Pearl Harbor. Two torpedoes and seven bombs struck the giant battleship before it sank. Nearly 1,200 officers and men were killed aboard the ship. Most of them (including eight Arizonans) died below deck and remain entombed there.

The *USS Arizona* had sailed a lot of seas after its launching in 1915. Miss Esther Ross, a high school girl from Prescott, had christened the ship with a bottle of water from Lake Roosevelt.

James Van Horn, a lanky freckled-faced sophomore at Tucson High, heard an inspiring recruiter and joined the navy. Six months later he went down with the USS Arizona during the Japanese attack on Pearl Harbor. Among the men sharing his watery grave is . . . the recruiter."

—Dudley Van Horn, brother

Several reminders of the *USS Arizona* are still on Arizona soil. The twenty-ton anchor rests on a memorial east of the capitol building. The ship's bell tolls in a tower at the student union building on the University of Arizona campus in Tucson.

A Time of Change

WORLD WAR II CREATED a "we" generation. "We are all in this together," people would say. Arizonans fully cooperated in the national war effort. Family life, of course, was disrupted as 30,000 Arizona men and several hundred women left to serve on war fronts all over the world. More than 1,600 of them were killed in action.

On the home front, the war ended the Great Depression. Everyone had a job and money in the bank. The wartime demand for copper got Arizona's mines in high gear again. Farmers doubled the amount of land they planted in long staple cotton. Cattlemen could sell all the beef they produced and then some. The construction industry was never so busy. New defense plants gave manufacturing its first big boost in this state.

Defense Contracts Give Business a Boost

The Del Webb Corporation kept the construction business humming with its big government contracts to build military *installations*. The military bases brought millions of dollars into the state. Businesses of all kinds prospered.

"Soldiers on leave walk through town and buy everything there is," said one pleased merchant. John Huber's jewelry store in Yuma had so much business, he posted a guard at the door to let in only a few customers at a time. Hungry and thirsty pilots from Falcon and Williams airfields turned Mick's quiet little cafe in Gilbert into a gold mine. Round-the-clock shifts in Phoenix defense plants kept downtown movie theaters and eating places open all night.

"I worked a swing shift at AiResearch on intercoolers for B-17s and B-29s. We had to make one of these each night. There was no letting up. When I was told to make one, I made two."

—Oleta Schlichting

Female Labor Force

During World War II, the role of women changed dramatically. Why? The need for workers in defense plants brought millions of them into the work force. Many a housewife traded her apron for overalls and welder's goggles. The women who couldn't change a tire before the war learned how to make airplane parts. By the war's end, women made up one-third of the labor force.

Women also joined the military services—WAC (army), WAVES (navy), SPARS (coast guard), and marines. As soldiers without guns, they piloted bombers and fighter planes across the Atlantic Ocean, repaired airplanes and other vehicles, drove trucks and jeeps, operated radios, and did clerical and technical work of all kinds. The war years changed the lives of women forever.

Anna Mae James was a WAC officer during the war.

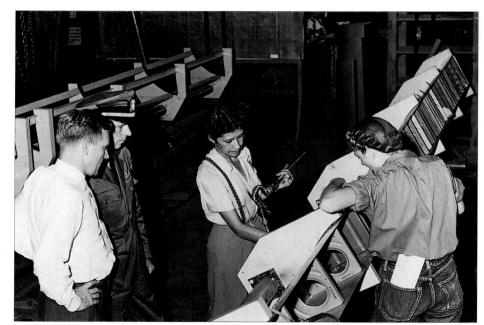

Goodyear Aircraft workers Mary Salazar and Roxie Barrett set rivets in a section of a flying boat wing in 1943.

Defense Plants

Most of the new factories sprang up in the Phoenix area. The Garrett Corporation led the way. Garrett made airplane components for B-17 bombers at its AiResearch plant near Sky Harbor Airport. Female employees worked side by side there with men on the assembly line. They made $1.25 an hour—the top wage for women then, but still not as much as men doing the same job.

Goodyear Aircraft Corporation made flight decks for the Navy's giant four-engine flying boats. The company hired thousands of people at its Litchfield plant. Among the many female workers at Goodyear were seven who car pooled daily from Tempe in a Model A Ford which they called "USS Arizona Jr."

Consolidated Vultee Aircraft built an important war factory in Tucson and brought B-24 and B-29 bombers to the plant and fitted them out with gun *turrets*, radios, and radar. Vultee also hired many women, saying "they were more efficient than men in wiring instrument panels in the planes." One woman who did electrical wiring was Molly Crouch. She was a four-foot-nine-and-a-half-inch-tall mother of twelve.

The Aluminum Company of America (Alcoa) operated the world's largest aluminum plant in Phoenix. Alcoa made aircraft *pontoons* and B-29 airframes. Allison Steel, an older company, made portable bridges during the war. Other smaller companies in a dozen Arizona cities turned out components for planes and tanks.

Arizonans Cope with Shortages

WARTIME INDUSTRY led to full employment. Workers flocked to Arizona from other parts of the country. A critical housing shortage in Phoenix made it difficult for workers to find places to live. To relieve the shortage, Phoenix built public housing near the Alcoa and AiResearch plants. In Tucson, Consolidated Vultee built houses for aircraft workers.

Housing was not the only shortage. Arizona civilians learned to sacrifice. They made do with less meat, sugar, coffee, dairy products, canned goods, tires, and gasoline. Ration books became a part of life. The *ration stamps* in each book were "points" that were needed to buy restricted items. The buyer had to turn in the points and also pay the cost of an item with money. Sometimes, no matter how much money you had, or how many points, grocers simply didn't have items on the shelves.

"Victory gardens" were encouraged so people could grow their own food. They sprouted up in many yards and were often watched over by a few egg-laying hens.

War Bonds

World War II was expensive. The government borrowed money to finance the war by selling war bonds to banks and private citizens. The bonds were paper certificates that could be turned in at a later time for more money than the people had paid for them. One of many ideas to promote the sale of war bonds caught the attention of Phoenix residents in 1943. They lined up to buy bonds and get an inside glimpse of a two-man Japanese submarine used at Pearl Harbor.

During the war, people stood in long lines to get sugar, meat, and canned goods.

"We stood in line to buy nylon stockings, Christmas tree lights, sugar, and meat. Many items were in short supply and we simply went without a lot of things."
—Mildred B. Sutch

These boys in Ajo helped win the war by bringing in scrap metal. The metal was used to make military equipment. Rubber was also gathered and recycled.

About 145,000 Americans trained in Arizona for service in World War II. This figure includes 61,300 pilots.

Pilot Training and Air Bases

THOUSANDS OF PILOTS and other military personnel were trained in Arizona. Nearly perfect flying weather made Arizona an ideal location for air bases. So many planes were in the air, "a red-tailed desert hawk had to look twice before going upstairs to stretch its wings," said one reporter.

Civilian aviation schools in Arizona taught beginners to fly for the U. S. Army. Ryan School of Aeronautics in Tucson trained 10,000 pilots during the war. Southwest Airways trained Americans and some foreigners at airfields in Glendale, Scottsdale, and Mesa. "From plow jockey to pilot in twenty-nine weeks" was the slogan of British cadets. "We were forbidden to buzz Camelback Mountain," recalled one cadet. "If they caught you scratching the camel's back, you would be washed out and sent back to England."

Chinese cadets were very serious about their training. But one day some cadets were given a one-hour walk as punishment for breaking minor rules. They laughed and laughed. As it turned out, they had walked 2,800 miles to join the Chinese Air Force.

The U. S. Army converted Tucson's city airport into Davis-Monthan Air Base. D-M bustled as the nation's largest heavy bomber base. Most of the ten-man B-24 bomber crews were trained there.

Luke Field spread out over land donated by the City of Phoenix. Clouds of dust from construction work greeted the first student pilots. Before long, however, Luke Field became the largest single-engine flying school in the United States.

Williams Air Force Base near Chandler trained pilots to fly bombers, the P-38 Lightning fighter, and other planes. After the war, Williams became the nation's first jet training base. Many other army and navy air bases were scattered around Arizona from Kingman to Douglas.

The Stearman biplane was a marvelous flying machine. Southwest Airlines trained many pilots to fly in this plane. After the war, the Stearmans served equally well as crop dusters in Arizona.

(Photos by Ken Long)

Thousands of pilots earned their wings flying the AT-6 advanced training plane.

The AT-6 was the primary advanced training plane at Luke Field. In this photo, Chinese pilots of the first foreign graduating class fly over Luke Field in 1942.

Desert Warfare Training

Airmen were not the only soldiers who trained for combat in Arizona. General George F. "Blood and Guts" Patton prepared his men for desert warfare in California and Arizona. Also, two infantry divisions endured the blistering summer heat at Camp Hyder and Camp Horn in Yuma County. "The desert can kill quicker than the enemy," Patton said, "but training will save hundreds of lives when we get into combat." As fate would have it, Patton's tank divisions fought in the deserts of North Africa and defeated the German Africa Korps. The infantry divisions fought in the steamy jungles on islands in the South Pacific.

Sgt. Art Benko (on top of the B-24) and members of *The Goon* crew.

The Bushmasters cross a stream during training in Panama.

Arizona's Soldiers Go to War

Bushmasters

The Arizona National Guard was ordered into active duty even before World War II broke out. Organized as part of the 158th Infantry Regiment, the guard went to Panama for training in jungle warfare. While there, the regiment became known as the "Bushmasters," the name of a deadly jungle snake.

During the war, the 158th shipped out to an island in the Pacific. "As soon as we arrived we faced the Japanese in pillboxes [shelters] made of coconut-palm logs. The pillboxes were no more than a foot or two above ground," said Colonel Fred Stofft of Tucson. "Some B-17s dropped bombs to no effect. I asked for some tanks. With tanks, flame throwers, and grenades, we cleaned them out."

The Bushmasters fought their way through the islands to the Philippines. They landed in Japan in October, 1945, two months after the atomic bombs were dropped on Hiroshima and Nagasaki and the war was over. "No greater fighting combat team has ever been *deployed* in battle," said General Douglas MacArthur.

> **The Bushmasters were the only regiment in the southwest Pacific who fought for four years of jungle combat without getting a rest in Australia or New Zealand.**
> —Colonel J. Prugh Herndon,
> *Arizona Daily Star*, March 26, 1995

Minority Groups During the War

American Indians

World War II brought many changes in Navajo life. Thousands of Navajos worked in war plants, shipyards, railroads, and mines. They were the principal source of labor at the Navajo Ordinance Depot near Flagstaff. The federal government built the huge plant for storage and maintenance of ammunition. Hopis and Havasupais also worked at the plant. Two towns, housing more than 4,500 workers, were constructed at the gates of the depot.

The Pimas knew how important their wartime work was. Some muscular Pimas were cranking airplane propellers at the Scottsdale field. Denied a raise which they asked for, the chief took an old crank, laid it on the boss's desk, and said, "You crank!" The Pimas got their raise.

Navajo Code was Foolproof

During World War II, Navajo radiomen in the armed services were used to send and receive "top secret" messages in their native language. Navajo code talkers had to be fluent in both their own language and in English. They invented a code that the Japanese never broke.

Most of the Navajo code talkers were in the Pacific. They used portable telephones and two-way radios. One Navajo would send a message to a second Navajo who would then translate the message back into English.

Navajo terms were applied to the letters in the English alphabet. Wol-la-chee (ant) stood for "a," shush (bear) for "b," and so on. The most common letters a, e, i, o, n, t were given three terms each to further confuse the Japanese. For example, "a" could be wol-la-chee (ant), tsenihl (axe), or bela-sanna (apple).

The code-talkers had special words for military items. They identified ships with Navajo words for different kinds of fish. Airplanes were birds—ginit (hawk) for dive bomber or ne-as-jah (owl) for observation plane. A hand grenade was nimasli (potato).

Code talkers, who were not allowed to speak Navajo when they were teenagers in government boarding schools, saved many lives during the war because they could speak it.

"Most of my U.S. Marine Corps buddies are gone," Ira Hayes said. "We hit the beach on Iwo Jima with 250 men in my company. We left with only 27 about six weeks later."

While on the island, Hayes and five other marines were ordered to raise a huge flag atop Mount Suribachi, so newsmen could take pictures of it. A photo of this event grabbed the nation's attention and made Hayes, a Pima Indian, famous. He appeared in newsreels, was honored by President Harry Truman, and was cheered at war bond rallies. A quiet man, Ira felt uncomfortable being called the "hero" of Iwo Jima. "This hero stuff is for the birds," he said. "I get sick hearing about the phony flag-raising."

Hayes, a combat survivor of bloody battles with the Japanese army, lost the biggest battle of his life—a struggle with alcoholism—after the war. He died a young man on the Gila Reservation. Hayes is buried at Arlington National Cemetery in Washington, D.C.

Lew Davis Builds Black Morale

During World War II, the U. S. Army enlisted Lew Davis, one of Arizona's most famous painters. Davis, who was white, was sent to Fort Huachuca, then an all-black post.

Davis did three things that improved the morale of black troops. He painted army posters with black faces, instead of the usual "smiling blond white men." His posters were silk-screened and sent to all black military bases. Then Davis started a world-wide newspaper for black servicemen. The paper was printed weekly at the *Douglas Dispatch*. Davis also painted a forty-foot mural, called *The Negro in American Wars*. The mural was sent all over the country with a light and music show.

"You know, when I got to Fort Huachuca, the 92nd Division was there. The 92nd was great. My *propaganda*—the posters, the newspaper, and the mural— instilled pride and a spirit in the 92nd," Davis said proudly in an interview.

Linking the past and the present

Today, people of all ethnic groups serve side by side in the military forces. It is hard to imagine things being different during other time periods.

African Americans

African American soldiers trained at Fort Huachuca. The 93rd Infantry Division departed for the Pacific in 1943 as the 92nd Division arrived to prepare for duty in Europe. For a time, black troops guarded vital points along Highway 66. The highway was an important link in military transportation.

Black civilians did important farm labor during the war. Trainloads of workers were recruited in Texas, Louisiana, and other southern states. Many of them stayed after the war. During the war years, the African American population of Arizona increased from 15,000 to 26,000.

Black soldiers at Fort Huachuca wait to see Sergeant Joe Louis, the world heavyweight boxing champion.

Soldiers of the 93rd Infantry Division parade at Fort Huachuca.

236   ARIZONA: A Journey of Discovery

Hispanic Americans

Hispanic Americans served in all branches of the armed forces. Early in the war, Epimenio Rubi of Winslow lost his life as one of the heroic defenders of Bataan in the Philippines. Many Mexican Americans fought on the Italian front as part of the 88th Infantry Division, called the "Blue Devils." Sergeant Manuel Mendoza of Tempe, known as "the Arizona Kid," won the Distinguished Service Cross for heroism. Lieutenant Mauricio Aragon of Avondale was an officer in the division.

Silvestre Herrera of Phoenix earned the Congressional Medal of Honor in World War II. His platoon was stopped by heavy German machine gun fire. The whole area was heavily mined but Herrera made a one-man assault on two different places. He captured eight German soldiers at the first position. In attacking the second machine gun, Herrera stepped on a mine and had both feet blown off. Despite the pain and loss of blood, he pinned down the Germans with rifle fire. Meanwhile, his fellow soldiers crept around the mine field and rushed in to capture the enemy gunners.

Silvestre Herrera

The governor proclaimed a "Herrera Day" to welcome him home. The proud people of Phoenix raised a fund to provide the hero with a house. The government of Mexico awarded Herrera, who was born in Chihuahua, the Military Medal of Merit, the highest decoration given to foreigners.

During the war, Hispanic American civilians answered the call for volunteers to help pick the cotton crop. There was a labor shortage and the cotton was badly needed to make parachutes, gliders, and blimps. On one occasion, 5,000 Mexican volunteers came to pick cotton.

Relocation of Japanese Americans

The bombing of Pearl Harbor was followed by a wave of anti-Japanese hysteria, especially in California where most of Japanese Americans lived. People were afraid that people with Japanese ancestors would have sympathy to Japan, might work as spies, and would not be loyal to the United States. President Roosevelt yielded to widespread fears and authorized the army to remove all Japanese from the West Coast.

The evacuation zone extended inland into Arizona. It included the area south of a highway that ran through Wickenburg, Phoenix, Tempe, Mesa, and Globe. The government made sure that Luke and Williams Air Bases were in the region. In the name of "military necessity," about 112,000 innocent Nisei (American-born Japanese) were relocated. The families were given short notice to leave their homes, farms, and small businesses.

"My parents, seven sisters, one brother, and I were given only twenty-four hours to get ready. Each of us could take whatever would fit in one suitcase."
—Nick Nakagawa, Phoenix Union High School student

Japanese Relocation Camps

Two of the ten relocation centers were in Arizona. Helen Takagi, age twelve, had to leave school in Safford. "Can this be true? Do we really have to go?" she asked at the time. "Everybody had to go. It was very sad." Takagi, born of an immigrant Japanese father and a Mexican mother, was sent with her two brothers and sisters to the hot, dusty camp at Poston. When they got there, each person was given a bag, like the one cotton pickers use, and told to fill it with hay for a mattress.

The camps consisted of wooden barracks grouped into blocks. Each block included a mess hall, recreation hall, and a combination washroom-toilet-laundry building. For the family-oriented Japanese it was not home, even though each family had a separate room. Furniture was made out of crates and scrap lumber.

"The confinement was outrageous," said Emma, Helen's sister. "Our immigrant father was so patriotic, he wouldn't let us speak Japanese at home. He said, 'We are Americans.'"

The Japanese Americans at the Gila Camp found life just as hard, but the soil was good. They dug irrigation canals and produced tons of vegetables. The people formed the Rivers Cooperative and got a license to sell the vegetables. The food produced by the Japanese Americans helped the war effort.

The Arizona state board of education did its best to provide teachers at the camps. Public libraries donated books.

Although a great many of us have overcome embitterment with understanding, others have not. . . . We must have faith in God, faith in democracy, and faith in ourselves.

—George Kataoke, Butte High School Yearbook, 1945
Gila River Relocation Camp

This was the Japanese relocation camp on the Gila River Reservation.

ARIZONA: A Journey of Discovery

Japanese American women harvest daikon at the Gila River camp.

"I was going to Glendale High School when a lot of Japanese vegetable farmers were moved out. It was sure lonely without my Japanese friends. . . ."
—Caroline McWilliams, teenager during World War II. Interview, *The Arizona Republic*, August 4, 1985

What do you think?

Mine Okubo wrote a book about her experiences at a relocation camp. Do you agree or disagree with her conclusions? Give some examples to support your opinion.

- "People everywhere have the same concerns for home, family, comfort, and loads of problems. That's all there is when you come to think of it."

- "Disaster always brings change both good and bad. Certain people get bitter, revengeful. Others show greater kindness, and they use their time to advantage."

Kazuo Hiyama, his wife, two children, and his aging parents occupied one room at the Gila River camp. "Dust came up through the cracks in the floor and settled on everything. We couldn't turn on the lights at night because there were no screens on the windows and the lights attracted blister bugs."
—James E. Cook
The Arizona Republic,
June 28, 1992

Japanese American children enjoy a card game at the Poston camp.

Japanese American school children march in a Harvest Festival parade at the Gila River camp in 1942.

World War II

Relocation Camps Close

Early in 1945, the government phased out the relocation camps. Many evacuees returned to California only to find their homes vandalized or in the hands of another owner.

The uprooting of the Japanese Americans proved to be unnecessary. Their loyalty and combat record during World War II were admirable. In fact, the 442nd Infantry Regiment, made up entirely of Japanese Americans, won more decorations fighting in Europe than any unit in the United States Army.

In 1988 Congress passed a law giving an apology and $20,000 each to 60,000 surviving Japanese Americans who had been confined in camps during World War II. There was no way, of course, that they could be fully *compensated* for the injustice and humiliation they had experienced.

Prisoner of War Camps

THE U. S. ARMY brought many German and Italian prisoners of war to the United States to remain until the end of the war. The Papago Camp in Phoenix was the largest in Arizona for German POWs. Other temporary camps dotted the state. The one big Italian camp was near Florence.

"Prisoners from the German POW camp north of Buckeye were bused to our farm to pick cotton. . . . Their leader would come up to the house to visit, play our piano, and sing. One of his favorites was a popular song, 'Don't Fence Me In.'"
—Marjorie M. Saroka,
The Arizona Republic,
August 4, 1985

Papago
(Phoenix)

Some of the captured Germans at the Papago POW camp pose for a picture.

German prisoners worked in forests, on irrigation projects, and in cotton fields. Before their capture, most of the prisoners of war (POWs) were sailors on ships and submarines. So why did the army ship them to desert country? Captain Jurgen Wattenberg, a navigation officer, understood. In broken English he said, "Dey put us out dere because ve vould be like fish out of vater."

Many of the POWs were young and strong. The worst ones seemed to feel no remorse when shown horror films of German *concentration camps*. Some of the POWs made anti-Semitic (anti-Jewish) propaganda leaflets which they tossed out of trucks on the way to work projects.

Phoenix school children started a fad of painting POW letters on their sweatshirts. But teachers and parents stopped this practice, explaining that a boy near adult size might be mistaken for an escaped prisoner and be shot.

Now and then a POW did escape from the Papago camp. The "great escape" came the night before Christmas Eve, 1944. Twenty-five men got out of the compound through a tunnel that had taken months to dig. Soon after arriving at the camp, the POWs discovered a blind spot. They strung a clothesline over the area and kept it full of blankets that looked like they were drying in the sun. With small coal shovels, cups, and screwdrivers, the POWs dug a 130-foot tunnel to the bank of a canal. They hauled dirt out in a little wooden cart and flushed it down toilets or scattered it carefully around the camp. Both the engineering and the deception were amazing.

The escape night was rainy and cold. Three men quickly gave themselves up to get out of the weather. One hitched a ride to the sheriff's office to surrender. Two others asked a surprised Tempe housewife to turn them in. The next day, Civil Air Patrol planes searched the desert for the other POWs. The state prison sent bloodhounds to help in the search. Gradually, the prisoners were rounded up. Only Captain Wattenberg remained free.

For days, Wattenberg hid in a cave north of Phoenix. He finally ventured downtown and ate a nice meal at a Chinese restaurant. His mistake was asking for directions to the train depot at a gas station. The attendant detected his German accent and called a policeman, who escorted the captain back to the prison camp. A few months after his capture, Germany surrendered.

What do you think?

"No country wins a war, some just lose more than others."
Explain why you agree or disagree with this statement.

"We had a farm and were thankful for the food we had. Dad got German POWs to clean the ditches, as all our help was gone. Also, Dad had problems getting gas for the tractor, so we put our plow horses back to use. . . ."
—Caroline McWilliams, teenager during World War II.
The Arizona Republic,
August 4, 1985

This is the entrance to the tunnel through which German POWs escaped from the Papago prison camp.

"Those stupid Americans put blue on their maps where there is no water!" said Wilhelm Gunther. He and two other POWs escaped through the tunnel with a raft built in sections. Finding only "little puddles" in the Gila River, they could not float to the Gulf of California as planned.
—*The Arizona Republic,*
August 27, 1989

The *Enola Gay* dropped the atom bomb on Hiroshima. The pilots trained on western deserts.

"The war was over. . . . My cousin and I rode the streetcar downtown [Phoenix] to join the festivities. . . . We formed a long snaky line, hundreds of us, dancing and singing. . . ."
—Helen Bays, *The Arizona Republic*

World War II: A Synopsis

Dictators who formed the Rome-Berlin-Tokyo *axis* were ruthless and seemed unbeatable. Hitler bragged that Americans could never outproduce Nazi Germany. He believed his young Germans, brought up in the Hitler Youth Movement, could outfight young Americans brought up in the Boy Scouts. But, as General Dwight D. Eisenhower said, "Hitler should beware the fury of an aroused democracy."

After entering World War II, the United States performed miracles. Working together, we quickly built our unprepared army and navy into a powerful military force. Civilian workers produced an unbelievable amount of war material—planes, tanks, ships, and weapons.

Arizonans took part in these miracles, joining with the nation in the struggle to save freedom and democracy. Arizona men and women served in all branches of the armed services in many parts of the world.

In the Pacific, American ground troops won bloody jungle battles on islands on the way to Japan. Our navy airplanes smashed a powerful Japanese fleet, sinking four aircraft carriers. By 1944, our big bomber planes were dropping their loads on Japanese cities.

Meanwhile, an American and British force, commanded by General Eisenhower, drove the shocked Germans out of North Africa and invaded Italy. In June, 1944, Eisenhower sent a large army across the English Channel from England. The soldiers landed on the beaches of Normandy in German-occupied France. From this hard-earned foothold, much tough fighting lay ahead. But Hitler was doomed. Stubbornly, he kept fighting while the allies bombed German cities, laying them to ruins. Finally, in May, 1945, Germany surrendered.

Franklin Delano Roosevelt died less than a month before Germany surrendered. The nation mourned his passing. The new president, Harry S. Truman, had a terrible decision to make. Should we invade Japan at the cost of several million American and Japanese lives? Or should we use a new weapon—the atomic bomb? President Truman warned the Japanese leaders "to surrender or be destroyed," but got no answer.

On August 6, 1945, a B-29 Superfortress flew over the hilly green terrain of southern Japan. The crew dropped an atomic bomb on Hiroshima. This seaport and rail center was the home of an army base. In a few seconds, Hiroshima was a flaming wreckage. In the words of historian Joy Hakim:

Dust makes the city as dark as midnight. The wind tosses people about. Thermal rays burn their bodies. An enormous mushroom cloud rises into the sky. . . . The second Japanese Army no longer exists. Thousands of civilians in the city are also dead.

Three days later a second bomb laid waste the city of Nagasaki. Finally, the Japanese surrendered on August 14, 1945. World War II was over.

Linking the past and the present

"World War II was a major turning point in Arizona history." Explain this statement, considering the contrast between pre-war Arizona and the ways the state began to change and grow during the war.

The Cold War (1945–1991)

THE UNITED STATES, leader of the free world, tried to stop the Soviet Union from spreading *communist* control over other countries. Without actually fighting a shooting war with each other, the two nations engaged in an expensive *arms race*, including nuclear bombs and guided missiles. In Arizona, Titan missiles were ready to be launched from silos south of Tucson. Defense plants prospered with government contracts.

During the hostile cold war, the superpowers also struggled to be superior in space technology. The Soviet Union took an early lead, launching the first satellite into orbit around the earth and causing American schools to put more emphasis on science and mathematics. Finally, in 1969, two Americans astounded the world when they stepped on the moon. The astronauts had done part of their training at Meteor Crater near Flagstaff.

The cold war ended in 1991 when the Soviet Union split into independent countries. In the face of an economic collapse of the communist system, dictator Mikhail Gorbachev surprised most people by granting reforms. He allowed free elections and began cooperating with the United States to reduce tensions.

During the cold war with the Soviet Union, the United States fought two wars in Asia to stop communist aggression—one in Korea and one in Vietnam. You will read about these wars in a later chapter.

In Arizona as elsewhere, fear of an atomic bomb attack by the Russians caused some residents in the state to maintain a supply of food, water, medical supplies, and other emergency equipment. Many adults who were in school in the 1950s and 1960s remember huddling under their desks in air raid drills. Public buildings often had a shelter area.

Chapter 12 Review

1. Who were the three "bad guys" that caused World War II?
2. When did the Japanese bomb Pearl Harbor?
3. Which industry got a big boost during the war, and why?
4. How did the war change the lives of women?
5. What was the job of the civilian airfields in Arizona?
6. List three important army air bases started during World War II.
7. What code did the Navajo code talkers use and how did it help the war effort?
8. Identify Ira H. Hayes and Silvestre Herrera.
9. List three things that artist Lew Davis did to build black pride.
10. Why did the U. S. government want to move Japanese Americans away from the West Coast?
11. Where were relocation camps built in Arizona?
12. What kinds of work projects were the POWs given?
13. What two events brought an end to World War II?
14. What country was "the enemy" during the cold war?

chapter 13

THE TIME
1945–1990s

PEOPLE TO KNOW
Dr. Daniel E. Noble
Governor Ernest McFarland
John F. Long
Del Webb
Mayor Margaret Hance
A. J. Chandler
Fred Harvey

PLACES TO LOCATE
Phoenix
Prescott
Litchfield
Mesa
Coolidge
Flagstaff
Snowflake
Miami
Sun City
Tucson
Casa Grande
Santa Cruz River
Yuma
Salt River Valley
Queen Creek
Tolleson
Willcox
Welton
Cochise County
Maricopa County
Castle Hot Springs
Safford
Chandler
Wickenburg
Winslow
Tempe

Each week the Cable Systems International plant in Phoenix makes more

1950s
Many electronics firms move to the Phoenix area.

1950s
Pima Mining Co. begins open pit mining.

1945   1950   1955   1960   1965

1949 Motorola builds its first plant in Phoenix.

1965 Anaconda begins digging an open pit mine.

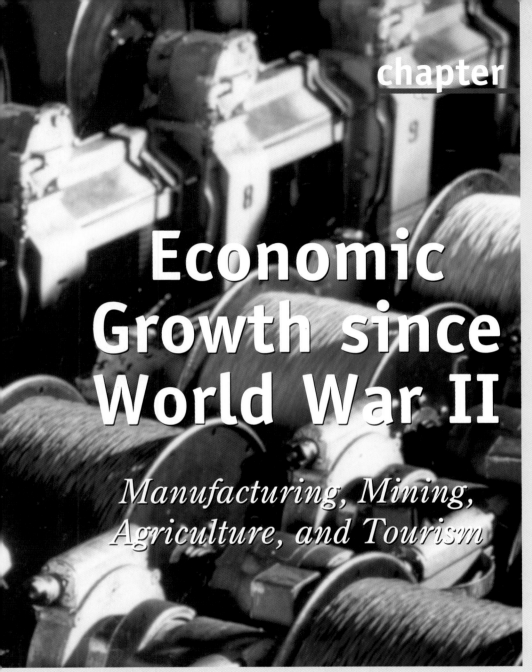

13

TERMS TO UNDERSTAND
repeal
refinery
lode
leach
percolate
rubble
cathode
byproduct
alloy
hydroponic
immunization
sojourn
conducive
subdivision
prefabricate
anchor store

Economic Growth since World War II

Manufacturing, Mining, Agriculture, and Tourism

copper wire than would be needed to connect the earth and the moon.

1984
First Apache helicopters are
manufactured in Mesa.

| 1970 | 1975 | 1980 | 1985 | 1990 | 1995 |

1970s
Some farmers plant
wheat instead of cotton.

1980s
More than half of Arizona women
have jobs outside the home.

Dr. Daniel E. Noble
1901–1980

Daniel Noble first visited Arizona when he was eighteen. He had been having trouble with his eyes, so his doctor advised him to take time off from his studies. He went to Prescott and led an outdoor life under the guidance of a mountain lion hunter.

Returning to school after a year, Noble became a scientist and a professor at the University of Connecticut. In 1940, Motorola in Chicago hired him as director of research. After helping the army and navy develop the walkie-talkie during World War II, Noble led a handful of Motorola engineers to set up a small research lab in Phoenix. His pioneer work in electronics made Motorola a leader in the field.

Noble served as president of the Phoenix Symphony Association. An outstanding painter, he did one-man art shows in Paris and other cities. He painted under the name of Elbon, his name spelled backward.

Manufacturing Balances the Economy

MANUFACTURING got a jump-start from wartime defense plants. Up to that time, the basic industries were the five C's: copper, cotton, cattle, citrus, and climate (tourism). Today, manufacturing is the number one source of income. Thousands of factories, located all over the state, produce everything from computers and missiles to doughnuts.

The Electronics Industry

"Phoenix will be attractive to scientists and engineers. Air conditioning has transformed Phoenix into a year-round city of delightful living. Refrigeration cooling is the complete solution to the Phoenix summer heat problem," said Dan Noble.

Noble visited several cities to choose a place where his company, Motorola of Chicago, might move into the emerging electronics field. Motorola built the first of many electronics plants in east Phoenix in 1949. The company expanded from making television sets to silicon rods, from which the all-important "chips" are shaved. Computer chips—those tiny bundles of circuits called semiconductors—are the heart of many modern gadgets. Your toaster has one. So do your iron

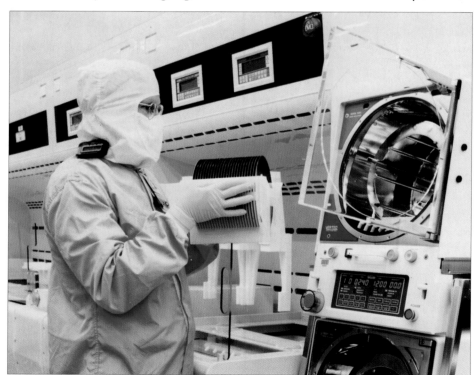

This Motorola researcher is using a wet chemical processor. Motorola manufactures wafers (chips) in Phoenix, Mesa, Tempe, and Chandler.

and TV set. The ever-growing number of chip-driven devices, especially the personal computer, fueled the expansion of Motorola.

Hundreds of other electronic companies sprouted and grew. General Electric arrived in the 1950s to do research and to manufacture computers. Intel Corporation, a large world-known high-tech company, opened plants where highly educated workers continue to make microprocessors, the brains of the modern computer. Intel developed the Pentium processor and does much ongoing research to stay ahead of skyrocketing demands for more computer memory.

Aerospace Factories

State officials have worked hard to bring "clean air" industries to Arizona. Governor Ernest McFarland proudly took credit for bringing Sperry Rand Flight Systems to Phoenix. The company would not build a factory in Arizona unless a two percent sales tax on goods sold to the federal government was *repealed.* McFarland persuaded the state legislature to do just that.

During the Korean War (1950–1953), Hughes Aircraft chose Tucson for a plant to build the Falcon missile. The Hughes company, a national leader in missile technology, was southern Arizona's success story. The company, now a part of Raytheon, has employed thousands of workers.

Several World War II defense plants reopened and were merged with larger companies during the age of business consolidation in the 1980s. AlliedSignal Aerospace Company, which specializes in aircraft engines, now controls Garrett's AiResearch and other plants in the Phoenix area. Goodyear Aerospace at Litchfield is now part of Lockheed Martin.

In 1984, Hughes Helicopters, Inc., completed years of expensive research and began manufacturing the AH-64 "Apache" helicopter in Mesa. The company soon became part of the McDonnell Douglas corporation, then Boeing, and finally Bell Helicopter Textron in 1998.

The Apache looks like a big insect on the prowl, but it is a lean, mean flying weapon. Designed to fly "low and slow" to avoid army radar, the Apache is the "ultimate tank killer." The helicopter is armed with a laser-guided missile system, rockets, and a 30 mm gun. The Apache is able to fly 225 miles per hour and climb in excess of 3,000 feet per minute. It is equipped for all-weather combat operations in total darkness—a truly amazing aircraft!

An AlliedSignal Aerospace associate puts finishing touches on an auxiliary power unit manufactured in Phoenix for a Boeing plane.

The AH-64D Apache Longbow multi-mission helicopter takes a test flight near Mesa.

Local Raw Materials

A lemonade tycoon (age seven) sets up a stand on a shady corner in Coolidge. He advertises "real homemade lemonade," and he means it. The lemons are from his backyard. The sugar is refined from Arizona-grown beets, and the water is from a local well. His first customer? The lady next door. From raw materials through processing to the consumer, it's an Arizona operation all the way.

Sawmills in Flagstaff, a paper mill in Snowflake, cement plants, brick factories, cotton gins, and copper wire plants—all of these factories and many more make use of local raw materials.

Making copper products is far more complex than squeezing lemons. The Inspiration Copper Company, for example, mines copper, refines it, and makes rolls of copper rod at its plant in Miami. Then Cable Systems International in Phoenix draws the rod into telephone wire for use in underground cables.

More than 200 firms in Arizona process food or beverages (even lemonade). You could prepare quite a Fourth of July picnic with products from Rosarita Mexican Foods in Mesa, Frito-Lay chips in Casa Grande, Kalil Bottling Company in Tucson, Shamrock Foods (dairy and meat products), and any of the many bakeries in the state.

Tortillas are cooked, counted, and packaged at the Rosarita food plant in Mesa. TV dinners are also prepared there.

(Photo by Cleve Langston, Rosarita)

The papermill at Snowflake now uses recycled material to make new paper.

ARIZONA: A Journey of Discovery

Copper Mining

Tucson is now called the "copper capital of the world." Most of the state's copper is mined within 125 miles of the city. Development came after geologists located a massive ore body that ran along the west bank of the Santa Cruz River. In the early 1950s, Pima Mining Company began open pit mining near Twin Buttes. Anaconda and other companies followed.

> **"Your mission, Jack, is to dig a hole more than 500 feet deep and half a mile wide. You are to move 220 million tons of dirt. Get the job done in four years. You're then down to low grade copper ore. Start mining. Remember the venture must be profitable."**

In this manner, the Anaconda Copper Company directed its man in charge to begin massive stripping operations at Twin Buttes, south of Tucson, in late 1965. To accomplish this fantastic job of earth moving, Anaconda bought giant bulldozers, scrapers, and trucks that haul 100 tons at a whack. A long conveyor system was installed to haul out 300,000 tons of rock and dirt a day. All of this work was to get a mere ten to fifteen pounds of copper per ton when the ore finally flows.

In addition to the mine, Anaconda built a multi-million dollar laboratory in Tucson. Scientists, engineers, and technicians at the lab now devote full time to developing new and improved methods of extracting copper from ores. Anaconda later combined with Amax to form Anamax.

Today's Problems

The good ol' days of bonanza copper mines are long gone. The old-timers searched for *lodes* with rich ores of maybe 150 to 400 pounds of copper per ton. Today's companies are mining large bodies of rock and dirt with clumps of ore scattered here and there like raisins in a pudding. The pudding part is waste. The raisins are ore that average one-half of one percent of copper per ton. Even the waste dumps in bonanza days were richer than that.

Today's ores are usually deep underground. It takes a team of geologists, chemists, and other scientists to find them. Some ore bodies have solid rock caps—too thick for either open pit or underground mining.

For several years, most of Arizona's copper companies were losing money because of low-grade ores, low copper prices, foreign competition, environmental pressures, and strikes. These companies and others expect to run out of easily accessible copper ore in Arizona by the year 2010.

> **"The mines in this state mean a lot to all Arizonians—and to all Americans too! Minerals are the keystone of our complex industrial society. Without them, this nation would no longer exist as we know it today."**
> —Arizona Mining Association

> **"Our coins are mostly copper, sandwiched between layers of nickel or silver. Coinage requires 50,000 tons of copper a year—equal to the output of one good-sized Arizona mine."**
> —Arizona Mining Association

> **"The Bagdad *refinery* makes powdered copper. . . . [It] is used in bearings, brake linings, disc brakes, and other items. So, a little Yavapai County town produces copper used the world over."**
> —Arizona Mining Association

Five Steps in the Solvent Extraction/Electrowinning (SX/EW) Process

Mine companies still grind copper ore into fine powder. The waste is removed in flotation tanks and by heating at a smelter. But some copper mines now *leach* low grade ores using the newer solvent extraction/electrowinning (SX/EW) process. The ore is first blasted into rubble for leaching; it does not have to be ground into powder or smelted.

Step 1. *Solvent Extraction:* Copper ore rubble is sprayed with acid solution for leaching. The acid dissolves copper as it *percolates* through the rubble.

Step 2. Acid solution containing copper flows from a leached *rubble* dump to a plastic-lined collection pond. This leach solution is then piped to tanks where chemical solutions remove the copper atoms. The acid is reused. (Silver Bell Mining, LLC)

Step 3. *Electrowinning:* Stainless steel starter sheets are lowered into the copper solution. An electric current drives the copper out of the solution and deposits it on the steel plates. (Silver Bell Mining, LLC)

Step 4. After about a week, the 200-pound plates are moved to a copper *cathode* stripping area. (Silver Bell Mining, LLC)

Step 5. Stripped copper cathodes, 99.99 percent pure, are ready for shipment at Phelps Dodge Bagdad. The cathodes are shipped to factories to make thousands of copper products.

Other Minerals

Gold and silver were the minerals that drew pioneer prospectors to Arizona. Today, these metals are mostly *byproducts* of copper smelting. Another important byproduct is molybdenum. Called "molly," this metal is used in making steel *alloys* and such things as spark plugs. Coal is plentiful in Arizona; most of it is on the Navajo Reservation. The coal is burned to generate electricity at several big power plants. Sand and gravel are another valuable source of mineral income in Arizona.

The Navajo generating plant near Page burns coal to make electricity.

The need for uranium to produce atomic energy caused a mining boom in northern Arizona. Navajos who worked in uranium mines later developed a high rate of lung cancer.

Agriculture Plays a Key Role in Arizona's Economy

FARMING HAS CHANGED GREATLY since pioneer days. Now it is called agribusiness. The typical Arizona farm is large and requires huge capital investments in land and equipment.

Only two percent of Arizona's land is farmed, but conditions have been favorable here for desert- grown products. Sunshine and irrigation are an unbeatable combination—if the water doesn't run out! Improved seeds, fertilizers, and insecticides help the farmers. Herbicides to control weeds, as well as better planting and harvesting methods, have also increased production.

Cotton is Arizona's Major Crop

Until the 1950s, most cotton was picked by hand. A person might pick 200 pounds a day. Now a cotton-picking machine can harvest 10,000 pounds in one day.

Technological changes have improved cotton planting too. "An electric eye on the planter feeds information to a computer in the cab, so the driver doesn't have to watch whether the seeds are dropping, and can concentrate on straight rows," said one farmer. "This is the most important operation we have. You can replant but it's less costly to do it right the first time."

Both Pima (long staple) and upland (short staple) cotton do well in Arizona. The average cotton yield per acre is more than double the national average. Today, the biggest market for Arizona cotton is in Asia. The chances are good that a cotton shirt or dress made in Taiwan or South Korea has cotton in it from Arizona.

> **"It's breathtaking the things (machines, pesticides, fertilizers) I have available to work with that my father didn't."**
> —Chuck Youngker, Buckeye cotton farmer

Machines made cotton picking easier.

Until the 1950s, cotton was picked by hand.

Forage, Grain, and Seeds

Alfalfa has been an important forage crop in Arizona since territorial days. The alfalfa is cut for hay and fed locally to livestock. In the 1970s, the high price of wheat caused many farmers to plant it instead of cotton. The average wheat yield per acre on an irrigated farm in Arizona is sixty-six bushels, more than double the national average. Arizona farmers grow some crops for seed. More than ninety percent of the nation's Bermuda grass seed is produced in the Yuma area. Most of the pearl millet seed planted in the southeastern states comes from Arizona.

Winter Vegetables

The warm desert climate is ideal for winter vegetables. Lettuce, called Arizona's "green gold," is the leading vegetable crop. At harvest time the iceberg lettuce is cut, boxed in cartons, hauled to cooling plants, and shipped in refrigerated trucks or railroad cars all over the country. Transportation is the biggest cost factor.

Birds can be a problem. "When the lettuce plants are real small, the birds pull them out till they get one without dirt on the root. Birds need green things," said one disgusted farmer. "We tried rubber snakes. They scared the birds away for about three days. Then the hawks swept in and carried the snakes away."

Deep orange-colored carrots and onions are grown in the Salt River Valley. Potatoes are planted at lower elevations, especially in the Queen Creek and Tolleson areas. The warm climate gets potatoes ready early for the heavy Fourth of July chip market. Frito-Lay at Casa Grande buys a lot of Arizona-grown potatoes, including those harvested later in the year at Willcox and Snowflake. The leading cantaloupe-producing area in the Southwest is at Yuma.

Irrigation water is vital to farming in Arizona.

Lettuce is harvested in the Salt River Valley.

Hydroponic Farming

Hydroponic farming is the agriculture of the future. The Eurofresh tomato farm, near Willcox, uses a high tech, state-of-the-art method to grow tomatoes in a glass-covered facility. Plants are grown in water, not soil. "We start the seed in soil, remove it early, and place it in rock wool. This soil-like substance absorbs the water and nutrients the plant needs," explained the grower. "We keep the temperature at a constant 70 to 72 degrees."

Bumblebees pollinate flowers on vines rooted in a fertilized water solution. Wasps and other insects keep the plants bug-free without the use of pesticides. The tomatoes, grown year-round, were judged the

Small onions are dug from the ground, trimmed, and wrapped in bundles.

"best-tasting tomato in North America" by the American Tasting Institute. Tons of vine-ripened tomatoes are shipped daily, mainly to markets in New York and the East Coast.

In the future, hydroponic farming may be a major industry, especially in Arizona's rural areas where people are looking for permanent, not seasonal, jobs.

Fruits and Nuts

Citrus has been an important Arizona crop since the 1880s. Grapefruit trees do well almost anywhere in the desert zone. Navel oranges grow mainly in the Salt River Valley. The Valencia, a late ripening orange that fills the need for fresh fruit in the spring, does best in the warmer localities of Yuma, Wellton, and the Salt River Valley. The Lisbon lemon produces heavily in the Yuma climate.

Most apple trees in Arizona are found in the cool Sulphur Springs Valley. The elevation there is about 4,500 feet. A packing plant in Willcox is designed to handle two million bushels or more when all the orchards are producing. Arizona apples have a higher sugar content and come on the market earlier than apples grown in Washington or Oregon.

Table grapes are another important fruit crop in Arizona. Grapes watered by drip irrigation use only about a fifth of the water needed for cotton. More than half the cost of grape growing is for labor.

Irrigated pecan trees are scattered over southern Arizona. The largest pecan grove in the country stretches out in the long green valley of the Santa Cruz River south of Tucson. Patient pecan growers wait about twelve years for a commercial crop. When harvest time finally comes, they shake the nuts off the trees by machine. Hershey's and other large companies buy most of the nuts. Stores such as Saks Fifth Avenue and I. Magnin sell the extra large pecans in fancy tins.

Oranges and other citrus fruits are important crops.

The Cattle Industry

TODAY, CATTLEMEN ARE CIRCLING THE WAGONS and fighting for survival. Not only do they battle the traditional foes—weather, predators, and the up-and-down beef market—but they face other problems too. First, how do they get enough land for their herds? A few fortunate families own a huge Spanish or Mexican land grant. But even they worry that their children will have to sell the ranch to pay inheritance taxes.

Most ranchers have to lease public land to eke out a living. Their ranches are hodge-podges of several different types of land. To get started, they have to own some land of their own to qualify for grazing permits on the federal forest reserves. The ranchers may also lease federal grasslands controlled by the Bureau of Land Management (BLM) or state school lands. Without leases on public lands, most cattlemen would go out of business.

About 1,500 ranches have survived in the state. The best grazing land is found in the Mountain Region. Cochise County has the most cattle on the winter range. Yavapai is second.

Cattle graze peacefully in the Mountain Region.

Cattlemen Have Other Problems

Livestock disease is not the problem it was in the early days. Many older ranchers say that disease prevention is the greatest change in the cattle industry. The modern cowboy, unlike the gun-toting stars of western movies, carries a hypodermic syringe to vaccinate livestock. Cattlemen find that their operating costs continue to rise. The price tags on good breeding stock, fencing, feed, and other purchases are high. The price for beef is uncertain.

Sadly, cowboys are a dying breed. Ranchers say they can't find good ranch hands. The reason may be the hard work and low pay. Cowboys often get housing, free grub, and a salary of about $1,000 per month.

Cattle Feeding

Cattle feeding is no longer a sideline to the Arizona range cattle industry. Today it is a separate business. Cattle are fattened in huge feedlots on hay, a variety of grains, cottonseed meal, and supplements. One feedlot in Maricopa County feeds 40,000 head in shaded pens. The animals walk single file down a chute, like an assembly line, for branding or ear tagging, dehorning, and *immunization*. Gradually, the feedlots were moved away from Phoenix because of the odor, flies, and high land values. The biggest market for fattened cattle is California.

Cattle are fed in this pen in central Arizona.

Tourism—A Growing Industry

THE TOURIST TRADE has been a source of income in Arizona since territorial days. J. Ross Browne even wrote a book about his visit, naming it *A Tour Through Arizona, 1864.*

"Our *sojourn* at Tubac was pleasant enough," he wrote. "Hunting and fishing, and bathing occupied most of our time. It was a lazy, vagabond sort of life, very *conducive* to health."

Health seekers, many with tuberculosis, were early on the scene. They pitched their tents in the desert to take advantage of the dry air.

Scottsdale, now an elegant city with art galleries and shops that attract tourists worldwide, was described in 1901 as a place with "thirty-odd tents and a half-dozen adobe houses."

Resorts

The rich and famous relaxed at Castle Hot Springs after it opened in 1896 northwest of Phoenix. Others visited Indian Hot Springs, near Safford, where Geronimo and his warriors soaked in the mud and drank mineralized waters at an earlier time. Another swanky resort was the San Marcos Hotel, built by A. J. Chandler in the town named after him.

The 1920s and early 1930s seemed to be the "golden age" of plush resorts: the Biltmore and Camelback Inn in Phoenix; El Conquistador and the Arizona Inn, run by Isabella Greenway, in Tucson. By the 1930s, more than sixty guest ranches entertained easterners who wanted to "go western" for a while. The first ranch was near Wickenburg, later called the "dude ranch capital of the world."

The Grand Canyon is our state's most famous tourist attraction. Scenic Airways of Phoenix took thousands of tourists on aerial trips over the Grand Canyon beginning in 1928. By the 1940s, American Airlines was spending $40,000 a month promoting Arizona.

(Photo by Tom Till)

"At the Flying E Ranch near Wickenburg, riding is our thing, with wranglers who enjoy horses and people! Lazy is an activity too."
—Arizona Dude Ranch Association

Tourists ride horses in the desert. (Photo by Bob Rink)

ARIZONA: A Journey of Discovery

Railroads Promote Tourism

The Santa Fe Railroad and Fred Harvey advertised northern Arizona, especially the Grand Canyon and Native Americans. Harvey operated restaurant-hotels, called Harvey houses, at stations along the Santa Fe. The Harvey Houses sold Indian jewelry, pottery, blankets, and other items to tourists. In the 1920s, the Harvey Company organized "Indian Detours," busing visitors in "Harvey cars and Harvey coaches." One popular Detour ran from the Winslow train station to the Hopi mesas. There, the guests camped in tents and attended the Hopi Snake Dance.

The Union Pacific opened Grand Canyon Lodge in 1928. The hotel was a stop on the railroad's five-day "motor bus" tour.

Harvey Houses were popular eating places. The food was excellent and it was served by Harvey Girls. They were attractive waitresses who were recruited in the East. There were very strict rules for the Harvey Girls. They had to be polite, clean, healthy, responsible, and moral.

Harvey cars brought many tourists to the Grand Canyon. This is a photo from the 1920s.

Tourism Today

Modern tourism is Arizona's second leading industry. It provides jobs in small towns and big cities. The millions of tourists who come here include vacationers, business travelers, conventioneers, campers, and people just passing through the state. They have a wide choice of accommodations ranging from wilderness campsites to luxurious resort hotels. Major convention centers are available in the larger cities. The Office of Tourism (OOT) promotes this industry with color brochures of interesting places to visit. OOT sends stories and pictures to newspapers and magazines around the country. Travel writers then write articles about Arizona.

Arizona Highways promotes our state all over the world. It encourages both local residents and out-of-state visitors to hit the road and see Arizona.

Economic Growth Since World War II

Construction Industry Booms

THE GROWTH OF MANUFACTURING after World War II and a steady stream of newcomers gave Arizona's construction industry a big boost. Carpenters, bricklayers, and other tradespeople found plenty of jobs. They built rows and rows of subdivision homes on the outskirts of the bigger cities. Other crews worked on shopping centers, factories, new schools, and retirement communities.

Del Webb, a millionaire who started as a carpenter, developed Sun City, a retirement community. He also built one of the new skyscrapers on North Central Avenue in Phoenix. Greyhound Bus Corporation, which moved its national headquarters to Phoenix, and other companies snapped up office space in the high-rise buildings.

Downtown areas changed after department stores began moving out in the 1950s—first to Park Central Mall in Phoenix and to El Con in Tucson. As suburbs grew in these cities, more malls sprang up. Metrocenter, along the Black Canyon Freeway in northwest Phoenix, opened in 1973 with 7,600 parking spaces. This large mall was the first in the nation with five *anchor stores* under one roof.

The downtown regions of larger cities became centers for banks, government buildings, conventions, cultural activities, and entertainment. Phoenix's forty-story, glass-covered Valley National Bank Center was quite a construction project. It towers over the twenty-six-floor Hyatt Regency Hotel, the city-county high-rise government complex, and the Civic Plaza. Symphony Hall, theaters, restaurants, America West basketball arena, and the huge Bank One baseball stadium have given our capital city a night life.

The growth of manufacturing brought many people to the cities. High rise buildings along Central Avenue in Phoenix reflected the changing economy.
(Photo by Bob Rink)

Homebuilder John F. Long and Ronald Reagan at a Maryvale model homes show in Phoenix, 1950s. Reagan, a future president of the United States, was doing advertising for General Electric.

Women in the Labor Force

Women have influenced the growth of Arizona's economy, both as workers and consumers. By the 1980s more than half of Arizona women were in the labor force. Like men, they realized that a good education often translates into higher earnings.

Traditionally, women in college chose a major in education, nursing, or the arts. Now many Arizona women are enrolling in the male-dominated, higher paying studies such as law, engineering, medicine, the sciences, and business administration.

Women are opening businesses in Arizona at a much faster rate than men. Many of the female-owned businesses provide services. Examples are health services, finance, insurance, real estate, legal work, and accounting. They also own a lot of restaurants and smaller eating places and a wide variety of stores.

Women, like men, often work at computers as part of their jobs.
(Photo by Bob Rink)

Chapter 13 Review

1. What is the number one source of income in Arizona today?

2. Why is Dan Noble important in the history of Arizona?

3. Explain why Arizona now has a diversified and well-balanced economy.

4. Make a chart with these headings: Electronics, Aerospace, Local Raw Materials, and Copper. In each column list companies that have factories in Arizona.

5. Why is Tucson called the "copper capital of the world"?

6. Explain "solvent extraction" as a means of removing copper from ore.

7. Define "agribusiness."

8. List five things that have increased farm production in Arizona.

9. Write a sentence on each of the following Arizona crops: cotton, lettuce, carrots, potatoes, apples, tomatoes, and pecans.

10. What is the basic problem faced by Arizona cattlemen today? How do they survive?

11. Explain how each of the following helped promote Arizona tourism: Fred Harvey, American Airlines, OOT, and *Arizona Highways*.

12. Explain how the downtown area of Phoenix was changed by the growth of the city.

chapter 14

THE TIME
1950—2000

PEOPLE TO KNOW
Senator John McCain
Cesar Chavez
Governor Raul Castro
Dr. Manuel Pacheco
Anna (Moore) Shaw
George Brooks
Lincoln Ragsdale
Dr. Ralph Bunche
Morgan Maxwell
Hayzel Burton Daniels
Wing Ong
Soleng Tom
Esther Don Tang
Sandra Day O'Conner
Edward Abbey

An

1953
Segregation in schools is declared unconstitutional by Arizona courts.

1960s–1973
Vietnam War

1963
Glen Canyon Dam is finished.

1966
Wing Ong is elected as the first Chinese state senator.

1950

1960

197

1950–1953
Korean War

1954
U.S. Supreme Court rules that school segregation is unconstitutional.

1964
Civil Rights Act outlaws discrimination in public accommodations.

1968
Civil Rights Act outlaws discrimination in housing.

1967–197
John McCain POW in Vietr

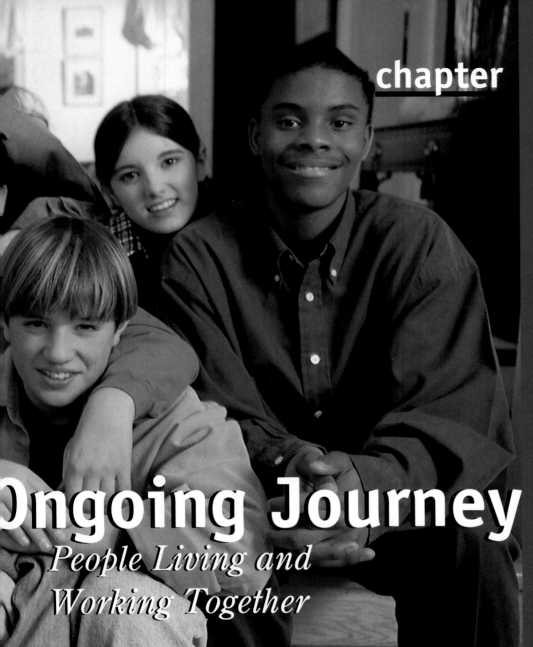

chapter

14

TERMS TO UNDERSTAND
suburbanization
urban sprawl
green belt
satellite city
emission
cold war
desegregate
barrio
integrate
alimony
resolution
repository

Ongoing Journey
*People Living and
Working Together*

The many faces of Arizona teenagers. (Photo by Scott Barrow)

1974
Raul Castro is
elected as the first
Hispanic governor.

1991
Persian Gulf War.
Manuel Pacheco becomes
head of University of Arizona.

1998
Senator John
McCain is elected
to a third term.

2000
Arizona's
population
is about five
million.

1980

1990

2000

1972
The Equal Rights Amendment
(ERA) passes the U.S. Congress.

1982
The ERA is dropped
after it is not
approved by enough
state legislatures.

1990
The Americans with
Disabilities Act (ADA) is
signed into U.S. law by
President George Bush.

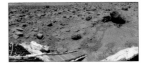

1997
U of A builds a
camera that takes
pictures of Mars'
surface.

> "I was among the first, . . . after World War II, to give up the swarming East. And so when Arizona began to grow, as they call it, it was as much my fault as anyone else's. Each of us wants to be the last to arrive."
>
> —Edward Abbey, environmentalist

Downtown Phoenix (Photo by Bob Rink)

Population Predictions for Phoenix

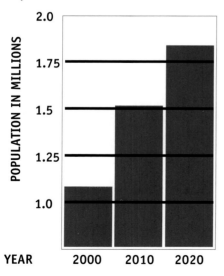

Source: Arizona Department of Economic Security, Population Statistics Unit

Arizona's Growing Cities Face Many Challenges

THE POPULATION OF ARIZONA IS SKYROCKETING. A World War II population of half a million grew to five million early in the twenty-first century. Families and individuals move here seeking a high quality of life in the Sun Belt. About three-fourths of the state's residents live in the Phoenix or Tucson metropolitan areas. A big part of the remaining fourth of the people live in the other cities. Arizona also has a small rural population.

Growth has brought opportunity and prosperity for many. More people, new industries, and jobs mean better business for merchants and housing contractors. More people also mean a wider choice of jobs, schools, recreation, and entertainment.

On the other hand, rapid growth brings many problems. It results in traffic congestion, air pollution, a strain on water and energy sources, and decay in inner cities. These problems threaten the environment and lifestyle that brought people to Arizona in the first place.

Suburbanization

Today much of the new growth is taking place in suburbs. The once-isolated farm towns of Tempe, Scottsdale, and Glendale have expanded to the city limits of Phoenix. These cities—along with fast-growing Mesa and about a dozen smaller places—are part of a complex community known as "greater Phoenix."

The spread of suburbs has taken over some of Arizona's best farmlands and open spaces. The building of interstate highways has added to this problem. When *urban sprawl* closes in on a farm, the market value and taxes go up. A farmer usually decides to sell to housing developers.

The real effects of what is happening to farmland can best be viewed from the air. High up, the new subdivisions look like spreading cancer cells under a microscope. Most city planners want to stop "cancerous" urban sprawl. One way is for cities to buy up farms and desert land and establish *green belts* (open spaces without buildings). The green belts would be wide enough to prevent new *satellite cities* from being built too close to the older cities.

Another way to stop urban sprawl is to allow more high-rise dwellings in the inner city. There is still building room left inside the city limits of most urban areas. One problem, of course, is that developers who want to build subdivisions prefer the large tracts of land found in outlying areas.

A word of caution—problems arise when the population density of inner cities is increased too much. For one thing, the crime rate usually goes up when more people are concentrated in a smaller area. Also, there never seem to be enough parking spaces in high-rise building districts. Noise pollution is another problem.

Transportation Problems

City dwellers in Arizona depend on the automobile for transportation. It is the only way that most people can get to where they are going. But some urban areas in Arizona do not have a system of freeways to move the traffic. During rush hours, the streets are often overcrowded.

Automobiles are a major cause of air pollution. Carbon monoxide from auto *emissions* cannot be seen or smelled, but it is especially aggravating to people with respiratory or heart conditions. The brown haze that hangs over the big cities during the worst pollution season, October to March, is called "smust." It is a combination of smog and desert dust.

Arizona cities do not have subways, elevated trains, or monorails. The urban areas are too spread out for rapid transit systems to operate efficiently. That was the opinion of voters in the Phoenix metropolitan area who defeated a mass transit proposal named "Val Trans." The plan called for 103 miles of high-speed elevated train service as well as more buses and freeways.

Many of the city's workforce go home each night to their homes in the suburbs.

This architectural drawing shows a traffic interchange that links interstate highways 17 and 40 at Flagstaff.

Heavy traffic in Phoenix is a maddening rush hour event for motorists.

Population Predictions for Arizona Counties

	2000	2010	2020
Apache	68,000	77,000	86,000
Cochise	122,000	137,000	150,000
Coconino	123,000	147,000	169,000
Gila	49,000	55,000	61,000
Graham	35,000	44,000	51,000
Greenlee	9,000	9,600	10,300
La Paz	20,000	25,000	29,000
Maricopa	2,954,000	3,710,000	4,516,000
Mohave	148,000	194,000	236,000
Navajo	89,000	100,000	112,000
Pima	854,000	1,032,000	1,206,000
Pinal	162,000	200,000	231,000
Santa Cruz	38,000	46,000	55,000
Yavapai	153,000	198,000	241,000
Yuma	138,000	172,000	210,000

Arizonans Fight in Korea and Vietnam

ARIZONA HAS BEEN GREATLY INVOLVED in national trends and events—the migration of people to the Sun Belt, the civil rights movement, and the *cold war*. In the 1950s and 1960s, the cold war erupted. The United States fought two "hot wars" in Asia to stop communist aggression.

The Korean War started when Russian-trained North Korean troops swept across the boundary into South Korea. A huge army from communist China jumped into the war later. The United Nations rushed to the rescue of South Korea, with the United States providing most of the soldiers and equipment. For the first time, Americans of all races fought side by side in the *desegregated* armed forces.

The first fights between jet planes took place in the skies over North Korea. Helicopters carried troops into battle—another first. On the home front, Arizona's air bases and defense plants hummed with activity. Fort Huachuca grew as the army's center for advanced electronic communications.

The Korean War ended in 1953. But, into the twenty-first century, the United States still has soldiers stationed along the two-and-a-half-mile-wide zone that divides the two Koreas.

What do you think?

The United States has troops stationed all over the world.
- **Do you agree or disagree with this practice?**
- **Why has our government taken on this costly responsibility?**

A memorial in Phoenix honors the brave men who served in the Korean War. About 250 Arizonans are counted among the thousands killed in battle. Can you identify the flags?

Vietnam War (1960s–1973)

The United States got involved in a war trying to save South Vietnam from a takeover by communist-ruled North Vietnam. Americans at home watched a war on television for the first time. They saw soldiers fighting in the rice paddies. The evening news brought pictures of anti-war protesters on college campuses. By 1973 the United States seemed to be in a no-win situation, both on the battle front and in this country. Our government signed a cease-fire agreement and withdrew the military forces from Vietnam. The longest war in American history ended with the United States on the losing side for the first time.

The sacrifices of Americans who died in the war were finally honored with the unveiling of the Vietnam Veterans War Memorial in Washington, D.C. on Veterans Day, 1982.

The names of 631 Arizona soldiers killed or missing in action are engraved on ten granite columns at the Vietnam War Memorial in Phoenix.

Civil Rights for Minorities

AFTER WORLD WAR II, minority groups increased their demands for justice, equality, and opportunity to achieve the American dream. It took many years of change, both in the minds of the people and in Congress, to bring about the equality we see today.

Hispanic Americans—the Largest Ethnic Minority

Hispanic Americans are the largest cultural minority in the United States and in Arizona. Some Hispanic families have lived here for generations. Newcomers, looking for opportunity in America, are rapidly expanding the population. "Hispanic American" is the label that some people

From POW to U.S. Senator

John McCain, flying a Skyhawk dive bomber, was shot down over Hanoi, the capital of North Vietnam. In 1967, while ejecting from the plane, he broke both arms and his right knee. He landed in a small lake and was pulled ashore.

An angry crowd of Vietnamese kicked and bayoneted him. McCain was locked in the Hoa Lo prison, better known as the "Hanoi Hilton." He remained a prisoner of war for five and a half years, much of it in solitary confinement.

After the war, McCain moved to Arizona. He served two terms as a U.S. representative before winning a U.S. Senate seat. McCain, a Republican, was re-elected in 1998 to a third term.

President Richard Nixon greets Lt. Commander (later U.S. Senator) John McCain at a reception for former POWs, 1973.

Anna (Moore) Shaw
1898–1976

Anna Moore grew up in two cultures. Born on the Gila Reservation, Anna learned the traditional customs of the Pimas. She then attended Phoenix Indian School, graduated from Phoenix Union High School, and married Ross Shaw, a Pima-Maricopa. The newlyweds chose to live off the reservation. "We must embrace the white man's ways which are good," she said, "while keeping our pride in being Indian."

Anna taught her three children the ancient customs of their Pima forefathers. She also wrote down the sacred stories for her book, *Pima Indian Legends*—one of the few authentic works on Indian culture told by a Native American.

When Ross Shaw retired, the couple moved back to the reservation. Anna taught the Pima language and culture to children. After her death, Anna Shaw was one of the first women admitted to the Arizona Women's Hall of Fame.

of Mexican ancestry prefer. Many, however, still like to be called "Mexican American," "Chicano," or simply "Mexican."

The people are caught between two countries and different cultures. They have the "old country" next door rather than across an ocean. Their original culture is strongly reinforced by Mexican films, newspapers, and Spanish language programs on radio and television.

A Turning Point for Hispanics

In earlier years, most Hispanic Americans were poor, usually living in *barrios*. They had little education and had to take low-paying jobs. Their health, school attendance, and political involvement were below that of the community as a whole.

World War II created a civilian labor shortage so, with the help of the mine union, Mexican American miners began to get equal pay for equal work. After the war, better-paying jobs in the mines and in construction work opened up. More Hispanics began to reach middle-class status and move out of the *barrios*. Going to college became an achievable goal.

In the 1960s, many Hispanics worked for *La Causa* (the cause)—decent wages, equality under the law, political representation, dignity, and a good self-image. One of the most militant leaders in this movement was Cesar Chavez, who was born in Yuma. Through marches, speeches, television interviews, and long fasts, Chavez inspired young Mexicans to seek *La Causa*.

Mexican Americans became more active in Arizona politics. They elected people to city, county, and state offices. Bert Romero was elected state mine inspector. In 1974 Raul Castro was elected governor. A year later, Alfredo Gutierrez was chosen as majority leader in the state senate. Hispanics have headed the police department in Arizona's two largest cities. Joel Valdez was Tucson's city manager for many years. In 1991 the Board of Regents chose Manuel Pacheco to head the University of Arizona.

Native Americans

"This is Indian country," as the saying goes. Arizona has more Native Americans and reservations than any other state. At least seventeen different Indian languages are spoken in Arizona today. There are also many dialects. The Bureau of Indian Affairs (BIA) divides the tribes here into five cultural groups:

Athapascan tribes (Navajo and Apache)
Pueblo Indians (Hopi and Tewa)
Desert Ranchería tribes (Pima and Tohono O'odham)
Yuman tribes (Yuma, Maricopa, Mohave, Chemehuevi, and Cocopah)
Plateau Ranchería tribes (Havasupai, Hualapai, Yavapai, and Paiute)

The Native American population in Arizona's towns and cities continues to grow as the people leave the reservations in search of greater economic opportunities. Indian leaders hope to develop reservation lands so young people will not have to leave. The BIA has helped by promoting industrial parks on several reservations to provide jobs. Some Arizona tribes have built gambling casinos, creating more jobs and income.

African Americans

"I am an Afro-American," said former U.S. Supreme Court Justice Thurgood Marshall. During three and a half centuries of slavery, segregation, and struggle for equality, blacks have been identified by many labels. They were kept out of the mainstream of American life solely on the basis of skin color and heritage. The Civil War gave them freedom, but the equality promised in the Thirteenth, Fourteenth, and Fifteenth Amendments to the Constitution came slowly.

Until World War II, blacks moved to Arizona mainly from the southern Cotton Belt states. Most of them were farm laborers. (A major exception was lumber workers at McNary.) After the war, use of machines decreased the demand for farm workers. Most blacks moved to the urban areas of Phoenix and Tucson. They soon learned, however, that job opportunities in the cities were scarce and low paying.

Segregation in Schools

Every elementary school "shall segregate pupils of the African race from pupils of the Caucasian race." That was the Arizona law until 1951, though not all school districts followed the law.

Blacks and whites attended the same schools in Prescott, Williams, Morenci, Hayden, and other towns. Douglas segregated Spanish-speaking students (including future governor, Raul Castro) as well as blacks.

Segregated high schools were permitted, but they were not required by law. Two black high schools were opened. One became known as Carver High in Phoenix. The other was Casa Grande-Eloy school. The school was held in an abandoned dance hall halfway between the two towns. The interesting thing is that white students at Casa Grande High School had voted in favor of black students attending their school.

In 1954 the U.S. Supreme Court ruled that segregation in schools is unconstitutional. A year before that decision, the Phoenix Union school board had opened all high schools in that district to all races.

The NAACP

In the 1960s the NAACP (National Association for the Advancement of Colored People) and other groups put pressure on businesses that had no blacks on their payrolls. George Brooks, a minister, and Lincoln Ragsdale, a local mortician, took the lead in Phoenix. They used picket lines and meetings with employers to persuade Woolworth's and other companies to hire blacks.

ARIZONA PORTRAIT

Hayzel Burton Daniels
1907–1992

Hayzel Daniels was one of five children of a black soldier stationed at Fort Huachuca. Hayzel graduated from *integrated* Tucson High School, where he starred in football. After graduating from the U of A, Daniels taught in segregated one-room schools and noticed how badly blacks were treated. "Blacks will never have equal education until the laws are changed," he said.

After service overseas during World War II, Daniels practiced law in Phoenix. In 1950, he and Carl Sims became the first blacks elected to the state legislature. They got a bill passed to amend Arizona's school segregation law. "We deleted the word Negro wherever it appeared in the law," Daniels explained. "The law still allowed segregation of pupils—not Negro pupils, just pupils."

Daniels was happy in 1953 when in two separate court cases the state's segregation law was declared unconstitutional. Later, Daniels served as the first black city judge in Phoenix.

In 1964 Reverend Brooks invited Martin Luther King Jr. from Atlanta, Georgia, to Phoenix. Dr. King called for nonviolent protest against "the many injustices of discrimination and segregation." He said that discrimination in public facilities is "one of the most humiliating situations that the Negro faces."

Civil Rights Acts of 1964 and 1968

The 1964 law was a turning point for civil rights. It outlawed discrimination in all public places—hotels, motels, restaurants, service stations, and places of amusement. No person could be denied access to a public place solely on the basis of race.

Most restaurants, movie theaters, and lodging places in Arizona had already opened their doors to African Americans. The Phoenix city council desegregated Sky Harbor Restaurant at the city airport in 1952. After black sit-ins at lunch counters, Walgreens Drug Store in Tucson began serving all races. During the 1950s, movie theaters stopped separating blacks and Native Americans from other people. Before that time, minorities had to sit in the balcony.

Until the 1960s, most low-rent housing in Phoenix and Tucson was segregated. Black soldiers at Luke and Williams Air Bases, for example, usually were unable to find apartments or trailer parks where they could live. In 1968, Congress passed a law against discrimination in the rental or sale of housing. This "open housing" civil rights law made it possible for blacks to rent or own property in previously all-white neighborhoods.

Chinese Americans

Chinese men came to Arizona to build railroads or dig ore in the mines. Many of them ended up cooking and doing the laundry for other workers. Even though the Chinese usually took jobs others would not take, some mines put up "No Chinese Need Apply" signs. The Birdcage Theatre in Tombstone did a play called "The Chinese Must Go." One newspaper ran the headline "Exit Pigtails." The territorial legislature passed a law forbidding marriages between Chinese and whites. In 1882, the U.S. Congress enacted the Chinese Exclusion Act, forbidding immigration of laborers from China.

Chinese Americans quietly survived in towns from Nogales to Flagstaff and from Yuma to Clifton. How? The Chinese had strong family, religious, and business ties. They fought prejudice with more hard work and education. Many became truck gardeners, producing cabbage, garlic, and other vegetables that the towns needed. Growing neighborhoods began to welcome the convenience of a Chinese grocery store on a nearby corner.

Slowly the Chinese gained acceptance. By 1960 "Chinatown" in Phoenix was gone. More than 1,100 Chinese were living throughout the city. The First Chinese Baptist Church had a large, active congregation. Family associations, however, still played a vital role in Chinese progress. The Ong, Yee, Wong, and other families raised money for business investments.

Esther Don Tang

Esther Don Tang prospers as a Tucson businesswoman and volunteers in dozens of community organizations. Mrs. Tang served as a Pima College board member. For many years, she directed a neighborhood center near her downtown birthplace.

Her father, Don Wah, came to Tucson as a cook for railroad workers. After saving some money, he went to China and brought back a bride. They had ten children—nine girls and a boy. Esther was born in a room connected to the family's small store in Chinatown.

"We didn't have much at first," Esther recalled, "but we always had food from our grocery store. We ate what we couldn't sell before it spoiled. I grew up speaking English, Chinese, and Spanish. The races intermingled but there was prejudice. At movie theaters, Chinese grownups had to sit in the balcony. The public pools were off limits to us, so we would go swimming in the irrigation ditches. After World War II, Chinese young people were becoming professionals. We had our first Chinese dentist and the first lawyers," she said with pride. Mrs. Tang is proud of her Chinese heritage, but she is very much a part of mainstream America.

Esther Don Tang

Soleng Tom

Soleng Tom stands out among many Chinese success stories. An immigrant from China, Tom learned English by memorizing a few words each day and singing them over and over.

Education took him from a laundry scrub board to a college degree in aeronautical engineering and his own pilot training school.

After World War II Tom turned to business, real estate, and cotton farming. In 1948 he opened Arizona's first supermarket in South Tucson. He also gave back to the community as Chinese were taught to do. For many years Tom was on the Tucson Board of Education. An elementary school in the district is named in his honor.

Other Asian Americans

Japanese Americans, few in number in Arizona, also value education and hard work. Many of the Japanese immigrants became intensive farmers, producing lots of vegetables and flowers on a small amount of land. The Japanese flower gardens in south Phoenix became a major tourist attraction after World War II.

Wing Ong was elected the first Chinese state senator in 1966.

In recent decades, hundreds of Vietnamese, Koreans, and Filipinos have settled in Arizona. Thuan VanTran and his family came to America as refugees after the Vietnam War.

(Photo by Kent Miles)

Rights for Women

WHEN YOU DECIDE ON A CAREER, what will you consider? Your abilities? Your interests? Your education? Yes, all of these factors. If you are a girl, should you have the same choices as a boy? Will you have a career or will you devote full time to home and children? These questions are important to your future and to the rights of women.

Women in Arizona and the rest of the country have been discriminated against just because they are women. If they worked outside the home, only low-paying jobs were open to them. They usually did not get equal pay while doing the same work as men. Very few women were bosses, business owners, government officials, or professional people. But by the 1960s, some women were asking, "Does equality of opportunity apply to women as well as men?"

In 1972 the U.S. Congress passed the Equal Rights Amendment (ERA) and sent it to the state legislatures. The purpose of the ERA was to give women equal status with men. But the amendment's one-sentence mention of "equality" was vague and gave no specifics. Arizona's two U.S. senators, Barry Goldwater and Paul Fannin, voted against the ERA bill in Congress and gave their reasons. "The ERA, if carried to extremes, could harm rather than help women," Fannin said. "Would women be subject to the military draft and combat duty? Would they lose *alimony* or child support [money] after divorce?"

During the next ten years, Arizonans who opposed the ERA said it was anti-family. "Equality of men and women means that husbands will no longer have to support their families," argued one anti-ERA woman to a committee of the legislature.

Pro-ERA people held rallies at the state capitol and imported well-known speakers from other states. Popular Arizona State Senator Sandra Day O'Connor said "the ERA is greatly misunderstood by the public." In her opinion, the amendment would not weaken the family. In 1981 Mrs. O'Connor introduced a *resolution* in the state senate to ratify (approve) the ERA. But the legislature voted down the amendment for the tenth straight year.

The ERA was never ratified by the required three-fourths of the state legislatures. Arizona and other states, however, passed laws protecting women's rights. The equal rights campaign also inspired both pro-ERA and anti-ERA women to get into politics. In 1998 Arizona became the first state to elect women to fill all the top executive offices.

Women demonstrated for and against the ERA.

People with Disabilities

RONALD GARDNER IS AN ATTORNEY. He often travels to Washington, D.C., to work for laws that will help people with disabilities. Mr. Gardner grew up in a family of nine children in Duncan. He attended public schools, participating in sports, dances, and other events. He graduated from college and then law school by listening to lectures and having other students read books and examinations to him. Mr. Gardner and two of his brothers have been blind since birth.

Ronald J. Gardner has been blind since birth. Today he is an attorney, helping other people with disabilities.

> When I was in school I couldn't read my textbooks. My mother read to me and my friends read to me, but I didn't like having to depend on others. Sometimes it was easier for the teacher to let me get by with less homework. I knew I could pass the tests, but sometimes the teacher would not make me do the work.
>
> Today, students with visual problems can get textbooks on cassette tapes. They can also get books on computer disks and have a computer read to them. Students with other disabilities can participate in school activities in wheelchairs. All of us have the desire to be independent, and these things are just one more step.
>
> —Ronald J. Gardner, Attorney

Rights for People with Disabilities

The Americans with Disabilities Act (ADA) of 1990 prohibits discrimination against disabled people in both jobs and services. What does this law mean to Arizonans? Ramps and special parking places must be provided for people with wheelchairs. Restrooms must accommodate people with different needs. An employer cannot fire someone just because of a disability as long as the person is capable of doing the work. A 1996 amendment to the law requires schools to provide every child with a visual impairment an opportunity to learn braille. The law means that disabled people can be more independent.

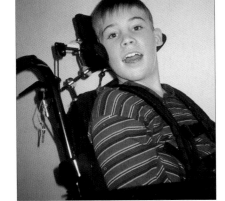

Aaron Slaugh has cerebral palsy and uses a wheelchair to get around. How did the new laws help him?

What do you think?

Review your regular day. Then think of a disability and what the same day would be like if you had that disability.

- What could you still do the same? What changes would you have to make?
- What changes could be made at your school to help people with a disability participate in more school activities?

The Colorado River and Glen Canyon Dam

OLDTIMERS CAN REMEMBER when melting snow in the Rockies transformed a slender Colorado stream in winter into a wild, mudgushing red torrent in the spring. Yuma and the low-lying valleys of California feared the mighty river as it rushed south from the Grand Canyon. Levees along the river didn't always hold back the raging flood waters.

The 1950s and 1960s brought many changes in the way the people of the West use the Colorado River. Now the spring runoff is stored in manmade lakes behind dams. The lakes behind Arizona's dams are world famous as water playgrounds. The water serves useful purposes. Glen Canyon can release water through turbines to generate the right amount of electricity for Phoenix and other cities in the West.

At first, nearly everyone liked the idea of building Glen Canyon Dam. When it was finished in 1963, water gradually backed up 186 miles to form Lake Powell— a huge storage and recreational reservoir. The gorgeous red sandstone cliffs of Glen Canyon and its surrounding valleys were flooded. The high water made new glens, rock formations, and canyons accessible by boat.

Before the dam, a few hundred adventurers drifted through the canyon each year on inner tubes, rubber rafts, or anything that floats. Is it worth sacrificing that kind of experience for the kilowatts the dam generates plus the opportunity for 10,000 people to stand under Rainbow Bridge on a summer weekend?

—William Smart, *Lake Powell: A Different Light*

ARIZONA: A Journey of Discovery

Glen Canyon Dam (Photo by Tom Till)

Shooting the rapids on the
Colorado River is a great sport.

Rainbow Bridge is one of nature's grandest accomplishments. Before Glen Canyon was flooded, only a few people could make the difficult trip overland to stand in the shadow of the largest natural bridge in the United States. Now tourists get within a short distance of the bridge by boat.

Today, however, few things rile environmentalists more than Glen Canyon Dam. Edward Abbey, an environmentalist who spent many years in Utah and Arizona, often expressed his feelings about the dam:

I was one of the lucky few who saw Glen Canyon before it was drowned. . . . here was Eden, a portion of the earth's original paradise. . . . Of course Glen Canyon will be restored eventually through natural processes (silt filling up the lake), but it may take a few centuries. Pray for an earthquake.

Why the Controversy?

Electricity, water storage for irrigation, flood control, water recreation—these benefits of the dam and Lake Powell are offset by flooding of Glen Canyon and damage to the ecosystem downstream in Grand Canyon. The clear cold water released from Lake Powell has wiped out several species of warm-water native fish. Rainbow trout do better but they can be left high and dry when the demand for electricity is low and little water is flowing through the turbines. On the other hand, a big volume of water erodes the sandy beaches. The clear water also leaches soil of nutrients needed for vegetation.

Lake Powell Photo by Tom Till

Arizona's three state universities are:
- University of Arizona (U of A)
- Arizona State University (ASU)
- Northern Arizona University (NAU)

Opportunities for Higher Education

Territorial pioneers had the foresight to establish schools of higher learning in Arizona. Modern educational leaders have guided the state's colleges to high national ratings in many academic fields. The three tax-supported universities rank among the best in the nation. They are trying hard to meet the current needs of students. They are developing outstanding research facilities.

There are other universities and colleges in Arizona. Grand Canyon University is a four-year private school in Phoenix. It is sponsored by the Southern Baptists. Another important private school, the American Graduate School of International Management in Glendale, enjoys a global reputation. Students come from all over the world to study economics, languages, and other subjects. The University of Phoenix tries to meet the educational needs of working adult students.

A two-year community college system provides a wide range of educational opportunities for high school graduates. In addition to liberal arts subjects, the community colleges offer many vocational and technical courses.

Off in Space

Faculty and students at the University of Arizona have been involved in the lunar (moon), Mars, Saturn, and other space programs. On July 4, 1997, the *Pathfinder* bounced several times on its air-bag cushion and rolled safely to a stop on Mars. Then the U of A camera beamed back striking color pictures of the red planet.

The world's best telescope mirrors are cast in a big spinning oven on the U of A campus. The spinning creates a convex lens that sees deep into space.

This picture is a mosaic of many snapshots taken by Imager and sent 309 million miles to Earth. Imager is a camera that was designed and built by the U of A Lunar and Planetary Lab.

ARIZONA: A Journey of Discovery

Preserving Our Rich Heritage

A STUDY OF THE PAST would be impossible without written records and artifacts of people who came before us. Much can be learned, for example, about native people from the diaries kept by Spanish explorers and missionaries.

There are dozens of local museums and historical societies throughout the state. The Arizona Historical Society in Tucson is Arizona's official *repository* for historical materials. Besides a huge library, the society also maintains a museum featuring colorful dioramas and displays. The Arizona Department of Library and Archives at the capitol in Phoenix houses the official government records of the territory and state.

A mariachi violinist entertains in Tucson. (Photo by Gill Kenny)

For years the Tucson Festival Society sponsored ethnic programs, highlighting the colorful songs, dances, and customs of Indian and Mexican people. (Photo by Gill Kenny)

Videotaping and Oral History Interviews

Videotaping is a modern way to leave a record for future generations. Hopi students at Hoteville have taped their Buffalo dance, basket weaving, a mother storing blue corn ears for winter, and other scenes from their culture. Navajos videotaped medicine men discussing tribal customs.

"We want young people to know why we believe in harmony with nature, why certain ceremonies are held," said Alfred Yazzie at the Navajo Curriculum Center.

"Ride 'em cowboy!" Prescott's rodeo offers thrills and excitement.

Modern-day students are a part of the Arizona journey.

The audio-taped oral interview is another popular way of recording history. A good example is the collection at the Arizona State University library called "The Lives of Arizona Women: An Oral History Project." Hundreds of "ordinary" women—with different racial, ethnic, and economic backgrounds—told their life stories. Each woman contributed to the development of Arizona by doing "just what the day brought."

You Are a Part of Arizona's Journey of Discovery

OUR STUDY OF ARIZONA'S PAST GIVES US an appreciation for the lives and achievements of people who lived before us. There were Indian leaders, fur trappers, soldiers, merchants, miners, ranchers, farmers, politicians, scientists, teachers, religious leaders, housewives, artists, industrialists, and many others.

Arizona's history has been shaped by outside influences, too. Wars, the Great Depression, the population explosion, and many modern inventions—automobiles, airplanes, radios, televisions, air conditioners, and modern computers—have contributed to our lives.

A knowledge of the past gives us better perspective to make decisions for the future. We should all remember the American Indian who never got lost because he always looked back to see where he had been.

activity

Problem Solving
The true test of character when problems develop (in government, in society, or in one's personal life) is what we do about them. What do you consider the five most important problems that Arizonans should face up to and try to solve?

1. List the advantages and disadvantages of population growth.

2. Explain why World War II was a turning point for Hispanic people.

3. What is *La Causa?* Explain.

4. List Arizona's five American Indian cultural groups.

5. Why do some Native Americans move from the reservations to cities?

6. What did the U.S. Supreme Court say about segregation in 1954?

7. What did the Civil Rights Act of 1964 accomplish?

8. List some Asian nationalities in Arizona.

9. What do the letters ERA stand for? What were some of the issues involved?

10. What do the letters ADA stand for? What did the new law do for people with disabilities?

11. List Arizona's three state universities and two of Arizona's other universities and colleges.

12. List several ways in which Arizona's heritage is being preserved.

Growth has brought first-class entertainment to Arizona. Dancer DeAnn Petruschke of Ballet Arizona performs in *The Nutcracker*.
(Photo by David Cooper)

Matt Williams, third baseman for the Arizona Diamondbacks, knocks a homerun in Phoenix's Bank One Ballpark.

chapter 15

PEOPLE TO KNOW
Governor Jane Dee Hull
Governor Sidney P. Osborn
Governor J. Howard Pyle
Governor Raul Castro
Governor Jack Williams
Governor Thomas Campbell
Governor Bruce Babbitt
Governor George W.P. Hunt
Councilman Calvin Goode
Justice Lorna Lockwood
Justice Sandra Day
    O'Connor
Justice Ernest W.
    McFarland
Congressman Morris Udall
U.S. Senator Barry
    Goldwater

In 1998 Arizona voters made national history by electing a woman to every top state office. The "Fabulous Five" (left to right) are: Governor Jane Dee Hull, Secretary of State Betsey Bayless, Attorney General Janet Napolitano, Treasurer Carol Springer, and Superintendent of Public Instruction Lisa Graham Keegan. (Photo by *Arizona Daily Star*)

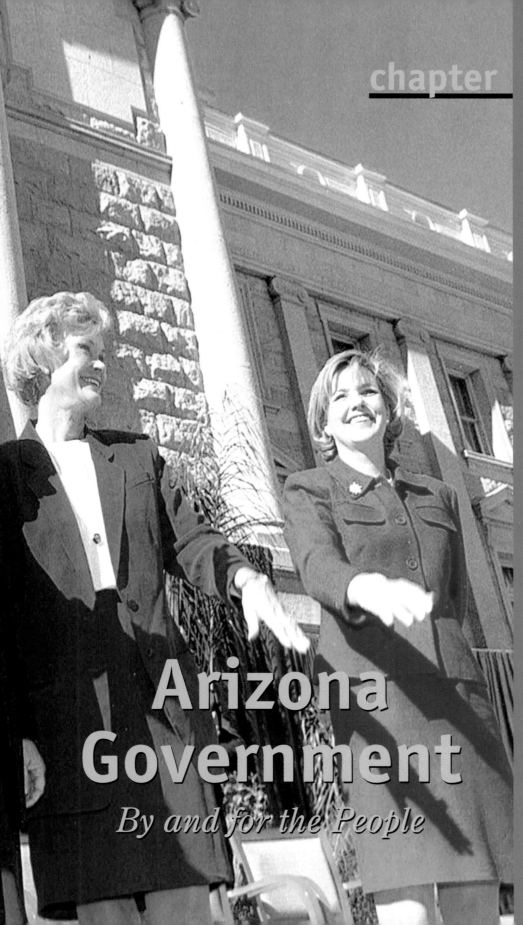

TERMS TO UNDERSTAND

revenue
representative democracy
direct democracy
bill
whip
absolute majority
veto
initiative
referendum
extradition
impeachment
felony
advisory opinion
commission
criminal case
civil case
plaintiff
defendant
misdemeanor
civil offense
magistrate
jurisdiction
arson
embezzlement
grand jury
petit jury
hung jury
charter
incorporate
direct primary
nominee
general election

Arizona Government

By and for the People

Arizona's State Capitol

The "Great Seal of the State of Arizona" must be on all official documents.

Our State Government

PEOPLE OFTEN TALK ABOUT "the government," but there are different levels and branches. The federal government works for all the states. Arizona's state government is concerned only with this state. A county, city, or tribal government deals with local matters.

State government affects our lives from the cradle to the grave. When a baby is born, the law says that the birth must be recorded with the state. Then the state pays part of the cost of educating students in the public schools. When a person is old enough to drive, he or she must have a state driver's license. Doctors and teachers must have state licenses to work in their profession. So does the undertaker.

There are three branches of state government—the legislative, executive, and judicial. This framework has not changed greatly since statehood.

State government, however, is much larger in size and functions today. Why? As the population grows, government is expected to provide more services. Highways, schools, law enforcement, health care, welfare, courts—these services and many more cost money. The annual state budget gets bigger every year to keep up with Arizona's growth.

To pay for services, state government has to raise *revenue* (money). That means taxes on income, sales, gasoline, and other things. As citizens who pay taxes, we should study government. We want our tax money spent wisely. A knowledge of government is the first step to good citizenship.

Political Parties

Political parties are groups of people who share many of the same ideas about government. Most people choose either the Democratic Party or the Republican Party. These are national parties. They are also the two main parties in Arizona. There are other parties, called third parties. As another choice, some citizens do not belong to any party. They run for office or vote as Independents.

The Republican Party is the Grand Old Party, or the GOP for short. Its symbol is the elephant. The Democratic Party symbol is the donkey.

What do you think?

"I pledge allegiance to the flag of the United States of America and to the republic for which it stands, . . ." A "republic," our form of government, is a representative democracy. What is that? How does it differ from a direct democracy?

Legislative Branch

ARIZONA'S CONSTITUTION gave the legislature most of the power in state government. The main jobs of the legislature are to make laws and to decide how the state's money will be spent. Its power comes from "control over the purse strings."

Arizona has two houses—the Senate and the House of Representatives. This system is called *representative democracy*. This means that instead of all the people voting for the laws, the people elect representatives to vote for them.

Districts

Arizona is divided into thirty legislative districts with about equal population. Every two years the voters in each district elect one senator and two representatives. More than half the districts are in heavily populated Maricopa County—metropolitan Phoenix.

What do you think?

• What did Chief Justice Earl Warren mean when he said, "Legislators represent people, not trees or acres . . ."?
• The "one-man, one-vote" rule does not apply to the U.S. Senate. If it did, would Arizona gain or lose U.S. senators? Why?

Officers and Committees of the Legislature

Each house has a presiding officer. The House chooses a speaker and the Senate elects a president. In each house, the majority party chooses a majority floor leader. Each house also has a minority floor leader. Each

"One-Man, One-Vote" Rule

Every state legislator must represent the same number of people, said the U. S. Supreme Court in 1964. To comply with this ruling, Arizona stopped electing two state senators from each county and divided the state into thirty equal districts. This change shifted the political power from rural counties to Maricopa County, where more than half the people live.
—*Reynolds vs. Sims* (1964)
U.S. Supreme Court decision

Sandra Day O'Connor was the first woman to serve as majority floor leader in the state senate. Later she became the first female U.S. Supreme Court Justice.

A Legislative Option

Here is what one former senator, Bill McCune, said about the legislature:

"First, the legislature is an amazing creation. Do you know any group with so many determined, active members that can reach a decision on any question? I don't.

"The only people who get shut out are those who expect everyone to look after their interests without lifting a finger. How many times have you written your representatives? Can you even name them? Do you then wonder why they don't always do what you'd like?"

of these leaders has the job of getting *bills* passed that his or her party wants. They also try to defeat bills they don't want. Each floor leader works with a *whip*, who rounds up as many votes as possible on each bill.

Most of the work on bills is done by committees such as the agriculture, education, transportation, and rules committees. A committee may hold public hearings on a bill. It may listen to lobbyists (persons hired by groups or companies to try to promote or defeat bills). Most bills are "tabled" or "held for further study" by the committee. This often means the bill is dead and will never be debated on the floor.

Special committees are set up to work on a single issue, and then they are done away with. The most common kind of special group is called a conference committee. It is used when the House and Senate pass different versions of the same bill. The conference committee, made up of members from both houses, tries to work out a compromise.

AzScam

A legislator can be expelled for "disorderly behavior" by a two-thirds vote of the members of the house to which he or she was elected. A legislator who is convicted in the courts of accepting a bribe also loses his or her seat and may get a hefty fine and a prison term.

In 1991, seven legislators were charged with accepting bribes to vote for legalized gambling in Arizona. The Phoenix police department videotaped legislators taking money from its undercover man. Six of the legislators resigned their seats before going to trial. A seventh was expelled by fellow senators. This bribery scandal became known as "AzScam."

How a Bill Becomes a Law

Any representative or senator can introduce a bill. The clerk gives the bill a "first reading" by number, title, and sponsor only. The bill is then referred to one or more committees. (For example, a bill to limit noise levels on motorcycles was sent to three committees—health, transportation, and rules.)

The powerful Rules Committee reviews every bill which has cleared all other committees. This group decides whether the bill will be sent to the Committee of the Whole for debate. The Committee of the Whole is an informal meeting of the House or Senate members acting as one big committee. Floor debate takes place here.

Sometimes a bill becomes a "Christmas tree." Many amendments and other bills are added to it like ornaments. In the end the bill will not be anything like it was in the beginning. The Senate once amended a bill by adding eleven other bills to make one law. When it came time to vote, the senator who had introduced the original bill showed his disgust. He voted "aye, aye, nay, aye, nay, nay." The members had a good laugh. They all knew how hard it was to get a bill through the legislature without change.

In the Committee of the Whole, only a simple majority (more than half of the members present that day) is needed to recommend that a bill be passed.

Next the bill is returned to the presiding officer and the Rules Committee. They decide if and when a bill will be placed on the calendar and given a "third reading" at a formal session of the full House or Senate. To pass, it must have an *absolute majority* (more than half of all the members). That would be 16 of 30 votes in the Senate and 31 of 60 votes in the House.

A passed bill goes to the other house and the same steps are repeated. Both houses must pass a bill in the same form before it goes to the governor.

If the governor signs it, the bill becomes a law ninety days after the end of the session. There is an exception, however. If the legislature attaches the emergency clause and passes the bill by a two-thirds vote, the bill becomes a law instantly.

The governor may *veto* the bill. That keeps it from becoming a law unless the legislature votes again and passes it by a two-thirds vote.

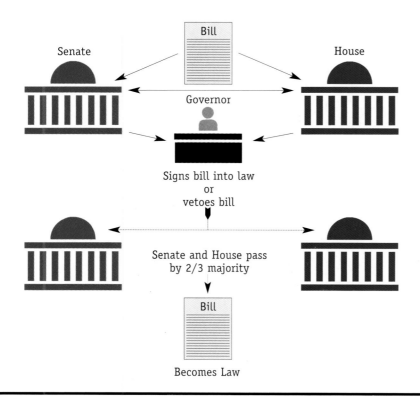

Impeachment Power

A majority of the House of Representatives can impeach (accuse) an elected state official or judge. In 1964 the House impeached two members of the Corporation Commission for bribery. The House chose William Rehnquist, than a Phoenix lawyer, to prosecute the commissioners. But the Senate, sitting as a jury, did not have the two-thirds vote needed to convict them.

A few years later, Rehnquist was appointed to the U.S. Supreme Court. As the chief justice in 1998, he presided over the impeachment trial of U.S. President William Clinton.

In 1988 Governor Evan Mecham became the first person in Arizona to be removed from office by the impeachment process. The House charged him with violating campaign finance laws by loaning money to his car agency from money donated to his campaign. Many Arizonans tuned in to watch the five-week trial.

"I guess they didn't like my politics," Mecham said, while admitting that some of his actions as governor were unusual. A tendency to "put his foot into his mouth" may have been the main reason for his removal from office. His careless, off-the-cuff remarks offended leaders of his own party, the news media, Afro-Americans, and other groups. Mecham's disruptive style of governing disappointed people who liked his program to trim the budget and cut taxes.

Secretary of State Rose Mofford completed Mecham's term. The first woman to hold the office of governor, she chose not to run for a full term in 1990.

Proposition 200

In 1982, Proposition 200 failed. Called the "bottle bill," this measure would have required a five-cent deposit on each beverage container. The idea was to cut down litter along roads and in parks by getting people to return bottles and cans.

The initiative was started by Steve and Betsy McKellar, a young Flagstaff couple. They found out that the legislature had turned down a bottle deposit bill eight times. They drew up a bill and held a Phoenix press conference.

More than seventy-five groups, including the Arizona Wildlife Federation and the League of Women Voters, said they would help. Together they got 77,000 voters to sign the initiative petitions—more signatures than were needed to get the measure on the ballot.

The opposition was strong, too. Beer and soft drink companies, grocery stores, and the Chamber of Commerce advertised against the bill. They said the bill would push prices up. Stores would have to hire more clerks and add storage space for the bottles people brought back for a refund. After a lively campaign, the people voted down the bill by a two-to-one margin.

Initiative and Referendum

The voters can make a law or change the constitution through the *initiative* or *referendum*. The initiative is the process by which a person or group may write a law or constitutional amendment and get it on the ballot for the voters to pass or defeat.

To get the initiative on the ballot, petitions must be signed by a certain number of voters. For a new law it takes 10 percent of the number of votes cast for the governor in the last election. A constitutional amendment takes 15 percent.

A referendum is a way to refer (send) a bill from the legislature directly to the people for a vote. There are two ways to get a referendum on the ballot.

The legislature may willingly place a bill on the ballot. The legislature in 1991, for example, put the Martin Luther King Jr. holiday bill on the 1992 election ballot. The legislature left it up to the people to decide if we should add a new state holiday.

Second, the people who are against an already-passed bill can force the legislature to put it on the ballot for another vote. Petitions to force this move must be signed by at least 5 percent of the number of people who voted for governor in the last election. The petitions have to be filed within ninety days after the legislature adjourns.

Ex-governor Bruce Babbitt addresses a joint session of the legislature. See the electric voting board above the Speaker of the House's platform.

ARIZONA: A Journey of Discovery

Executive Branch

THE EXECUTIVE BRANCH is charged with enforcing state laws and administering the state government. This branch is headed by five elected officers: governor, secretary of state, attorney general, treasurer, and superintendent of public instruction. They are elected to four-year terms. To perform their duties, the executive officers are assisted by numerous state agencies and thousands of state employees.

The Governor is the Chief Executive

The Arizona governor "wears many hats." As an executive it is his or her job to see that all laws passed by the legislature are put into operation. Another important duty is to appoint department directors, judges, and about 500 members of boards and commissions.

The governor supervises agencies over which he/she has authority. In this regard, the governor appoints administrators to carry out his/her policies. The governor puts together a budget each year and presents it to the legislature. The governor is commander of the Arizona National Guard in peacetime. As the symbol of state government, the governor appears at all kinds of ceremonies to make speeches and cut ribbons.

The governor's most important duty is to work with the legislature. He or she gives the "State of the State" address at the opening session of the legislature. Bills become laws when the governor signs them. Or, the governor may veto a bill. The governor has some judicial power. For example, he or she may grant a pardon to someone. A pardon is the legal release of a person from being punished.

The governor has sole authority in *extradition*—the return of a fugitive to the state from which he fled. Governor Jack Williams once agreed to extradite a man to Arkansas only if that state promised to treat him fairly. The convict had escaped from an Arkansas prison farm with only a short time left to serve. He had settled in Tucson, where he had a job, a family, and was living as a good citizen.

Secretary of State

The secretary is the acting governor if the governor is out of state. He or she is the chief elections officer. Candidates for state office must file at the secretary's office. Initiative and referendum petitions are filed there, too. The office prepares the publicity pamphlet which explains the propositions (initiatives and referendums) that will be on the ballot. The secretary gets state laws printed and performs many clerical duties.

The secretary of state is the first in line to take over if the governor dies, resigns, is removed by the *impeachment* process, or is found guilty of committing a *felony*.

ARIZONA PORTRAIT

Jane Dee Hull

Jane Hull was born in Kansas. A former teacher, she served fifteen years in the Arizona House of Representatives. Her fellow legislators there chose her as the first female Speaker of the House. Then, in 1994, the voters elected her secretary of state. She modernized and computerized that office.

Secretary of State Hull took the oath as Arizona's twentieth governor after Governor Fife Symington resigned in 1997. A year later, Hull became the first woman elected governor of Arizona by the voters. In fact, for the first time in any state, women candidates won all five top executive offices in the 1998 election.

Governor Hull brings together people with different views to improve education and school financing. She gives priority to children's programs, job training for high-tech jobs, and lower taxes.

Sidney P. Osborn
1884–1948

"Sidney P. Osborn, Governor of Arizona." Osborn wrote this in one of his sixth-grade books at the old Central School in downtown Phoenix. He knew what he wanted to be. After several defeats, Osborn won in 1940. He was the only governor to be elected four terms in a row.

While Osborn was governor, the legislature finally joined six other states in the Colorado River Compact. The federal government then allowed Arizona to take its share of Colorado River water. In 1946 the voters approved the "right to work" initiative which permits a person to work without joining a union. Osborn and the labor unions opposed this initiative.

Governor Osborn did not finish his fourth term. He was slowly dying of Lou Gehrig's disease. When he could no longer speak, he talked to his secretary by pointing with a pencil in his mouth to letters on an alphabet chart. Osborn died in 1948 while still in office.

Attorney General

The attorney general heads the Department of Law. The attorney general is the legal adviser for all state agencies. His or her *advisory opinion* has the effect of a law until a court issues an opinion that is different.

The attorney general supervises county attorneys. The Department of Law handles a few criminal cases itself. In the 1970s, for example, the attorney general prosecuted the major milk and bread companies for fixing prices. The court made them return money to customers.

The attorney general can form a state grand jury to consider evidence and decide if a person should be charged with a crime and brought to trial.

Treasurer

The treasurer is in charge of all state funds. It is the job of this officer to receive revenue collected by state agencies and to account for money spent.

Superintendent of Public Instruction

The superintendent heads the Department of Education. This department gives money to school districts as directed by the legislature. An important duty of the superintendent's office is to see that schools offer the courses required by the state constitution and laws.

State Mine Inspector

The state mine inspector is an elected position, but is not classified as an executive officer. The state mine inspector sees that state health and safety rules are followed in the mines.

State Government Reorganized into Departments

The state constitution gave the governor little power. Then, after 1912, the legislature created many new boards, commissions, agencies, bureaus, divisions, and departments. For more than half a century, however, the governor had little authority over all of the government boards and agencies. (One exception was Governor Sidney P. Osborn. He had each of his appointees sign an undated letter of resignation before starting to work. Later, if Osborn was not happy with the employee's work or attitude, he dated the letter and announced the person had retired.)

By the time Jack Williams took office in 1967, the number of agencies had grown. Governor Williams began grouping them into departments. The agencies were reduced by a third.

The line of authority now goes through the governor, who appoints a director to run each department. The governor, with some exceptions, may also remove a director for just cause.

Departments in the Executive Branch

Here are a few departments that answer to the governor. Match the title of each department with the job it does:

Administration	a. Keeps highways safe
Commerce	b. Builds and repairs state roads
Corrections	c. Helps to control diseases
Economic Security	d. Its work includes child welfare programs
Environmental Quality	e. Helps the governor to prepare the budget
Health Services	f. Collects income and other taxes
Public Safety	g. Keeps convicts in prison
Revenue	h. Promotes business for Arizona companies
Transportation	i. Keeps consumers from being cheated
Weights and Measures	j. Is concerned with clean air and the proper disposal of hazardous wastes

Weights and Measures

Do you always get what you pay for? Maybe not if you buy it by the pound, gallon, minute, or mile.

Some years ago, a newspaper reporter set out to see if measuring devices used in Arizona were accurate. He sold a bag of aluminum cans to a recycler. He had his gold ring weighed at a pawn shop. He bought ten gallons of gas. Later he had the octane rating of the gas checked. In every case the reporter was cheated. All the businesses were violating state law.

Today Arizona has a Department of Weights and Measures. Its job is to inspect scales, meters, and other measuring devices. It tries to protect consumers.

How important is the Department of Weights and Measures? Make a list of ten things that your family buys which have to be weighed or measured. Look at a grocery store scale or a gas meter; what do you see that shows its accuracy?

An inspector checks a gasoline pump for accuracy.

ARIZONA PORTRAIT

J. Howard Pyle
1906–1987

"I was elected governor because I am not a politician," said Howard Pyle, a popular Phoenix radio man. A Republican, Pyle was first elected in 1950. At the time, Democrats in Arizona outnumbered Republicans by more than four to one. His friend, city councilman Barry Goldwater, flew him all over the state to campaign.

Pyle's KTAR radio program, "Arizona Highlights," had made him the state's best-known voice. Every year he broadcast the Easter sunrise service at the Grand Canyon for NBC radio. During World War II Pyle had gone to the Pacific to tape interviews with Arizona men in the service.

After two terms as governor, Pyle worked for President Eisenhower in the White House. Later he headed the National Safety Council where he fought for seat belts, a defensive driving course, and a campaign against drunk driving.

Some State Commissions Are Still Independent

Some *commissions* have not been brought under the control of the governor. The Corporation Commission has important duties that affect nearly every Arizona resident. It regulates public utilities that are not owned by cities and towns. Electric, natural gas, telephone, and telegraph companies must get the commission's approval to raise rates. The commission also licenses corporations that do business in Arizona.

The Industrial Corporation is in charge of the Workmen's Compensation Fund. This money comes from the tax paid by all businesses that hire three or more workers. The money is used to pay workers who get injured on the job.

Judicial Branch

THE WORD "JUDICIAL" IS TIED TO THE WORDS "judge" and "justice." It has to do with courts. The courts protect the rights of all citizens. They guarantee justice based on the law. The state court system was set up by the Arizona Constitution.

There are two kinds of court cases. In *criminal cases* the court decides if an accused person is guilty or innocent. In *civil cases* the court settles many kinds of disputes between persons. A civil case might be a claim for damages following an automobile accident. It might be over a broken contract or a request for a divorce. It could be over someone's will and how an inheritance should be divided.

The Judicial Branch in Arizona Has Four Levels of Courts

- Supreme Court
- Court of Appeals
- Superior Court
- Lower Courts (Justice of the Peace and municipal courts)

A Justice of the Peace Court

Justice of the Peace Courts

These are the people's courts. Each county in Arizona is divided into justice of the peace precincts (regions). A justice is elected in each precinct.

The JP courts give the most people easy access to the justice system. These courts handle civil suits if the amount of money in question is under a certain amount. The amount in the year 2000 was $5,000. The *plaintiff* is the party in a lawsuit who sues another party—the *defendant*.

Every JP court in Arizona has a small claims division that settles most civil claims up to $2,500 very quickly. There is no jury. Landlord-renter disputes are a common type of case in a small claims court. The judgment of the JP or hearing officer is final.

Misdemeanors, however, can be tried in a JP court. These are lesser crimes such as petty theft, disturbing the peace, or speeding more than 20 miles per hour over the limit. Less serious traffic violations are called *civil offenses* instead of crimes. They include running a red light or speeding less than 20 miles per hour over the speed limit. The fines for civil offenses are lower.

Municipal Court

Each town or city in Arizona has a municipal court. It is also called the police court or the city court.

Magistrates (judges) hear cases that arise out of the breaking of a town or city ordinance (law). Traffic laws bring the largest number of people to this court. A person found guilty of a misdemeanor in a municipal court can appeal to the Superior Court.

Superior Court

The Superior Court is the great trial court in Arizona. Each county has at least one Superior Court judge. To qualify, Superior Court judges must be lawyers. They serve a four-year term.

The Superior Court has *jurisdiction* in civil suits where the amount in question is more than a certain amount—$5,000 in the year 2000. Divorce cases keep some judges busy. All felony cases arising under state law are also tried in Superior Court. Felonies are major crimes such as murder, robbery, *arson*, *embezzlement*, or check forgery.

Juvenile cases are also handled by the Superior Court. Youths may have a lawyer and all other rights in court. The U.S. Supreme Court decided that juveniles have these rights in the famous *Gault* case. This case started when a fifteen-year-old boy in Globe was accused of making an obscene call. He was put in detention without being told his rights. These are the right to have a lawyer, the right to be silent when arrested, and the right to cross-examine witnesses.

ARIZONA PORTRAIT

Raul H. Castro

"I was a typical Mexican boy in a border community," said Raul Castro, Arizona's first Mexican American governor. Born in a mining town in Mexico, Raul grew up in Douglas. He was one of fourteen children of a poor copper miner and a midwife.

After finishing high school he hitchhiked to Flagstaff, got a job in the college kitchen, and earned a teaching certificate. Castro became a professional boxer. He later taught Spanish at the University of Arizona while working on a law degree.

In a few years, Castro was elected the first Mexican American county attorney and then superior court judge in Pima County. A natural for foreign service, he accepted an appointment as ambassador to El Salvador and later to Bolivia.

In 1974 Castro won the governor's office with the slogan "This man is a leader." Three years later, he resigned when President Jimmy Carter chose him to be ambassador to Argentina.

A Case Study: *Miranda vs. Arizona*

A Maricopa County Superior Court case in 1963 resulted in a famous U. S. Supreme Court decision three years later. Ernesto Miranda was convicted on kidnap and rape charges and sent to prison at Florence. He had not been told his rights, however, at the time of his arrest. He had the right to remain silent and the right to have a lawyer present when asked questions. These rights are guaranteed in the Fifth and Sixth Amendments to the U. S. Constitution.

While Miranda was in prison, a well-known Phoenix criminal lawyer appealed his case all the way to the U. S. Supreme Court. In the *Miranda vs. Arizona* decision, Miranda's rights were upheld. The Miranda decision forced every police officer to advise each suspect of his or her rights at the time of arrest.

Miranda was released from prison. Later, however, he was arrested again, retried on new evidence, and convicted.

Juries

A *grand jury* holds hearings to find out if there is enough evidence to bring a person to trial. The grand jury is not used much in Arizona.

The *petit jury* is the trial jury. Most Superior Court juries have eight members. In a criminal case the jury members decide what the facts are. Is the accused person guilty or innocent? All jury members must agree on a verdict. If they cannot, it is a *hung jury*. In that event, the county attorney can retry the person with a new jury or drop the case. The judge determines the sentence and/or fine if the accused person is found guilty.

A lawyer summarizes his case to a petit trial jury in Superior Court.

The Court of Appeals

The Arizona Court of Appeals can review all cases appealed from the Superior Court except one kind. That is the one in which the person has been sentenced to life in prison or death. This kind of appeal is sent directly to the Arizona Supreme Court.

Each Court of Appeals case has three judges and no jury. (Notice that the higher the court, the more judges there are.) The Arizona Court of Appeals is divided into two parts. Judges in Division One hold court in Phoenix. Division Two courtrooms are in Tucson. As the caseload grows, more judges are added to each division.

The Arizona Supreme Court

The Arizona Supreme Court is the highest state court. This court has five justices (judges) appointed by the governor. The justices choose one of their members to be chief justice. Cases are decided by a majority vote of the five justices. No jury is used.

The Arizona Supreme Court has final jurisdiction in cases appealed from the lower courts. It gets some difficult cases from the Superior Court. A 1976 case involving water rights illustrates the point. The case arose out of a groundwater shortage problem in the Santa Cruz Valley south of Tucson. Too much water was being pumped. The water was needed by farmers, several copper companies, and the City of Tucson.

By a four-to-one vote the Supreme Court upheld a Pima County court decision that a farmers' group had "prior rights" to the water for irrigation. The mining companies and the City of Tucson were ordered to cut down the amount of water that they pumped from the Santa Cruz basin so there would be more water for the farmers. The Supreme Court said, however, that the legislature could decide which economic interests were most important to Arizona. This part of the decision gave hope to the people in Tucson who must solve a water shortage problem for the city.

ARIZONA PORTRAIT

Ernest W. McFarland
1894–1984

"The job I really enjoyed the most was judge of the Superior Court in Pinal County," said Ernest McFarland. He is the only person who has served in the top office in three branches of government: U.S. senator, governor, and chief justice of the Arizona Supreme Court. While he was in the U.S. Senate, his fellow Democrats elected him majority leader.

A former math teacher in Oklahoma and World War I Navy veteran, McFarland earned a law degree at Stanford University. He started practicing law in Casa Grande and later moved to Florence where he specialized in water law.

"Mac," as he liked to be called, is honored by McFarland State Historical Park, a museum housed in the old adobe courthouse in Florence.

Lorna Lockwood, the first woman to serve on the Arizona Supreme Court, is shown in this 1973 photo.

Local Government

A LOCAL GOVERNMENT IS ONE that is "close to home." It serves the people in counties, cities or towns, and single-purpose districts such as school districts.

County Government

Arizona is divided into fifteen large counties. Everyone in Arizona lives in a county. One city in each county is the county seat. A courthouse in the county seat is the center of most activities of county government. Extra buildings for office space, courtrooms, or jails are needed in some counties.

There are two major purposes of county government. First, county officers do many things for the state. They keep a record of property and collect taxes. They conduct elections. They arrest people who break state laws. They hold court.

Second, the counties provide many services. People outside of towns are protected by a sheriff. Roads in these outlying areas are built by the county. A county government may provide parks and libraries. Pima County even operates a sewage disposal plant north of Tucson.

The most important duties of a county's board of supervisors are to approve a yearly budget and set the property tax rate. This tax is reduced by revenue received from the state. A county gets a share of the state sales, automobile, and gasoline taxes.

The Future of County Government

County government was created in horse and buggy days when Arizona was a rural area with few people. County courthouses were little more than branch offices of territorial government. Through the years, counties have been saddled with more state burdens. They must pay most of the cost, for example, of the criminal justice system.

Today, Arizona is a fast-growing state with modern problems. But county governments are limited legally in what they can do. They have to seek approval of the state legislature for nearly every change. This process is slow. It creates delays in providing needed services for the people.

Some political scientists favor "home rule" county government. Then the people in each county could choose the best form of government for them. The county supervisors could take action without first going to the legislature to get power to act. In 1992 a statewide proposition passed that gave each urban county the right to draw up its own *charter* and have home rule if voters in the county approve the charter.

The sheriff has been an important county officer since territorial days. In this photo, Sheriff George C. Ruffner of Yavapai County is shown relaxing in 1897.

Yavapai County Courthouse

Your County

It might be interesting to find out how much money your county is spending this year. What is the county property tax rate? How many people work for the county?

Match the title of each elected county officer below with the job each does.

1. County Attorney

2. Sheriff

3. Assessor

4. Recorder

5. County School Superintendent

6. Treasurer

7. Supervisors

a. Keeps a record of property deeds (including one on the moon in the Maricopa County office) and other legal papers.

b. Approve the county budget.

c. Enforces laws outside of incorporated towns and cities.

d. Must have a teacher's certificate.

e. Figures the value of property in the county.

f. Collects taxes for the county, cities, and school districts.

g. Prosecutes persons accused of breaking state laws.

Arizona Counties and County Seats

Calvin Goode

Calvin Goode is Phoenix's longest serving city councilman. He served eleven consecutive terms (1972–1994). The former City Hall is named in his honor.

"I have never considered myself a typical politician," said the soft-spoken, dignified, but persistent Goode. "The mayor told me I'd never get the 16th Street Bridge over the railroad tracks. It took me nine years, but I did it."

One of eight children in a poor family, Calvin graduated from all-black Carver High in 1945, earned a college degree, and started a career in the Phoenix Union High School District. On the side, he owned an accounting business and became a leader in the city's anti-poverty programs. He and his wife, Georgie, raised three sons.

After retiring from the city council, Goode helped to start the Carver/PUCH Museum in the old high school building. He also won a seat on the Phoenix Elementary Board of Education.

Calvin Goode set goals to improve the community and stuck with them. "I was taught that people should be fair, just, and decent."

Town or City Government

Arizona is fast becoming a state where most of the people live in towns and cities. The change from a rural to an urban state has come mainly since World War II. Electronics, manufacturing, and tourism are now the leaders in employment, so most of the new jobs are found in the cities. Town and city governments in Arizona try hard to keep up with population growth. They have to plan and add new services at a fast pace.

The lives of people are directly touched by what town or city governments do or don't do. The local government usually tries to furnish water, repair streets, build a sewer system, and improve parks. It provides police and fire protection, hauls away garbage, and gives many other services.

In many places, people expect local government to do more to improve the quality of life. They want libraries, streets with trees and sidewalks, a zoo, and a civic center. Larger cities hope for an airport, a sports arena, programs for the young and elderly, and many other projects.

Three plans of government are used in Arizona's towns and cities:

- **Weak mayor-council.** In this plan the mayor is a member of the elected council. He or she is the "first among equals" and has little power. The job is part-time. The pay is low.
- **Strong mayor-council.** This plan gives the mayor more power. He or she does more than preside over council meetings. The strong mayor is also the administrative head. There is a clear line of responsibility in this system. The Nogales strong mayor, for example, has real power—he or she can fire appointed officials.
- **Council-manager.** A well-paid expert is hired to be in charge of city departments.

Helicopters get Tucson police to crime scenes in a hurry.

City services include fire protection.
Photo by Bob Rink

Incorporation

A town with 1,500 or more people may *incorporate*. That means the town becomes like a business. It can own land and make contracts. When a town has 3,000 or more people, it may call itself a city. A town or city with 3,500 people may draw up a charter, which is like a city constitution. Charter cities have home rule. They can act more on their own.

Tombstone was given home rule in 1881 during territorial days. The people have added amendments to the original charter and still use it. In some ways, however, it is out-of-date. For one thing, it allows the council to license gambling places though state law forbids it.

Sometimes a charter city wants to change its government in some way. It can do this without asking the legislature. Before 1983, for example, Phoenix elected all council members from the whole city. Then the city grew so big, it needed a plan that would give every part of the city a voice in the council. Phoenix voters chose to divide the city into eight wards. Each ward now elects one member of the council. Only the mayor is elected by the whole city.

> ### What do you think?
> City and county services sometimes overlap. In some places (Denver, San Francisco, and Philadelphia) the city and county governments are one.
> - Would this system be a good idea for Tucson and Pima County or for Maricopa County and its cities?
> - Why do you think political parties tend to favor having both county and city governments?

Special Single-Purpose Districts

- **School Districts.** The school district is the most common type of single-purpose district in Arizona. There are more than 200 districts in the state. Each is governed by an elected board of education.

- **Salt River Project.** This district brings water and electricity to homes, farms, and factories in the Salt River Valley.

- **Central Arizona Water Conservation District (CAWCD).** This district has an elected board. Its main job is to repay the cost of building the Central Arizona Project. This project was built to bring water from the Colorado River to central Arizona and Tucson. The CAWCD board charges water users and then pays the federal government.

- **Other:** Single-purpose districts are formed for fire and police protection, flood control, or sanitation. Many of these districts are outside the boundaries of towns or cities.

Charter Cities

City	Charter Date
Tombstone	1881
Phoenix	1913
Yuma	1914
Nogales	1926
Tucson	1929
Glendale, Winslow	1957
Flagstaff, Prescott	1958
Avondale	1959
Scottsdale	1961
Tempe	1964
Chandler	1965
Mesa	1967
Casa Grande	1975
Douglas	1982
Peoria	1983
Bisbee, Goodyear	1988
Holbrook	1994

Phoenix City Hall
(Photo by Bob Rink)

Morris K. Udall
1922–1998

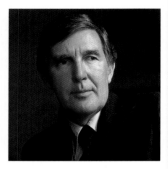

Morris Udall grew up in St. Johns, where life was simple and everybody knew everybody else. Mo, as he was called, lost an eye in a childhood accident, but went on to play professional basketball, earn a law degree, and serve thirty years in the U.S. Congress.

An effective and popular lawmaker, U.S. Representative Udall pushed through bills protecting the environment. The Alaska Lands Act alone added millions of acres to the National Parks system and wilderness areas. Udall also worked to reorganize the postal service and helped get the Central Arizona Project bill enacted. He brought high ideals, honesty, and civility to politics.

Famous for homespun humor and his gangly, "Lincolnesque" appearance, the 6' 5" Udall often poked fun at himself. After losing the campaign for the Democratic presidential nomination in 1976, he said, "I drew more laughter than votes." Mo later compiled many of his jokes and stories in a book named *Too Funny to Be President.* He used humor to get people in a frame of mind to listen to him.

Citizenship Responsibilities: Voting and Elections

VOTING IS THE MOST IMPORTANT WAY that citizens take part in a democracy. Arizona has had elections since 1864. In that year, the pioneers voted for members of the first territorial legislature. Today there are hundreds of jobs filled through the election process.

The election process begins with the nomination of candidates. This is done in the *direct primary election.* Each party tries to choose a *nominee* for each office. The party nominees then run against each other in the *general election.* The winners in this election take office a short time later.

To register as a voter in Arizona, a person must be eighteen years of age and live in the state at least fifty days. Most people register in one of the two major parties—Democratic or Republican. Others register in a third party or as "Independents."

Every vote counts. In the 1916 governor's race, for example, there was only a thirty-vote difference between the candidates in the whole state. Thomas E. Campbell, the Republican, appeared to be the winner. He served a year before the Arizona Supreme Court threw out the ballots that were marked wrong. That made George W. P. Hunt the winner. He finished the term.

U. S. Senators and Congressmen

Like people in other states, Arizona voters elect two U. S. senators. These are people who represent Arizona's interests in Washington, D.C. They help make laws for the entire country. The number of representatives varies from state to state according to population. The size of the U. S. House of Representatives is frozen at 435 members. After each ten-year census, the 435 seats are reapportioned. Arizona, a fast-growing state, has been gaining seats. In the 1990s Arizona had six seats. Each congressman represented a district with about equal population. Do you know who represents your district?

Voting is a privilege.
It is not a "must" duty of citizenship like obeying the law and paying taxes. Voting is a "should" responsibility.
You should vote if you want democracy to work.

1. Why does the legislative branch have great power in state government? Into how may legislative districts is Arizona divided? How many representatives and senators does each district elect?

2. What is the job of a Senate floor leader?

3. After a bill is introduced, it is studied by one or more_____.

4. What is the Committee of the Whole? What sometimes happens to a bill in this committee?

5. Define: simple majority, absolute majority, emergency clause.

6. Name the five elected executive officers.

7. What is the most important duty of the governor?

8. Why is the Corporation Commission an important agency?

9. What are the four levels of courts in Arizona?

10. Explain the two different kinds of juries.

11. Explain how the small claims division of the JP court works.

12. Define: misdemeanor, civil offense, felony.

13. Which court is the great trial court?

14. Why did the *Miranda* case become so important all over the country?

15. Why was the Court of Appeals created?

16. What kind of jurisdiction does the Arizona Supreme Court have in most cases? How many judges are on this court? By what vote is a decision reached?

17. What are the two main purposes of county government?

18. What is the main problem faced by many town and city governments in Arizona today?

ARIZONA PORTRAIT

Barry Goldwater
1909–1998

Barry Goldwater was the most famous Arizonan of all time. Born in Phoenix on New Year's Day, 1909, Goldwater was a third–generation Arizonan. Descended from pioneer merchants, Barry also ran a clothing store. As a young man, he enjoyed operating a ham radio, photographing Native Americans, and flying. He was a pilot during World War II.

Goldwater, a Republican, won a seat on the Phoenix city council in 1949. Three years later he won a seat in the U.S. Senate. Successful and charismatic, Goldwater attracted voters to the Republican Party. Many conservative Democrats switched parties.

In the Senate, Goldwater became a national leader and wrote a widely-read book, *Conscience of a Conservative*. In 1964, his party nominated him for president. Though defeated, Goldwater went on to serve five terms—thirty years in the U. S. Senate. Throughout his career he was respected for his honesty and courage.

Motivating Projects and Activities

Individual and group projects can be used with almost every chapter in this book.

Map and picture postcards: Put a map of Arizona on the bulletin board. Pin or thumbtack Arizona postcards around the map. Run a string between each picture and its location on the map. For a more limited project, use only pictures on one topic.

Explorers map: Use colored yarn or string to show the routes of explorers on a modern highway map.

Jigsaw puzzles: Use Arizona scenes found on calendars, magazines, or posters. Political campaign posters might be used. Road maps or an enlarged map of Arizona's counties would make a good puzzle. Cut the pictures into puzzle pieces and trade with classmates to put them together.

Murals: Create a mural to illustrate some event, person, movement, or era in Arizona history. Use posterboard or a long piece of butcher paper.

Poster drawings or mosaics: Use an opaque projector to make enlargments of the state bird, flower, and tree. For a mosaic, glue small pieces of colored paper or beans, nuts, macaroni, or other materials to fill in the drawing.

Cartoon posters: Decorate the classroom with cartoons that are related to state or local topics. Use an opaque projector to make enlargements of the cartoons.

Scrapbook: Clip newspaper articles, pictures, editorials, and cartoons on Arizona's history, geography, recreation, and government. Summarize the main points of each clipping in a few sentences and write down its source and date. Organize the clippings by main subjects in clear plastic sheets in a scrapbook.

Current event reports: Choose a significant happening in the news related to Arizona. Use as many newspapers and other media sources as are available, including the Internet.

Primary sources research paper: History is a record of people's lives as it is written in diaries, letters, public documents, and newspapers. History is also shown on gravestones, buildings, and in photographs. Choose a topic related to Arizona history and do a research paper or oral report, using as many primary sources as possible.

Cowboys: Collect poems, songs, and pictures relating to the life of Arizona's cowboys and ranchers.

Arizona history in place names: Make lists of Arizona towns, counties, rivers, or streets that have Indian or Spanish names. Make a list of places named after people who are important in Arizona history.

History in advertising: Check the yellow pages for the names of businesses that use historic names. Write a list or make a collage with these names, pictures, letterheads, etc.

Ethnic studies: Research one of Arizona's ethnic groups and present a class report using pictures, tape recordings of ethnic music, dances, and language.

Native American crafts: Visit a museum or other place that has handicraft exhibits. Learn how to weave a basket or yucca sandals, make a pot, grind corn or wheat with a stone, construct a model of a Native American pueblo, wickiup, or hogan, make a bow or an arrow with a stone arrowhead, etc. Bring your project to class.

Contribution (Show and Tell) Day: Bring to class a family heirloom—old photo, letter, diary, postcard, magazine, or document. Show the class a barbed wire collection, an antique tool, an old Arizona automobile license plate, soldier's uniform, or stamps. A taped or written interview with an older person would be a good contribution. Show pictures or slides of historic sites. Wear a costume from an historic era.

Original poem, letter, or song: Pretend that you are present at some important Arizona historical event. Find out all you can about the event and write a poem, song, or letter about your experience.

A war project: Do a research paper, class report, or bulletin board display about a war in which Arizonans took part. Use books, interviews, pictures, maps, songs of the time, timeline, drawings, etc.

Committee study of legislative bills: For a class project, get copies of important bills being considered by the state legislature. Divide the class into committees. Study a bill and report on it to the class.

Write a letter to your legislator: Study a bill in the legislature and write to your senator or representative about it. Be brief and courteous. Cover one topic and give reasons for your opinion. Point out facts that support your point of view. Address the letter to Senator (name) for a Senate member or Representative (name), for a House member. The rest of the address is 1700 West Washington, Phoenix AZ 85007.

Copper mining project: Do a research paper, a collage of mine pictures, an interview of a miner, or drawings. Free materials for classroom use may be available at the Arizona Mining Association, 2702 N. Third Street, Suite 2015, Phoenix, AZ 85004. Write to the educational director.

Stamp collecting: Collect stamps related to Arizona and American history—wildlife, plants, transportation, art, science, sports, etc. Your family, friends, and neighbors can help you. Cut cancelled stamps from the corners of envelopes. A stamp collection could become an ongoing project for future classes. A helpful book for collectors is *The Postal Service Guide to U. S. Stamps.*

Name the Faces. Find pictures of five prominent Arizonans (governor, U.S. senators, a Congressman, mayor, television or music celebrity, or other important person). Place the pictures on cardboard and number them from 1 to 5. Count the number of students who can identify each picture. Several years ago, a newspaper reporter did a similar survey at a shopping center. Some of the wrong answers proved to be interesting.

Games for Review

Who Am I? This game can be used for a break in the usual classroom procedure and for review. Names of people studied are drawn from a hat. Each student writes down three clues, arranged progressively from the most difficult to the easiest. Each class member, in turn, comes to the front of the room, gives the first clue, and asks, "How many know who am I?" Give the scond clue, then the last, seeing each time how many more students can guess correctly.

Team Review. Appoint two teams of about equal ability with four students on each side. Ask one side a question which they discuss quickly and quietly before giving a team answer. If right, that team gets one point and the second team is given a different question. If wrong, the second team gets the same question. Each side is given the same number of chances to answer questions. Then choose two new teams and continue.

Open Book Review. Divide the class into two groups. One student from each side goes, in turn, to the chalkboard to represent his/her side while her team looks up answers to questions asked by the teacher. Answers to questions are written on the chalkboard by each team leader. A record of points is kept on the board above the answers.

Jeopardy. Write out the questions for each of several categories about Arizona. Value each question according to difficulty—maybe 80, 60, 40, 20 points. Two teams compete for points. Each side, in turn, chooses a category and a point value. When a question is read, the team that puts up a hand first (or presses a buzzer) gets to answer. A penalty may be assessed for each wrong answer. The other team is given a chance to answer a missed question.

Glossary

The terms are identified according to their use in the chapters of this textbook.

AAA: Agricultural Adjustment Administration

abolish: to do away with

absentee owner: someone who owns land but does not live on that land; someone who controls his/her land from another place

absolute majority: more than half of the people eligible to vote

adobe: sun-dried brick

advisory opinion: the legal opinion of an attorney general which has the effect of law until a court gives a different opinion

agile: able to move quickly and easily

agitator: one who disturbs or shakes things up

alimony: money paid to a divorced person by his/her former spouse

alkali: a mixture of salts in the soil of dry regions; a bitter substance that neutralizes acids

alloy: a mixture of melted metals

amateur: someone who is not an expert; someone just learning something

amendment: a change or alteration

anchor store: the largest business, usually a department store, in a mall

annex: to add or incorporate

apostle: the first important missionary or priest to a group

apprentice: a person learning a craft or skill from a master

aqueduct: a channel or ditch built to move water from a distance

arable: suitable for farming

archaeologist: a scientist who studies ancient people by studying the things they left behind

arid: very dry

Arizona Rangers: a group of lawmen whose job was to keep the peace in early Arizona

armistice: a truce or arrangement for peace

armory: a place where arms are stored

arms race: the race to build up more or more powerful weapons than another country

arson: burning property on purpose

artifact: an object made by people long ago

artillery: large guns mounted on bases, such as cannons

assault: a violent attack or threat

assayer: someone who examines ore to determine its quality

aviation: the operation of planes and other aircraft

axis: an alliance between major powers

barracks: a building or group of buildings for lodging soldiers

barrio: a Spanish-speaking section or neighborhood

battalion: a large body of troops organized to act together; a military unit

battery: the act of beating or using force on a person

bill: a written idea for a law

boll: a seed pod

bounty: a reward

"buffalo soldier": a nickname for African American soldiers in the West during frontier days

bureaucrat: one who works for the government, an administrator, or under several levels of authority

byproduct: a sometimes unexpected product or result produced in addition to the main product or result

cathode: a refined copper plate (sheet) 99.99% pure

cauterize: to burn to prevent infection

cavalry: troops mounted on horseback

CCC: Civilian Conservation Corps, an agency formed during the Great Depression to help put people back to work and improve national parks, roads, and bridges

chaparral: a dense thicket

chaplain: a priest or minister attached to a certain group, such as the army

charter: an official document granting rights or privileges

civil offense: less-serious violations of the law, such as minor traffic violations

civic: relating to a city or citizenship

cold war: an intense rivalry with another country; a war without weapons

colonizing: done in order to establish a colony or settlement

commerce: the buying and selling of goods; business

commission: a group of people charged with performing a certain duty

communal: in common; sharing property and responsibilities

communist: having to do with communism, a way of government in which all the goods are held in common by the state

compensate: to make up for; to pay back

concentration camp: a camp where people, usually prisoners of war, are confined and often treated badly

conducive: leading to a particular result

Confederate: a term for the Southern states during the Civil War that tried to form their own country and wanted slavery to be allowed

consolidate: to combine or unite

constable: a public officer who keeps the peace

contractor: a person who signs a contract to erect buildings, supply materials, or do other work

controversial: open to argument; involving opposing viewpoints

convene: to meet

converge: to approach a common center or point

convert: to change another person's beliefs

cultivate: to prepare for raising crops

cured: prepared

defendant: a person required to defend himself/herself in a lawsuit

defraud: to cheat

delegate: someone who speaks and acts for a group of voters

denomination: a particular religious group

dependent: one who relies on others for support

deploy: to spread out so as to form a line or front

depression: a period when business, jobs, etc. decline or remain at a low level

desegregate: to eliminate racial segregation (separation by race)

desert refrigerator: an outdoor cabinet that keeps food cool as water drips over it

desolation: loneliness, sadness, grief

dictator: a leader with absolute power

direct democracy: a type of government in which the people vote directly (instead of through representatives) and majority rules

direct primary: an election in which each party's candidate is decided

discrimination: treating people unjustly because they are different

dispatch: a message

divert: to turn away from a purpose or course

domesticate: to tame or raise at home

drought: a long period of dry weather

elevation: how high or low a place is in relation to sea level

embezzlement: stealing by changing the records dishonestly

emission: a substance given off into the air

empire: a group of countries under one ruler

engraver: someone who cuts figures, letters, or designs for printing

eradicate: to eliminate

erode: to wear away gradually

etching: a design on a hard surface made by wearing away part of the surface, usually with acid

ethnology: the study of human ethnic groups or races

evaporative: able to turn water into vapor

evict: to kick out legally

excavate: to dig out

exceed: to go beyond

exile: banishment

expedition: a journey for a specific purpose

exterminate: to destroy; to do away with

extradition: return of a captured fugitive to the state from which he or she has fled

farce: a ridiculous sham

FDIC: Federal Deposit Insurance Corporation, an agency formed during the Great Depression to insure the money people deposited in banks

felony: a serious crime punished with a heavy sentence

firebrand: a piece of burning wood; a torch

"fireside chat": the name given to the radio talks President Roosevelt delivered to the American people during the Great Depression

flint: a hard kind of stone used to start a fire

fluted: cut in grooves

foliage: the leaves of plants

forage: to search for food

foray: a quick, sudden attack or raid

general election: an election in which the nominees of one party run against those of the other parties

geography: the study of the earth and the people, animals, and plants living on it

geology: the study of the history of the earth, including its rocks and physical changes over time

glen: a small, narrow, hidden valley

gorge: a narrow valley or canyon

grand jury: a jury that considers evidence against a person to determine if he/she should be charged with a crime

grant: an agreement or transfer

green belt: an open area of land without any buildings

guerrilla: one who engages in irregular warfare, such as surprise raids

gunnery: the science of making and managing large guns

homestead: to settle on public land

Howell Code: laws that Judge William T. Howell made for the Arizona Territory before the first legislature met

humanitarian: practicing goodwill and charity toward people; one who practices goodwill and charity

hung jury: the situation when a jury cannot reach a verdict

hydroelectric: relating to the production of electricity by waterpower

hydroponic: growing in a nutrient solution instead of soil

ideal: the best imaginable

immigrant: a person who moves to a new country to live

immunization: an injection of antibodies to help a person or animal resist disease

impartial: not taking sides; fair

impeachment: to bring a formal accusation against a public official by the House of Representatives for a trial in the Senate to possibly remove him/her from public office

impregnable: strong enough to resist attack

inaugural: relating to a person taking office

incorporate: to become one legal body

Indian agent: someone who has the job of dealing with American Indians and keeping peaceful relations

indict: to charge with a crime

induct: to admit as a member

infamy: an extremely bad reputation

infantry: soldiers who fight on foot

ingot: a mass of metal formed into a block or bar to be sold

initiative: a process by which the people can write a bill (law) and get it on the ballot for the voters to pass or defeat at an election

inoculate: to give a shot against disease to a person or animal

installation: any military establishment such as an air base or fort

installment: part of a total amount; the division of a debt for easier payment

insulation: a covering or extra layer to keep in heat or cold

integrate: to bring together different races as equals; to bring together as a whole

integrity: sticking to one's values; soundness of moral character

IRA: Indian Reorganization Act

irrigation: watering land by use of canals or ditches

IWW: the Industrial Workers of the World, a union of workers

joint statehood: the idea of two territories joining the Union as one state

junket: a trip for pleasure

jurisdiction: the power or right to interpret and apply the law in a given area or case

justifiable: able to be proven just or right

kiva: a religious structure built by American Indians, often underground

land deed: a document recording a transfer of land and proving ownership

leaching: to cause water to pass through a material full of pores

legislator: a lawmaker

levee: a river landing place

liberty bond: an interest-bearing certificate sold by the government to raise money for the war effort

lode: a vein-like deposit of ore

lye: a harsh substance used for washing and making soap

magistrate: in Arizona, a town or city judge

Manifest Destiny: the idea that America was meant to expand from coast to coast and was blessed by a higher power

marauding: roaming about and raiding

martial law: the law imposed by military forces when the regular civil authority has broken down

martyr: someone who dies for what he or she believes in; someone who suffers because of his or her religious beliefs

menial: lowly, humble

Mexican Cession: the term for the land Mexico gave over to the United States

misdemeanor: a crime less serious than a felony

mission: a religious settlement

Moor: a Moslem person from Arabia or North Africa

moral: relating to right and wrong

morale: the mental and emotional state of someone or of a group

mural: a large painting on a wall

musing: thinking quietly

mythical: from a legend or story

navigate: to steer on or through water

niche: a space or position that is suitable for a person or thing

nominee: a candidate chosen by his/her party to run for an office

notoriety: the state of being well known

obsolete: no longer in use

opportunist: someone who takes advantage of opportunities or circumstances

organized labor: workers who organize or work together so they can better bargain with the owners

overgraze: to allow livestock to eat too much of the plant life in one area

overproduction: making more than can be used

parish: a local church community

pelt: the skin of a fur-bearing animal

percolate: to cause a liquid to pass through a material full of pores

persecution: causing people to suffer because of their beliefs or race

petit jury: a jury that tries cases

petroglyph: an ancient carving on rock

pious: showing religious devotion or reverence

pit house: a home made by digging a pit in the earth

plaintiff: the complaining party in a lawsuit

politicking: political discussion or activity

poll tax: a tax a person has to pay in order to vote

polygamist: a person who is married to more than one wife or husband at the same time

pontoon: a flat-bottomed boat or float to support a temporary bridge

porter: someone who has the job of carrying baggage; an attendant in a railroad car

posse: a group of men called by the sheriff in an emergency to help keep the peace

POW: prisoner of war

precipice: a steep cliff

prefabricate: to make the parts of something beforehand to be put together later

prehistoric: before written history

presidio: fort or military post

primary source: something made or written by someone who was there at the time; an original record

profitable: able to make money

progressive: moving forward toward reform; relating to the Progressive political party

propaganda: information or ideas spread to promote or hurt a particular cause, nation, or group

prospector: someone who explores for mineral deposits

PWA: Public Works Administration, an agency formed during the Great Depression to help put people back to work

quarantine: to isolate in order to prevent the spread of disease

radical: extreme; someone who wants quick and sweeping changes in laws and ways of government

ratify: to approve and accept

ration: food that is divided up in order to use it sparingly

ration stamps: stamps given to families with which to buy rationed food during World War II

Rebel: a name for Southerners during the Civil War

recall: the process of removing an official by popular vote

recession: a mild but widespread slow-down of business activity

referendum: the process of submitting legislative bills to the people to vote on

refinery: a plant for refining crude or raw materials such as metals

regiment: a military group

relocation: the moving of people to another place

renegade: a person who deserts one cause or group for another

repeal: to cancel by official authority

repository: a place where things are kept or put

representative democracy: a type of government in which representatives are elected by the people to vote for the people in the law-making body

republic: a government in which the people hold the power and elect the officials; a representative democracy

resent: to dislike or be annoyed with

reservation: an area of land set aside for American Indians

resolution: a formal statement of opinion or intent

resurrection: rebirth; revival

revenue: money collected by the government

reverence: a feeling of respect or awe

riotous: noisy, violent, disorderly

rostrum: a platform for a speaker

Rough Riders: a term for a cavalry unit led by Theodore Roosevelt that fought in the Spanish-American War

rubble: broken pieces and trash

rustler: a person who steals cattle from the range

sanction: approval

satellite city: a city that branches out from or is part of a larger city

scarcity: something that is not plentiful or easy to get

secede: to leave one country to form another

sediment: material such as stones and sand deposited by water, wind, or a glacier

self-sufficient: able to support oneself

sentinel: a guard

silt: fine earth or sand floating in rivers, ponds, or lakes

skirmish: a minor battle

smelter: a place where ore is melted to separate or refine metals

sociable: friendly; liking companionship

sojourn: to live in a place temporarily

speculator: a person who takes a business risk

subdivision: an area of land divided into home lots

stockmen: people who own and raise livestock

suburbanization: the process of more and more people moving to the suburbs, causing housing developments to be built quickly

suffragette: a woman who wanted women's right to vote

supplement: to add to

surveyor: someone who measures the land

symbolic: standing for something else; representative of something else

syndicated: distributed or published in a number of publications

tandem: one behind another; a carriage with horses hitched one behind another

tabernacle: a house of worship

teamster: one who drives a team of animals

terrace: to cut the land into wide levels or steps

territorial legislature: a group of law makers in a territory

"thieving thirteenth": a term for the thirteenth territorial legislature, which spent more money than the law allowed

thrift: careful management of money

"Tin Lizzie": a nickname for early automobiles

title: a legal right to ownership

transcontinental: going across a continent

transient: passing through a place; one who stays for a brief period of time and then moves on

treason: going against one's country, especially by trying to overthrow the government

trestle: a supporting framework

turret: a low armored structure on which guns are mounted; a small tower

ultimatum: a final demand in a dispute

undaunted: not shaken or discouraged; brave

Union: a term for the Northern states during the Civil War

unproductive: not productive, not producing a lot

urbanization: the process of becoming more like the city

urban sprawl: the spreading of a city outward onto rural land

vegetation: the plant life of a place

venture: something involving risk or chance

veto: to reject a bill

viceroy: the governor of a territory who rules in place of the king or queen

vitality: liveliness, energy

whip: a member of the legislature who tries to gather support for his/her party's ideas or bills

women's suffrage: women's right to vote

WPA: Works Progress Administration—an agency formed during the Great Depression to help put people back to work

Yankee: a name for Northerners during the Civil War

Index

Credits

Photography

Allied Signal Aerospace 247 (upper)
Arizona Capitol Times 284
Arizona Daily Star 228, 278
Arizona Department of Library and Archives 15 (upper right), 113, 140 (lower), 182 (lower), 187 (upper right), 190 (middle left), 191 (lower right), 212, 214 (right), 217 (lower), 286
Arizona Department of Transportation 263 (mid)
Arizona Diamondbacks 277 (right)
Arizona Gazette 191 (upper mid)
Arizona Highways 222 (upper), 234 (upper left), 234 (lower left), 257 (lower right)
Arizona Historical Foundation 102 (upper left), 106 (left), 112 (lower left)
Arizona Historical Society 14 (lower mid), 15 (lower), 42, 47 (all), 48 (lower left) 52, 56, 58 (left), 60, 65, 68, 76, 80, 87, 92 (all), 93, 94 (all), 97 (upper), 98 (left), 99 (all), 101, 102 (lower left), 108 (upper left), 112 (lower left), 115, 116 (right), 117 (all), 119 (lower), 123, 126 (lower), 127, 131, 133 (upper), 143 (upper), 146 (lower), 149 (lower left), 150 (right), 151 (middle right), 153 (upper), 154, 155, 156, 157 (right), 161, 162, 171 (upper right), 172, 175 (left), 176 (lower), 177 (all), 180 (all), 181 (all), 184, 186, 187 (left), 190 (middle center), 191 (lower left), 193, 195 (left), 202 (all), 216, 218 (upper), 220 (upper left), 231 (left), 257 (upper right), 292 (upper)
"Arizona Joe" 178 (upper)
Arizona Judiciary, The 290
Arizona National Guard 234 (upper right)
Arizona Office of Tourism 20 (all), 63, 109, 148, 171 (left), 273 (right insert), 275 (lower right), 292 (lower)
Arizona Public Service 107, 149 (upper), 168 (lower), 183, 200 (upper left), 208, 221 (upper right)
Arizona Republican, The 187, 188 (upper left)
Arizona State Museum 32, 38 (upper left), 38 (lower left), 40 (lower), 266
Arizona State University 235 (upper)
Arizona State University Department of Archives and Manuscripts 190 (left), 190 (far right), 201
Arizona State University Libraries 116 (left), 142, 164, 170 (left)
Artifacts from the Pueblo Grande in Phoenix 49

ASARCO Silver Bell 250 (upper left, lower left, and upper right)
Ballet Arizona 277 (left)
Bancroft Library, University of California Berkeley 72
Bank One 125, 129, 134 (left), 179, 211
Barrow, Scott 260
Bisbee Mining and Historical Museum 151 (upper), 169, 170 (right), 199, 233 (lower)
Boeing Company 247 (lower)
Bureau of Reclamation, Dept. of Interior 26 (lower), 253 (left)
Cable Systems International 244
California Historical Society/Title Insurance and Trust Company 153 (lower)
Chamberlain, Lynn 25 (lower right), 77 (lower)
Church of Jesus Christ of Latter-day Saints, Historical Dept. Archives 49, 136 (lower left)
Church of Jesus Christ of Latter-day Saints, Museum of Church History and Art 85
City of Tucson, Community Relations 294 (lower left)
Collection of the Utah Museum of Natural History, University of Utah 32, 40 (upper)
College of Eastern Utah 34
Columbia Pictures 224
Cooper, David 277 (left)
Coronado National Memorial 54 (upper), 55
Cundick, Maryella 12 (all), 22
Cyprus Bagdad Copper Corporation 250 (lower left)
Daniels, Lois 267
De Wald, Bud 197
Department of Weights and Measures 287 (lower)
Detroit Publishing Company 159 (upper)
Don Tang, Esther 269 (upper)
Fannin, Paul 221 (lower left)
Fort Huachuca Historical Museum 53, 130, 236 (all)
Fort Apache Museum, University of Arizona 137, 219
The Frank Lloyd Wright Foundation 23 (lower left)
Galeria de Historia 73
Gilchriese, John D. 173 (left)
Goodyear Aircraft Corporation, Arizona Division 230 (upper)
Heard Museum, The 105 (top right), 135, 257 (left)
History and Archives Division Department of Library, Archives, and Public Records 150 (left)
Hughes, Mark 200 (lower)
Jennings and Thompson Advertising 257 (lower right)
John F. Long Properties 258 (upper left), 258 (lower right)
Jorgenson, Larry, Mr. and Mrs. 240 (right), 241

Kansas Historical Society 204 (right), 226
Kenny, Gil 14 (lower left), 25 (upper left), 66 (lower right), 67, 275 (left), 275 (upper right)
Langston, Cleve 248 (upper)
Library of Congress 96, 119 (upper), 231 (right)
Long, Ken 232 (all)
Los Angeles County Museum of Natural History 90
Los Angeles Department of Water and Power 192
Lowie Museum of Anthropology, University of California Berkeley 57
Luck, Hal 113, 121 (left)
Markow Photography 289, 291 (right)
McCain, John 265 (right)
McLaughlius, Mrs. 70
Mesa Tribune, The 282
Metropolitan Tucson Convention and Visitors Bureau 13 (upper), 14 (lower left), 25 (upper left), 66 (lower right), 67, 275 (left), 275 (upper right)
Miles, Kent 269 (lower)
Mora, Jo 74 (all), 82
Motorola Inc. 246 (all)
Museum of New Mexico 84 (upper left), 104 (upper left)
Museum of Northern Arizona 48
National Park Service 50
National Archives 84 (lower left), 97, 104 (lower right), 133, 155 (lower left), 159 (lower), 176 (lower), 194 (all), 195 (right), 215, 220 (lower right), 235 (lower), 238 (right), 239 (upper, lower right)
Nielsen, Ric 10
Office of the Secretary of State 280 (lower left)
Palmer, Oscar 222 (lower)
Phelps Dodge Corporation 198
Phoenix Chamber of Commerce 151 (lower right)
Phoenix Gazette, The 165 (upper mid)
Pinal County Historical Society 204 (left)
Preston, Tom 204 (left)
Rink, Bob 23, 200, 256 (lower), 258 (lower left), 259, 262, 294 (upper), 294 (lower right), 295
Rosarita 248 (upper)
Salt River Project 143 (lower), 158, 252 (right), 253 (lower right), 255 (lower)
Sharlot Hall Museum 118 (upper), 122 (upper) 160
Smithsonian Institution 105 (lower right)
Southwest Forest Industries 248 (lower)
SRP 4, 21, 26, 27, 39, 223 (upper), 251, 252 (left), 253 (upper right), 255 (upper), 263 (upper), 263 (lower), 280 (upper)
State Parks Board 203

Tally, Steve 240 (right), 241
Teiwes, Helga 32, 38 (upper left), 38 (lower left), 40 (lower), 219, 266
Till, Tom front cover, back cover, Arizona portrait, 1, 6, 11, 18, 19, 21 (upper), 38, 41, 45, 256 (upper), 272, 273 (left insert)
Tombstone Epitaph 157 (left)
Tumacacori National Monument 58, 61 (upper right)
U. S. Postal Service 14 (upper left), 81, 108 (lower right), 126 (upper), 165 (right), 173 (right), 178 (lower left), 205, 217 (upper)
U. S. West 168 (upper)
U.S. Air Force 233 (upper)
University of Arizona Library 118 (lower), 128, 165 (lower left), 188 (lower right), 239 (lower left)
Utah Historical Society 145 (upper right)
Utah State Historical Society 230 (lower), 242
Wagoner, Jay 264, 265 (left)
Washington National Records Center 121 (right)
Weekly Gazette 291 (left)
Weeks, Tim 288
Wupatki National Monument Museum 43

Other photographs and art not listed are the possession of the author or the publisher.

Art

Bayless, Gigi 6, 28
Beaugureau, Francis H. 125, 129, 134 (left)
Browne, J. Ross 102, 103
Cohen, Peter Zachary 144 (all), 145 (lower)
Coze, Paul 80, 106 (lower right), 140 (upper)
Dixon, Maynard 56
Hale, Bob 167
Kemp, Charles E. 110
Kemper, Charles O. 30, 37 (upper left)
Mollhausen, Balduin 96
Ottinger, George 80
Perceval, Don 173 (left)
Peters, Cal 50
Remington, Frederic 78, 122 (lower), 179
Wieghorst, Olaf 138
Wright, Harold Bell 213